Marilyn Lawrence has worked as a psychiatric social worker and as a university lecturer. She began working with anorexic women when she was employed in the National Health Service. She later set up a voluntary counselling service for anorexic women and their families in Leeds. She now works in London as a psychotherapist and has close links with The Women's Therapy Centre, where she runs workshops and teaches on training courses.

Her book *The Anorexic Experience* was published by The Women's Press in 1984 and revised in 1989.

MARILYN LAWRENCE, EDITOR

Fed Up
and Hungry

Women, Oppression & Food

With a foreword by Susie Orbach

First published by The Women's Press Limited, 1987
A member of the Namara Group
34 Great Sutton Street, London EC1V 0DX

Reprinted 1989, 1992

British Library Cataloguing in Publication Data

Fed up and hungry: women, oppression and food.
  1. Eating disorders
  I. Lawrence, Marilyn
616.85'2   RC552.E18

ISBN 0-7043-4008-9

Typeset by MC Typeset Ltd, Rochester Road, Wouldham, Kent
Printed and bound in Great Britain by Cox & Wyman Ltd, Reading,
Berks

Contents

Acknowledgments   2

Foreword   *Susie Orbach*   3

Introduction   *Marilyn Lawrence*   8

1 Eve Was Framed: Food and Sex and Women's
   Shame   *Annie Fursland*   15

2 Women's Anger and Compulsive Eating
   Bunny Epstein   27

3 Boundaries: One-Way Mirror to the Self
   Mira Dana   46

4 Anorexia and the Family   *Gill Edwards*   61

5 Anorexia and Adolescence   *Wil Pennycook*   74

6 Compulsive Eating: Issues in the Therapy
   Relationship   *Tamar Selby*   86

7 Bulimia: A Feminist Psychoanalytic
   Understanding   *Carol Bloom*   102

8 Self-Help Groups: The Agony and the Ecstasy   *Katina
   Noble*   115

9 Putting the Issue on the Boards   *Clair Chapman*   136

10 Images and Eating Problems   *Mary-Jayne Rust*   145

11 'Going for the Burn' and 'Pumping Iron': What's Healthy
    About the Current Fitness Boom?
    Jean Mitchell   156

12 Anorexia and Bulimia: The Political and the
    Personal   *Troy Cooper*   175

13 'Poison is the Nourishment that Makes One Ill': The
    Metaphor of Bulimia
    Mira Dana and *Marilyn Lawrence*   193

14 Education and Identity: The Social Origins of
    Anorexia   *Marilyn Lawrence*   207

15 Food, Need and Desire: A Postscript   *Tamar Selby*   226

Biographical Notes   233

Cartoons by Jacky Fleming

Acknowledgments

First and foremost, I would like to thank the authors who have contributed to this book for their patience with each other, and with me, and for their real dedication to the task of making the book come about. Nothing could have happened without the Women's Therapy Centre, whose very existence makes it a focus for all our work. In particular, I would like to thank Jose Nicolson. One of her many roles is to liaise with those of us who operate outside the Centre, and she has consistently and generously supported and promoted our work, always reminding us of the common goals we all share.

I would like to thank my friend and colleague Mira Dana, who has given me so much support and indeed continues to do so. My thanks also go to Clair Chapman, Lesley Day and Geoffrey Pearson, who have each helped me in specific ways with the task of editing. Christina Dunhill has been a most considerate and creative editor and it was with her help that the book was finished.

Finally, I would like to thank Luise Eichenbaum and Susie Orbach, whose pioneering work on women's psychology forms the background to so much of what we have written.

Foreword

Susie Orbach

In 1970 I discovered that I was a compulsive eater and – it goes without saying – a compulsive dieter. Finding myself scrambling in the fridge looking for something to soothe my appetite, resolving not to buy or keep 'fattening' foods at home, finishing a packet of Jaffa Cakes I didn't even know I'd started, waiting for Monday so that I could start a new diet and feel cleansed and righteous: all such thoughts, behaviours and activities were a part of my life I took for granted and assumed would be with me always. It was my personal problem and my personal failure. I had no basis for imagining that I could really stick to a 'sensible' eating plan. Even as I planned the next diet, I knew I would not be able to stay on it. The inherent illogic of the diet–binge syndrome had not yet penetrated my consciousness.

It was only the experience of sitting with 40 women and hearing their individual stories that allowed me, and them, to think differently about the pain and distress as well as the irrationality of the acts that we were engaged in. It became possible to name the activity – compulsive eating – and it became possible to see that our individual experiences with food were comprehensible if we had on a different set of eyes. It became possible too to consider not living our lives in daily dread of the scales or of clothes suddenly becoming too tight.

In 1970 I not only discovered that I was a compulsive eater but with the other women in my group I came to realise that compulsive eating is an individual response to a complex set of social circumstances that women find themselves in. In other words, we began to locate our eating problems within the political. We began to see that the way we felt about food, our confusion about appetite and satiety, our preoccupation with fat and thin, our love of food and our fear of it, our need for bulk, our need for soothing, our need for a reliable way to respond to a variety of emotional situations were indicators that all was not well where women lived. The bodies we inhabited – bodies that carried the load of self-definition – were places we were rarely comfortable in. We could not rejoice or celebrate in the female form: we were busy remodelling it to fit in with the aesthetic standards of the day.

In that first group, we looked at the particular role food plays in the lives of women. We looked at the contradictory messages about eating we had received while growing up: 'Eat, eat, my darling,' and 'Watch yourself now, don't get fat.' We looked at how the organs of mass culture depicted women's relationship to food and we saw how we had all internalised the message that we should prepare food for others but be wary of it ourselves. We looked at when we ate and discovered that hunger was a rare trigger. We ate when we were happy and we ate when we were sad; we ate when we were bored and we ate when we were angry; we ate when we were sexually frustrated and we ate when we were sexually satisfied; we ate at mealtimes and we ate when we passed a bakery. We ate with our children and we ate to keep our husbands/friends/lovers company. As long as we weren't dieting, we could be eating at any moment. Eating was a punctuation point between activities, an accompaniment to activities, a way of being in the world and a way of withdrawing from the world.

The more we talked, the more we recognised how food and our obsession with the body dominated aspects of our emotional life. And the more we talked we realised that this was a social phenomenon affecting lots of women. Food and body-image issues, far from being trivial, could now be seen as the language of women's inner experience. As such we could dignify what had clearly become an area of enormous difficulty for many women. We could take it out of the arena of personal failure and simplistic dietary solutions into the realm of women's psychological and social existence. Once located there, we could begin to develop practices that helped us change the distressed or disordered ways we had of being with food. We could explore the conscious and unconscious ideas we held about body-size; we could begin the process of speaking rather than stuffing; we could begin to assert our bodies as they were rather than as they should be, and so on.

What we discovered in that first group and the subsequent ones that Carol Munter and I went on to run together and separately was powerful and enabling. Although the first group was the essence of self-help, we then went on to lead groups and to see people with eating problems in individual therapy. It was with the opening of the Women's Therapy Centre in London in 1976 and the oversubscription for workshops for women with eating problems that I thought back to the original group and remembered how important self-help had been. It simply wasn't possible to offer enough ongoing led groups or individual sessions to cope with the demand. A simple mention of the fact that 'interesting work was going on in this area at the Women's Therapy Centre' in *Woman* magazine would bring a postbag so heavy with enquiries that the already overstretched administration we carried at the time was in danger of collapsing. Something had to be done. I devised a format within which I hoped that women who had never been to a workshop before could embark on the exciting (and painful) process of working through their food problem and changing their often tortured relationship to their bodies. We mimeographed sheets and sent them all over the country, and when people initiated work on their own and sent in queries it became clear that something more polished and thought through needed to be prepared.

Fat is a Feminist Issue[1] was that project. I debated between a pamphlet and a book and decided that the latter would have wider distribution. At that time there was sufficient evidence to suggest that this was a problem that affected significant enough numbers of women to warrant wide readership. I wanted to convey the real and substantial knowledge we had generated in the women's liberation movement – a knowledge as legitimate as the knowledge acquired in conventional educational settings. And I wanted to share that knowledge in an accessible form, I wanted the book to reach the range of women who attended the Women's Therapy Centre – middle-class women who had careers, middle-class women who stayed home to look after the children and the household, educated working-class women, school dinner ladies, skilled and unskilled workers, mothers, grandmothers, women too young to think of bearing children, women who excluded reproduction from their agendas.

The process was a personally agonising one. A whole book needed to be written and I was someone who had never managed to complete a school essay! But I was motivated by the hurt I saw expressed every day by women with eating problems. I was angry that women should suffer so and hopeful that this way of looking at things could provide the kind of relief for them that it had provided for me. I wanted to give back to a wider community of women what I had been able to learn in the rich creative spirit of the women's liberation movement. And so I went to my desk and wrote *Fat is a*

Feminist Issue. It was an attempt to provide pointers to the world of the psychological, guidelines for the setting up and running of self-help groups and the situating of women's eating problems within the context of their socialisation process.

But even though I knew that the subject of the book might be of interest to many women, I never imagined quite how large that number would be. I never expected the Pandora's Box it would open. I never anticipated that almost 10 years on I would still be receiving letters from women all over the world who write to tell me about the experience of compulsive eating. I never anticipated that *Fat is a Feminist Issue* (or rather that I) would be seen by some to be condoning fat and arguing that it was okay for women to be fat (of course it is – fat is not the issue *per se*, compulsive eating is) and that others would read *Fat is a Feminist Issue* as a diet book urging women to be thin. I never imagined that I would still be working in the field and would have written two more books focusing on women's eating problems,[2] because *Fat is a Feminist Issue* was also my way of saying goodbye to this piece of work, of sharing with women in the UK and USA what I had learnt so that I could give it up – or so I thought!

And so, as I write this foreword and read the essays in this book, I feel both tremendous pleasure and tremendous concern. The last 17 years have seen the development of the ideas first taken up in that women's group. Compulsive eating (and bulimia and anorexia) is now part of the vocabulary; an understanding of women's body-image distortions is commonplace; the pattern that sees women providing food for others but withholding it from themselves is recognised. And it is now understood that the dominant aesthetic of the day – an elusive and ever-changing aesthetic – insinuates itself into each woman's feelings about herself. Women have come out of the closet about their eating and their not eating and they have bravely told one another about the ways they feel about their bodies. Feminism has enabled a whole field to develop, a field with a distinctive contribution, a field in which the psychological is entwined with the social rather than one being tacked on to the other.

But, as I say, I am also full of concern. I am full of concern because it seems that there is no let up in the amount of women who are reporting eating problems. Women's preoccupations with their bodies continue now with no less insistence, and indeed the problem would seem to be intensifying, affecting girls at younger and younger ages[3] and extending into old age as a proper area of concern for elderly women. Surely, one feels, this can't be the case. And yet it is. There is hardly a woman in the West between 15 and 55 who doesn't fret about her body, who doesn't wish to change something about it, who doesn't imagine that things in her life would be better if only her body were different.

The insistence with which food and body-image problems press themselves on women has meant that an area of work I previously saw as just a 'sideline' to my work as a therapist has continued to occupy a great deal of my time and my interest. Eating problems aren't something that are at a tangent to women's other problems; they are integral to so many women's lives that they are almost the normal experience. The more women I encounter with eating problems, the more I listen to what they are saying about themselves through their food and through their body-image, the more I realise how central women's relationships to food are in the development and shape of their pyscho-social existence.

Food is a metaphor through which women speak of their inner experiences. Until we have a real voice in the body politic, individual women are likely to use their bodies as their mouthpieces to express the forbidden and excluded feelings we carry inside. A collection such as this which takes up so many different aspects of women's body-image and eating problems will be of tremendous help both to women who suffer with eating problems and to those who try to help them. As workers in this field we share our understanding with women in general and with other clinicians so that those who do seek help will have a greater chance of a compassionate encounter.

Notes

1. Orbach, S., *Fat is a Feminist Issue*, Paddington Press, New York and London, 1978.
2. The two books are *Fat is a Feminist Issue II*, Hamlyn, London, 1982, and *Hunger Strike: The Anorectic's Struggle as a Metaphor for Our Age*, Faber and Faber, London, 1986.
3. See 'Fourth Grade Girls These Days Ponder Weighty Matters', *Wall Street Journal*, 11 February 1986.

Introduction

There are a number of reasons why this book came to be written. Perhaps the most important was my own growing realisation that among feminists in the helping professions, in academic life and in the arts there was a continuing lively interest in women's relationships to food, eating and our own bodies. I became aware that a great deal of original work was going on in this area and that there was a need to write it down and collect it together. The other major impetus for the task came from the continual flow of requests from the UK and beyond for information, knowledge, advice and understanding about ourselves and our relationship to food.

At the time that this collection was conceived I was a member of a supervision group at the Women's Therapy Centre, where those of us involved in work with women with eating problems met together to share our work. It was this experience more than anything else which gave me some insight into the range of work that was actually going on and the level of skill and expertise that had been developed. At the same time, I was on the receiving end of the needs of and demands for help with food-related problems from not only women who themselves had difficulties but also, and ever increasingly, their friends, parents, doctors, social workers, counsellors – all seeking to understand the problems and to respond more effectively.

The Women's Therapy Centre has for the past 10 years specialised in dealing with women's eating problems, and although this is only one aspect of the Centre's work it does form a considerable proportion of it.

While only one of the contributors to this anthology is a staff member at the Centre, many others of us are associated with the work there, either as sessional workshop leaders or through having participated in courses. All of us to a greater or lesser extent have been influenced by the Centre's ideas and by the non-punitive, woman-centred approach which has been developed there. In spite of the serious limitations imposed upon the Centre by lack of funding, it is still possible to offer women with eating problems a variety of treatment options ranging from self-help groups through to long-term individual therapy and including short-term intensive workshops, analytic groups and short-term counselling.

Fat is a Feminist Issue, Susie Orbach's book which did so much to set the Centre's ideas on course, was first published in 1978.[1] Influential though this book has undoubtedly been, many of the women who approach the Centre for help with their eating problems are still caught up in the endless cycle of dieting and overeating. Some of our clients approach the Centre in an attempt to break out from this self-destructive and humiliating spiral. They know that an 'alternative' approach is available and are actively seeking help which they feel is not available from the more traditional and medically dominated agencies. Other clients, however, do not choose to come to us because they especially like our approach; they come because we are a last resort. Most of the women who come for help in an anorexic episode have already been hospitalised, usually several times. They have been discharged, are once again losing weight and feel desperate to find someone who might be able to help. While some of our clients come to us because of our feminist understanding of psychology and eating problems, others come in spite of it.

The women who approach us for help are of different ages and come from a wide range of backgrounds. A number of our clients are lesbians and some belong to racial minority groups. At one end of the spectrum might be the 50-year-old woman, married for 30 years and bulimic for 25 of them, who has never before told anyone about her problem. Her marriage is by most standards highly successful, her children are at university, but just recently she has heard that what she has always regarded as her 'bad habit' – making herself sick several times a day – is now thought of as a sign of distress and emotional difficulty. She comes to us to see if we really do understand what terrible feelings her eating behaviour conceals. At the other end we might be approached by a 25-year-old woman who is a feminist and a lesbian. She is a creative woman who is struggling (successfully) to earn her living and live her life outside many of the established structures. Her political consciousness makes it difficult for her to acknowledge how painfully caught up she still feels with issues to do with weight and food and how, much as she dislikes her own attitudes, she cannot give up her obsession with being thin.

The challenge for those of us interested in understanding eating problems in their context is to acknowledge that those two women are similar in terms of their socialisation and development in a patriarchal culture but very different in terms of their current relationship to that culture.

The authors of this book have tried throughout to draw attention to the aspects of experience which women share while at the same time honestly highlighting and exploring the differences between us.

While we feel we are offering women an approach and perspective which is often lacking in more traditional settings, our optimism has not always been shared by other health-care workers. Initially much of the opposition to our work was couched in terms of 'what can mere women know about women's problems'! This has now been largely overcome, but we still find hospital settings which regard our work as 'useful for self-help' but find it hard to take us seriously as genuine alternatives to what they have to offer. Having said that, we do receive a lot of referrals from doctors and hospitals, and health-care professionals make up the majority of participants on our courses. We often find that while nurses, dieticians, social workers and psychologists are actively using our ideas in their own work settings, the medical ideology which they are supposed to service is quite opposed to what we say. For my own part, I feel both pleased at the progress which has been made over the past decade in changing the prevailing views about women's eating problems and also frustrated at the resistance we still encounter.

This anthology came together out of the work and experience of the authors. It makes no attempt to 'cover the field' in a systematic way. Authors were not commissioned to write a chapter on a particular topic which it was felt should be explored. Rather, we have all written about our own current interests and preoccupations.

I have not attempted to impose a uniformity of style or presentation. Quite apart from the impossibility of such a task, uniformity seemed to me to be unnecessary. I had thought at one point during the process of assembling the material that I should at least insist that we all use the same terminology to describe our subject-matter – either 'eating disorder', 'eating problem', 'disturbed eating' or some other such term. On reflection, and after discussion with the authors and others, I decided against it. Some women felt uneasy with the term 'eating disorder', on the grounds that it is the traditional medical form of description and thus tends to medicalise something which is such a common experience for so many women. Other women felt they wanted and needed to use this terminology. In their work, they are often told that they work with a different 'population' – the less severe 'cases'; they wanted to make the point that we as feminist therapists work with the same group of women as doctors, although we do different work. My own feeling is that at present an adequate feminist terminology simply doesn't exist: 'eating disorder', 'eating problems', 'disturbed eating' – all of these describe a symptom which we recognise as related to a much more profound and serious malaise. I have therefore decided to leave each author to use the terminology with which she feels most comfortable.

It is traditionally the task of an introduction to spell out what it is that the various chapters have in common, to direct the reader to the common core of shared assumptions and perspectives, to integrate the fragments, make a whole out of the parts.

In this anthology, it is clear what the different chapters have in common. It is less clear what is common to the women who have written them. When I think about the authors of this book, I realise that we are as diverse a group as the women we work with.* We don't all know each other and in fact we originate from and live in very different parts of the world. Some of us began our professional lives within the state-funded services, such as health, education and social work. Others of us have our original training in psycho-therapy. Others again have found our way through the self-help movement and would shy away from the title 'professional'. Some of the authors hold academic posts, others are unemployed. Some of us are full-time parents, students, writers or actors. I think we would all call ourselves feminists, although I suspect this does not mean the same for all of us. For some, our feminism is located within a socialist framework, while for others it has developed out of our understanding of the distinctive nature of women's inner psychological world. Some of us write from within a feminist psychoanalytic understanding, while others have a background in the feminist self-help movement.

The interesting question, perhaps, is why it is that problems to do with food, eating and women's bodies have become such a central

*A brief biography of each author can be found on pp. 233–6.

interest for us all. To answer this question is to begin to explore the common perspective which we share.

The writers of this book begin with the assumption that eating disorders and food-related problems are problems for all women. Some women produce very severe and even life-threatening symptoms around food, but most of us merely spend our lives feeling troubled and uneasy about our bodies and the amount of food we eat. The woman who eats in an unselfconscious way, without worries and concerns about putting on weight, is an unusual woman indeed. Even she will probably have had periods in her life when she was unable to meet her physical needs in such a straightforward way. We can say very simply that we all take women's eating disorders seriously. We know, both from our own experience of such problems and from working with other women, the enormous pain and despair which we can feel as women because we feel fat, unable to control our eating and as though life will never be bearable until we are the right size. As well as taking this desperation seriously, we are able to see beyond it. The woman who can never be satisfied with her own body is expressing her despair about her relation to the world.

It is the exploration of the many aspects of this disturbed relationship which women have to a world which should be their own, which forms the real theme and unity of this book. We do not understand or describe eating disorders as mental illnesses, symptoms of individual 'pathology' or signs of 'maladaptive coping behaviour'. On the contrary, we know very well that women develop problems around food and eating in response to readily identifiable social demands. Further, we know that to develop such a problem in response to sad, depressed or angry feelings is, for women, a socially adaptive response. That is not to say that the women who become trapped in these responses are not disturbed and ill – psychologically and spiritually. But it is the understanding of the context of such 'illness' which transforms it.

We understand the problems which women have with food and eating as meaningful expressions of women's inner psychological reality. Eating disorders for us are not merely troublesome symptoms which need to be eradicated.

The first three chapters point specifically to some of the issues which underlie women's difficulties with food, eating and our own bodies. Annie Fursland's reflections on the parallels between food and sex remind us that eating problems are the late twentieth-century manifestation of a form of oppression which has been around for a very long time. It is a suggestion, right from the start, that if we want to understand the true nature of our difficulties with food, we have to cast the net very wide indeed.

Bunny Epstein examines the central importance of anger in women's lives and the way in which our difficulties in expressing it can lead us to produce self-destructive symptoms instead.

Mira Dana's Chapter 3 is a theoretical account of certain aspects of women's inner experience which is a clear reflection of our social condition. In Chapter 4, Gill Edwards traces the origins of anorexia through a social and family structure which are both patriarchal. She looks critically at what has been said and written about the families of the young women who develop anorexia and provides a re-evaluation of their roles and responsibilities. In the next chapter, Wil Pennycook suggests that anorexia is very often connected with depressed feelings, which, although quite reasonable and under-standable, are often not accepted and tolerated in young women.

Tamar Selby analyses some aspects of the relationship which women who eat compulsively tend to set up with therapists who specialise in working with this problem. Far from romanticising the therapeutic relationship, Tamar is concerned to draw attention to the hostility and need to control which many women experience in relation to their therapists.

Carol Bloom's chapter on therapy with bulimic women follows the life of one particular woman and illustrates not only how she came to develop her eating problem but also how she was helped to recover from it.

The next two chapters are concerned with innovative ways in which women have tried to help themselves. Katina Noble provides an invaluable guide to the ups and downs of self-help groups. Drawing on her extensive experience of setting up and supporting such groups, she tackles the practical, emotional and political difficulties head on. Clair Chapman's account of the genesis and development of Spare Tyre is a lightly written and moving piece of history which records some aspects of women's changing conscious-ness of ourselves and our bodies.

Chapter 10 looks at the potential of art therapy as a means by which women can use our creativity to combat the oppression which surrounds us and which we have internalised. Mary-Jayne Rust uses detailed material from the women she has worked with to suggest ways in which we might move forward.

Jean Mitchell looks at the way in which the current preoccupation with fitness and physical perfection for women is yet another variation on the familiar theme of our having to keep our errant bodies under control. She suggests that far from offering women power and freedom the new fitness boom simply reproduces the kind of oppression which anorexia and bulimia also represent.

Troy Cooper's Chapter 12 contrasts anorexia and bulimia in terms of the message they give to the world and how this message has been perceived by the medical and helping professions. She shows how they have been ready to applaud the highly controlled anorexic and despise the bulimic whom they wrongly consider to be indulgent and out of control. These unhelpful responses actually reinforce the bulimic woman's self-image and so compound the difficulties.

Mira Dana and I consider eating problems as metaphors of an inner reality which they attempt to conceal. Viewed in this way, bulimia begins to make a very different kind of sense.

My Chapter 14 examines the connection between the onset of an anorexic phase and a high level of educational achievement. I suggest that there is not yet an easy way for women to be successful in the world, and that a self-destructive disorder such as anorexia might be one of the prices which we pay.

Tamar Selby has the last word in a short paper which questions the way we eat and the way we relate to our eating and to other pleasures in our lives. She suggests that we belong to a generation seduced by the fantasy of the idea, which can often spoil our capacity to be engaged with and enjoy the real.

Notes

1. Orbach, S., *Fat is a Feminist Issue*, Paddington Press, New York and London, 1978.

1
Eve was Framed: Food and Sex and Women's Shame*
Annie Fursland

The double standard

I have been under the misapprehension all my life that Eve tempted Adam to eat the apple and God punished her for this. I now discover that the *serpent* tempted Eve and all she did was share the fruit with her male companion – no mention of temptation. As a result, God punished all three (according to the Bible). Such is the power of myth, not only the original story but the overlay of misinterpretation. We are left with the vivid image of forbidden fruit and Eve the evil. Like poor Eve, women in our society get blamed – framed? – *for actions we didn't commit*. Our behaviour is evaluated in such a way that it is frequently seen to be wrong, and we internalise these prevailing norms so that we end up believing we *are* in the wrong. How and why do we let this happen?

In any system, people in power make the rules and it follows that these rules will suit them. Since we live in a world ruled largely by men, it is men who benefit; women (together with women's behaviour and notions of guilt) are evaluated in relation to male-defined norms. Throughout our culture there is a double standard in operation favouring men, and nowhere is this seen more clearly than in the areas of food and sex – e.g. 1. pre- or extra-marital sex, where men's exploits are discussed with much pride and elbow nudging, while a woman's activities still get her labelled 'promiscuous'; 2. large bodies, which are accepted in men

*This paper was first presented at the National Conference of the Association for Women in Psychology, in Oakland, California, on 7 March 1986.

but despised in women. And in the areas of both food and sex, boys/men are encouraged to have 'healthy' appetites, but girls/women mustn't be 'greedy'.

The irony is that, despite being regarded as inferior (less intelligent/ important, etc.), women are often placed by men on pedestals. This is deemed to be a desirable position, a mark of respect, but we find that it's lonely up there, and there's further to fall. Women are supposed to maintain and uphold moral standards – we are made to feel guilty for not living up to these prescribed standards and end up feeling ashamed of our 'inadequacies'. So women strive to reach the often unreachable heights without questioning the unreasonableness of the goals or the unfairness of the demands. There is continuous pressure on us, for even when our behaviour does get the okay, we are never really sure if we have succeeded or if the rules have changed. For example, we cut our hair in the latest bob only to read that long hair is back, or we stay at home to bring up the children only to be told that it wasn't necessary and why hadn't we got a job and contributed to the housekeeping? We are kept constantly on our toes, dancing to somebody else's tune which isn't even clear to us. We cannot relax, we have to remain vigilant, aware of ourselves and our image. We are after all, the *seen* sex, and there is power in the gaze. As John Berger[1] puts it:

> A woman . . . is continually accompanied by her own image of herself . . . she has to survey everything she is and everything she does because how she appears to others, and ultimately how she appears to men, is of crucial importance for what is normally thought of as the success in her life . . . *Men act and women appear*. Men look at women. Women watch themselves being looked at. This determines not only most relations between men and women but also the relation of women to themselves.

This self-consciousness relating to our image permeates our entire lives. Women have felt guilty and shameful, especially regarding sexual matters, for many years, culminating in the puritanical values of the nineteenth century. It now appears that food is replacing sex as the focus of guilt in women's lives. With women's ambivalence towards food being discussed more openly now, it seems timely to examine the links between food and sex in the search for the roots of our unease.

Food and sex – some links

A few days after I'd begun this piece, I came across an article in the *Guardian* newspaper entitled 'No Sex Please We're Hungry'. It asserted:

> Food has come back to Soho. *Boudin noir* is replacing bondage, pasta bars are taking over from peep shows. A quarter of the sex-related premises that have changed use in the last two years have gone over to food. (*Guardian*, 23 November 1984)

It wasn't the statistic of 25 per cent which surprised me (after all, given the location, it didn't sound very high) but rather the tone, which seemed to suggest that eating and sex were interchangeable pleasures. A novel idea? Not really, but rarely are the two pleasures so explicitly linked.

There *are* examples though. A scene from the film *Tom Jones* comes to mind in which the hero and a woman tear into chicken legs and guzzle down their meal in an overtly sexual, lascivious manner. A more exploitative instance of highlighting the sexual aspects of food is the book *Rude Food*, a series of photographs of various foods posed with parts of living human bodies.[2] A typical example (from the cover) is a woman's torso, her crotch decorated with curly lettuce, with salad dressing being poured over it.

But mostly this connection between eating and sexuality is made unconsciously or, if it is made overtly, its relevance is taken in subconsciously. An obvious example is the pre-seduction dinner routine where the man buys food and expects to receive sex from the woman in return. Although this convention has been current for many years, the meaning of the exchange (food for sex) is rarely acknowledged openly.

It is some years since Freud's original proposal of the oral stage as the first stage of sexuality in humans. His focus was on the oral cavity, the mouth – an object closely involved with the taking in of food. Although the mouth is most commonly associated (consciously) with food, it is rarely considered as a source of *pleasure* in relation to food; when thought of as a pleasure zone, it is more often associated with the taking in of parts of other people's bodies (especially nipples, tongues, genitals). When the pleasurable aspects of the mouth (related to *food*) are recognised, they are usually associated with sex, an obvious example being the advertisement highlighting the phallic qualities of a Cadbury's Flake, and oral pleasures of a sexual nature are often linked with food. Our language reflects this, not only with such descriptions as 'tasty', 'crumpet' and 'dish', but with the more explicit, 'I want to eat you', referring to a desire for oral sex. This is women being objectified, and – in a male culture like ours – objectified by men.

Thus oral *pleasures* (and therefore food through association) are often linked with sexual images, especially oral sex, which is regarded as distinctly exciting and prohibited,* and in particular fellatio – the sexual act involving a penis entering another person's mouth (which in our predominantly heterosexual and heterosexist culture is generally assumed to be a female mouth). This image of a woman's mouth taking in what is dangerous and prohibited is reinforced in advertising, where women and women's sexuality are used to sell products. Our mouths are not our own. Frequent emphasis is put on the female mouth: moist, open, red, ready, and so on. It is no coincidence that this is reminiscent of another specifically female orifice in a sexually aroused state.

No wonder that attitudes to women eating reflect attitudes to women's sexuality. And no wonder that there are injunctions regulating our eating as well as our sexuality – extremes are not tolerated. In sexual activity celibacy and 'frigidity' on the one hand and 'promiscuity' on the other are taboo, while in eating behaviour anorexia and 'obesity' are treated. Sex and eating are, however, about *meeting needs*. And whereas men are encouraged to meet their needs, women are defined as 'need meeters' whose own needs are usually denied or subverted. But we *do* have needs; it's only that we aren't allowed to acknowledge them. Faking orgasms is like saying we've had enough to eat when we haven't. And both are the result of feeling ashamed of having these needs.

It will be helpful to consider food and sex separately in their relation to women's shame, but first let us look at a source of shame among women which is crucial to both issues, women's relationship with their bodies.

Women's shame: (1) our bodies

Girls are brought up to be ignorant about their bodies. This is usually explained by the assertion that boys'/men's genitals are more visible and obvious, and seems to ignore our most vital sexual organ, the clitoris, which is easily visible and easy to locate if you

---

*Oral sex was widely considered a perversion only a generation ago, and is still illegal, even between wife and husband, in some states in the USA.

know where to look! The trouble is that many of us didn't and many males don't. Sex education and biology diagrams always detail the male sexual parts: the penis, testicles, etc. In the case of women, however, the only sexual organs which are described are the reproductive organs, i.e. the ovaries, womb and vagina. The clitoris is invariably omitted, despite its being, together with the labia, comparable to the penis in both importance and size.[3] This emphasis on reproduction rather than sexual pleasure is a clear denial of female sexuality.

Girls' examination of their genitals reveals the undisclosed truth, but leaves girls confused and uncertain, since their experience of their own bodies doesn't match what they've been told. It is hardly surprising that many women grow up fearing they are deformed and abnormal, with two sets of labia and a clitoris that the textbooks haven't mentioned!

Furthermore, sexual exploration in females is regarded as taboo and frequently results in extreme guilt. Not only girls but adult women are discouraged from self-examination (woe betide any woman who admits to her doctor that she has obtained a speculum* and seen her cervix). We are treated as though ignorance concerning our own bodies is best for us, which leads us to suspect that there is something terrible and shameful about our bodies.

Menstruation is a further source of shame. While in some cultures a girl's first period is celebrated, in our society it is shrouded in secrecy and referred to in whispers, which adds to our suspicions that something is wrong and unacceptable. Euphemisms reinforce this, and one of the most widely used, 'the curse', aptly describes how we learn to consider our normal monthly bleeding. Menstrual blood itself is thought of with disgust, as if tainted. Publicly, menstruating women are regarded as impure – in some cultures prohibited from preparing food and in this country, in the not too distant past, banned from the dairy in case the milk turned sour! Privately, girls and women internalise this public disgust and conclude that our genitals are dirty and smell bad – not only during our periods.

The feeling of failure about our bodies is not confined to our genitals. There is a constant war being waged – and lost – against natural female features, i.e. curves. The 'ideal' female body that we read about and see displayed in the media is that of an adolescent, smooth and sleek (body hair is regarded as unsightly). This is yet

*A device used for internal examinations. It is inserted into the vagina and holds the vaginal walls open.

another example of double standards: whereas the ideal male image is *mature* (hairy, muscular) and teenage boys yearn to develop these qualities, teenage girls and women desperately work to keep our bodies looking *immature*. We are surrounded by images equating thinness and youth with success, fame and glamour. Advertising uses young, thin models; most film stars are young and thin. We inevitably compare ourselves with them and inevitably feel failures. This is a tremendously sensitive area in women's lives. It is not mere vanity but a more fundamental self-consciousness which demands constant self-monitoring and camouflage of our 'bad' points to avoid stigma and shame. We cannot be ourselves; we feel that we have to be an image.

Certainly, many women are conscious of feeling unhappy about their bodies. But the picture is not that simple: it has been suggested (initially by Susie Orbach[4]) that women unconsciously break diets and 'choose' to be large as it helps us feel secure, powerful and respected. Consciously, however, women experience a common disgust at female (our own) flesh, which is echoed in emotive language, e.g. floppy, flabby, saggy. Such self-hatred (for that is what it is) is sad, and reflects a denial of our femaleness. Kim Chernin[5] movingly and powerfully describes this:

> I realised that what I had called fat in myself, and considered gross, was this body of a woman. And it was beautiful. The thighs, too large for an adolescent boy, were appropriate to a woman's body. Hips rounding, belly curved, what had driven me to deny this evidence that I was a woman?

Women's shame: (2) sex

One result of the unease that women feel about the female body is, not surprisingly, that we develop ambivalent feelings about our sexuality. If we don't like our own body, after all, how are we ever to relax and enjoy sharing it with another person?

Furthermore, we have to contend with society's ambivalence about women's sexual feelings. The message we receive is unclear: girls/women who won't 'do it' are still labelled 'frigid', yet a girl/woman who shows uninhibited sexuality is written off as a whore, a nymphomaniac, an 'easy lay'. It seems that sexual desire is taboo and that we can't win either way. As a result we easily feel failures.

As recently as the end of the last century, female desire at

tomorrow at eight then

menopause was regarded as an illness and 'cures' included surgery. Could it just be that men find women's sexuality a threat? Certainly, women have been kept in the dark about our sexual potential. The clitoris has been denied (ignored in most texts) or invalidated (as in Freud's theory of clitoral orgasms being 'immature' and inferior to vaginal ones). Some of us may know better now, but we cannot be complacent while in other parts of the world clitoridectomy is widespread.*

There is a universal taboo on female sexuality outside the conventional marriage, not only on pre- and extra-marital sex but on lesbianism and masturbation. Society seems to have silenced us into invisibility and shame in its denial of female sexual activity, especially autonomous sexuality which does not include (or need) men. Lesbianism has never been considered unlawful (in compari-

*Many Moslem cultures in northern Africa practise this, referring to it as 'female circumcision'. However, the operation bears no resemblance to the male version. It is usually carried out without anaesthetic on four- and five-year-old girls. There are several versions, the most common (but not the worst) being the cutting out of the entire clitoris and labia minora. For further discussion of this and other misogynistic practises, read Mary Daly.[6]

son with strict laws against male homosexuality) – as if it didn't exist! And while male masturbation is widely acknowledged, female masturbation is hardly ever mentioned. All this means that if we do have desires in areas other than those approved by society for us, there is a higher tendency to feel abnormal and ashamed. Many girls and women don't know how to masturbate, or even that it is possible! Those who do are often furtive and feel guilty.

The treatment of females who are raped is another appalling example of double standards and a further means of controlling women's sexuality. When a boy is raped there is a tremendous outcry – rightly – and he is dealt with sympathetically as an unquestionably innocent victim. In contrast, sexual assault of girls and women doesn't raise many eyebrows and is often met with, 'What do you expect, walking alone at night? wearing a dress like that? flirting?' Female rape victims are often considered guilty, of being responsible for the assault. As women internalise these prevailing ideas, we feel guilty and ashamed (not to mention frightened) of our sexuality, which we fear might be held responsible for a man's violent, criminal sexual behaviour.

To a limited extent, women's sexuality was allowed to come out of the closet in the 'sexual revolution' of the 1960s. 'Free love' was the order of the day, but with hindsight it looks rather as if men wanted free *sex* and wanted women to satisfy their urges. Women were at last recognised as sexually active – though still in relation to men – but the straitjacket of chastity was suddenly replaced by the demand that we were constantly sexually available. Women who hesitated were labelled 'uncool' or prudish and women's reluctance to fit into this new mould was ignored.

Another area which has helped the recognition of women's sexuality but which has proved a mixed blessing is the body of research conducted by Kinsey, Masters and Johnson, and Shere Hite.[7] On one level, it has been liberating for women to have our capacity for sexual pleasure validated, and a positive experience to read about other women's sexuality. It has also come as a great relief to many women to learn that we are not abnormal, e.g. masturbation is common and the majority of women do not orgasm during intercourse (penetration). However, these studies also provide women with further standards to live up to and a further sense of shame and failure if we don't.

Repressive sexual morals for women still abound. The shame persists, whether it is related to being sexually active at all or not being sexually adventurous enough. Yet again, it feels as if we can't win.

Women's shame: (3) food

When we feel ashamed of our bodies and our sexuality, it is no surprise that we find the satisfying of another kind of physical need, hunger, a difficult and troubled activity. Women's relationship with food is all too often ambivalent, and frequently fraught, reflecting our feelings about our bodies and our sexuality. And on top of this, there is the cultural link between morality and eating: the 'sins of the flesh' include eating, which is seen to be on a par with law-breaking and sexual transgression. (Pleasurable activities are often advised against with expressions such as 'it's illegal', 'it's immoral' or 'it will make you fat'!)

Fasting and asceticism are found in cultures with a dualistic philosophy (e.g. Christianity, Judaism) where the body is seen as corrupting the soul. The soul must overcome the body, its 'prison', before transcending the sinful world. Purification by denial (e.g. not eating) is seen as good, particularly in women, because we are thought of as more prone to moral weakness and our bodies are thought of as especially unclean. Self-denial of food therefore offers a route to a kind of 'moral kudos'.[8] Women who do not practise such self-denial (either by refusal or 'lack of willpower') are considered self-indulgent and lacking *self-control*.

The notion of self-control used to be bandied about as an injunction to women concerning pre-marital sex. Although it is rarely heard in that context nowadays, it is currently the weight-watchers' catchphrase. Women are made to feel guilty when we are shown to 'lack self-control' with regard to food. In slimming clubs, punishment takes the form of humiliating those women who have put on weight (proof of their 'guilt'). This varies from public weigh-ins and announcements of 'failure' to having to wear humiliating pig masks. Even outside slimming clubs, women are made to feel 'piggy' if we eat heartily rather than pick daintily at our food. A woman eating in public – especially if she is large – will be met with 'can't she restrain herself?' or 'she's revolting'. So strong is this image that it is diffcult for us, even as women, to conjure up in our minds a positive image of a woman eating heartily. We all experience hunger, yet we find the satisfying of that physical need unacceptable in women.

Indeed *the urge to eat reminds us of our other appetites and brings with it feelings of shame associated with our bodies and sexual desires.* This is clearly described by Kim Chernin:[9]

My hunger filled me with despair. It would always return, no matter how often I resolved to control it . . . I had these same feelings about masturbating when I was a little girl. Then too it seemed to me that a powerful force would rise up from my body and overcome my moral scruples and all my resistance. I would give in to it with a sense of voluptuous release, followed by a terrible shame. Today I begin to see that there is a parallel here. A woman obsessed with losing weight is also caught up in a terrible struggle against her sensual natures . . . She is attempting to govern, control, limit and sometimes even destroy her appetite. But her body and her hunger are, like sexual appetite, the expression of what is natural in herself; it is a futile, heartbreaking and dismal struggle to be so violently pitted against them.

As in sexual desire, our appetite for food is often satisfied in secret. Eating, seen as shameful, will frequently be restrained in public but indulged in private. Yet even then it will not be enjoyed in a relaxed manner: it will tend to be furtive binges or pickings. As in sexual desire, there is a taboo on women satisfying oral appetites. More than men, women are discouraged from smoking and drinking alcohol, but it is food which poses the severest problem since eating is not a luxury but a necessity for life. However, girls are taught that it is 'lady-like' (i.e. desirable, but to whom?) to eat only small amounts and are encouraged to do so, even if it means remaining unsatisfied. And when there is not enough food to go round, it tends to be the woman who goes without, despite her hunger. This is reminiscent of sexual practice, where a woman still tends to feel that a male partner's sexual satisfaction is more important than her own.

Food is presented to us in the media at its most tantalising: beautifully arranged and photographed, often accompanied by recipes to tempt us. We are seduced by the image, encouraged to fantasise, and then – we turn the page and are exhorted to diet. Crash goes the excitement, out pops the guilt. This 'food pornography'[10] mirrors sexual pornography, with its explicit aim of exciting; however, the implicit message is that we're allowed to look and dream only, not to play out our fantasies on the real thing, which is *forbidden*. Because we are the consumed, not the consumers.

The forbidden qualities of food are usually associated with the idea that food will make us fat. This tends to overlook the fact that we need food to survive, and in any case, eating *per se* does not make us fat. It is almost as if someone is trying to make us feel miserable and guilty! It is also noticeable that it is at women that this message is aimed (when did you last see an article listing calories in *Playboy*?).

Women are associated with the provision of food – with buying, preparing and serving it. This is another problem area for us. If we feed our families healthy foods, we face rejection of not only the food but of ourselves ('Where's the white bread?' 'Why don't you ever give us what we like?'), but if we pander to them and give them their favourite foods, we are often conscious that this is unhealthy. Either choice leaves us with a sense of failure and riddled with guilt. Could it be that fatness for women is bad because it means we are pleasuring ourselves, rather than men?

Women as providers of food are easy targets; the association also taps our vulnerability (as mentioned earlier) over the fear of putting on weight. The thought of food automatically reminds us of weight and size, which makes it hard for us to enjoy the pleasures of eating. Even when we aren't on a specific diet, how can we ever enjoy food when we are so uncomfortable with our bodies?

The way forward

As I see it, eating is a problematic subject for women because our hunger for food is linked to another hunger, the hunger for sex, and both remind us of our bodies, which we dislike for not conforming to male-defined norms. This actually reflects the way in which we learn to dislike our *selves*, trying and often failing to mould ourselves in accordance with male definitions. But we must see these patriarchal double standards for what they really are, and realise that *women are labelled for being normal*.

Only if we accept this can we see ourselves in a positive light and begin to love ourselves as we are, not aim for what we're told we should be. We will then be free to delight in the femaleness of our bodies. We will be able to accept our hungers and desires as natural instead of shameful, and look to satisfy them with joy in place of guilt.

None of this will be easy, of course, since women have for so long internalised woman-hating values. Wanting to change is not enough; individual effort will be dogged by doubts. What is needed is for women not to be afraid to speak out about our problematic relationships, not only with food but with ourselves. Beyond that we need to look to the roots of our unease and challenge any system or theory which devalues women. We need to revalue ourselves, supporting each other in our refusal to be blamed, framed or shamed any longer.

Notes

1. Berger, J., *Ways of Seeing*, Penguin, Harmondsworth, 1972, pp. 46–7.
2. Le Poste, P., *Rude Food*, Macmillan, London, 1981.
3. Federation of Feminist Health Centers, *A New View of a Woman's Body*, Simon & Schuster, New York, 1981.
4. Orbach, S., *Fat is a Feminist Issue*, Paddington Press, New York and London, 1978.
5. Chernin, K., *Womansize: The Tyranny of Slenderness*, The Women's Press, London, 1978, p.18
6. Daly, M., *Gyn/Ecology: The Metaethics of Radical Feminism*, Beacon Press, Boston, 1978; The Women's Press, London, 1979.
7. Kinsey, A.C., Gebhard, P., Pomeroy, W.B., and Martin, C.E., *Sexual Behaviour in the Human Female*, W.B. Saunders, Philadelphia, 1953; Masters, W., and Johnson, V., *Human Sexual Response*, Little, Brown & Co., Boston, 1966; Hite, S., *The Hite Report: A Nationwide Study on Female Sexuality*, Macmillan, New York, 1976; Collier Macmillan, London, 1977.
8. Lawrence, M., 'Anorexia Nervosa: The Control Paradox', *Women's Studies International Quarterly*, Vol 2, 1979, pp. 93–101.
9. Chernin, *op. cit.*, pp. 9–10.
10. Coward, R., *Female Desire*, Paladin, London, 1984.

2
Women's Anger and Compulsive Eating
Bunny Epstein

In this paper I would like to explore some of the ways in which women's anger and women's eating disorders are connected. I start from the premise that anger is a useful and important part of our emotional capacity. Anger can be used appropriately and constructively, or it can be used destructively. To cite but a few examples of its positive use, it can summon quickly our reserves of energy in the cause of self-defence, it can be used to right social wrongs and it can mobilise the powerful forces needed to produce change. On a more personal level, we can use our awareness of our anger constructively to assert, confront or negotiate our demands and needs.

Anger derives from and implements the aggressive impulse. The aggressive impulse finds its origin in movement itself, in the reaching out of the infant in its mother's womb. This reaching out and making contact begins a process of definition which will have truly dramatic consequences for the developing individual. It will lead the infant to distinguish its self from that which is not its self. It will lend itself to a distinction between the boundary of self and others, particularly in intimate relationships. It will enable the infant to start the lifelong process of separating inner and external reality. It plays an important role in the individual's adult capacity for erotic love and tenderness for the beloved.[1] The aggressive impulse first experienced as movement is a preliminary to those aspects of activity we value highly such as purposeful work, accomplishment and achievement. Thus anger, with its roots in the aggressive impulse, can be seen as a resource. It is a useful, sometimes essential, part of an individual's capacity to reach out, move, master and achieve in the world.[2]

This is in no way meant to deny that many of us have great difficulty in feeling and appropriately using and expressing our anger. Indeed, if this were not the case, there would be no need to write this paper. The large majority of the women I see who come to me to work on their eating problems feel (if they can feel their anger at all) that their anger like their eating is out of control, a menace to themselves and to others. It is no accident that women are puzzled and bewildered, if not terrified, by their anger and its consequences. The public image – the dominant media image of woman (which is only now changing) – has not been that of an integrated person, a person with rights fully equipped to act purposefully and decisively when the need arises. The damaging psychological and social myth of femininity as passive and receptive places vigour, assertion and potency out of the realm of the feminine. It is feminine to pout, whine, nag, sulk, placate, manipulate and be generally childlike; it is unfeminine to be angry, confronting, direct, powerful and adult. This unwelcome distortion has persisted long since women stopped being the property of men. It is one which encourages women to act roles which deny fundamental aspects of themselves.

I do not share the view of a number of my contemporaries who call anger a redundant or negative emotion. Anger is part of our basic emotional equipment[3] and women must reappropriate it and make it work for them. Anger can be seen as a problem or a resource depending on how and when and to what purpose we use it. Anger which serves our needs I call potent anger and anger which is destructive to us and to those we encounter I call impotent anger. In this paper I will explore the connection between impotent anger and compulsive eating and the bridge that can be built from impotent to potent anger.

How is the compulsive eater's relationship to her food and to her anger connected? Let us first look at what compulsive eating is about. The compulsive eater says, 'I am out of control around food.' If we stand on our heads and look at what compulsive eating is *not* about, it is not about eating when we are physically hungry and stopping eating when we are physically full. The woman who eats compulsively has lost touch with her hunger and with her fullness, the basic biological controls of her eating. If we accept Susie Orbach's exciting hypothesis that there is an unconscious motivation for weight gain (that our eating and our fat, although consciously hated and despised, serve us in some way of which we are unaware), then we must understand that although compulsive eating feels out of control, on another and deeper level it is a way of controlling something which the woman may find more frightening, more distressing even, than eating when she is not hungry.[4] The 'something' to which I am referring is a woman's feelings. Anger is one particularly disturbing feeling for women, although many other so-called 'bad' feelings such as jealousy, envy, competitiveness, loneliness, sexuality or sorrow may be avoided by the compulsive eater in much the same way that she avoids her angry feelings. Ironically, two of the few permissible feelings for the compulsive eater are loathing for her fat and disgust with her greediness, which link with her feeling of being out of control.

Women deny their own anger and it is denied by others. Often I have heard a woman's anger dismissed with a slur, 'She hasn't been getting enough lately', or 'It must be her time of the month!' When a woman tries to avoid her own anger, it is often diverted in a dangerous way: I worked briefly with a family who brought this issue vividly to my attention. The family came presenting their son as 'the problem'. He certainly had a problem with anger and violence, but he rightly protested that he was not 'the problem'. 'My mother is even more violent than I am,' he said, without much hope that he would be heard. What could not be acknowledged in the family was the mother's violent and out-of-control anger. The father wanted peace at any price, was frightened of conflict and of his wife's anger being unleashed at him. The mother stopped coming and so counselling ended when it became apparent that what needed to be looked at were the dynamics of anger within the family, particularly the violent interaction between mother and son – the result of the anger she could not express to her husband.

Since women's anger is such a frightening phenomenon that others cannot bear to see it and acknowledge it, it cannot be surprising that the individual woman will deny, avoid, disown and suppress her own anger. Those parts of ourselves which we cannot acknowledge take on a power and ferocity out of all proportion to their origin. They erupt, and when they erupt they feel and are totally out of our control.

If we agree with Winnicott and Freud that anger derives from the aggressive impulse and that the aggressive impulse is an essential and functional part of our psychological make-up – without it we could not distinguish self from other, or reach out and grapple and achieve in the world – then why are women so frightened of their own anger and others of women's anger? What is so disturbing about women's anger?

The answer is intimately connected with our socialisation. Traditional polarised images of women contrast the good wife and mother with her erotic counterpart, the 'loose', sexually provocative, aroused and arousing woman. No need to discuss which image has been held in highest esteem in our culture, and yet both are essential to womanhood. Space has been widening for the 'career' women of our time. Such women move and advance within the well-defined structures already existing within our society. They have the capacity to outdo men at their own game, but are expected to neglect the possibility of developing new and more hopeful structures for human interaction. There is very little space or goodwill for the woman who feels uncomfortable with the role/s allowed her and who agitates for social change.

Feminists today, like their suffragette sisters of yesterday, find themselves scorned and reviled. It is the anger behind their actions and demonstrations which alienates people, not just their ideas. It is the outraged anger behind feminist demands for an end to sexual discrimination, sexual harassment and the right to walk the streets at night which is threatening. Women's anger expressed potently in action, that is what is at the root of men's complaints about feminists.

Yet anger is optimistic: it reflects the presence of hope whereas despair reflects its absence. Anger energises. Witness a mother trying to retrieve her young from a predator, or the accounts of Bowlby in his study of maternal deprivation describing the young child separated from the mother reacting first with anger and rage in an attempt to get her back and then sinking into despair (and ultimately apathy and detachment) when hope for her return fades.[5] The anger of feminists is fed by their hope that the situation of women can be improved, and provides the raw energy to back that hope with action.

When anger is too frightening for a woman to experience, she can use food to cut herself off from it. She does not feel the bad or upsetting feelings which she stuffs down her throat and numbs with food. An extreme example of this was a young woman who came to me with a severe compulsive-eating pattern she had had since early adolescence, bingeing to obesity followed by dieting to gauntness. Her recollection was of being overweight as a child and young girl. Her relationship to herself and to her body was full of loathing and recrimination. Curiously, however, she felt no anger whatsoever towards her mother, who was a drug addict. Her childhood had been a misery: the mother had been unable to care properly for her daughter or to prevent the sexual advances of one of her lovers to her child. As is not infrequently the case in severe childhood deprivation, the child blames herself for not being good enough to deserve the mother's goodness or love. In this instance, my client kept herself aloof from her contemporaries and had no access to her angry feelings – except in relationship to herself and her eating. Her eating was out of control. Later she discovered that she feared her anger would be murderously out of control if she let herself feel it.

In sessions, my client relived her childhood experiences of having to cope day in and day out with chaos and unreliability – the nightmare of a drug-addict mother. She didn't know her father, as he had left her mother when my client was two years old. Her mother might, for instance, drop her at a friend's house and forget to collect her, or she might come home from school and find the door barred from the inside with her mother too zonked to be able to respond to her pleas to be let in. Meals were catch as catch can. The one bright spot was her warm relationship with her mother's sister, who lived nearby and loved her and encouraged her to make something of herself.

The compulsive eater comes to the counsellor saying, 'I have a terrible problem with my eating and my weight. If you can only help me to get over it, then everything in my life will fall into place.' Paradoxically, the first steps towards insight begin when the client realises that her compulsive eating is itself a solution to a problem. The therapeutic task is then to uncover the underlying problem and look for other ways of resolving it.[6] By encouraging my client to take on the role of Sherlock Holmes and assisting as Watson, we can together track the evidence and clues of her inner world which are inevitably expressed in her actions in the world and in our relationship. We seek the source of the problem to which her compulsive eating is but one (and a very unhappy) solution. It must not be forgotten that this solution was once a very imaginative and creative one, reached at an early age when the younger person did not have the many options of an adult. My client's impotent rage and fury towards her mother led to an intolerable conflict in childhood – however awful her mother was, she was all the child had, and needed to be preserved in the interests of her survival. She also, of course, loved her mother. My client's early and creative resolution of this desperate and horrible conflict was to find a safe haven, which was with no bad feelings towards her mother. Her own bad feelings could be safely contained in her disgust for her body and its relationship towards food.

Any solution which runs away from the problem is an imperfect solution. The denial of one's bad feelings may help in the short-term, but in the long-term it is a disaster. Although my client worked with others she lived alone in a bed-sit and had virtually no friends. In running away from her angry feelings, she had lost touch with other feelings, including her loneliness. She needed to rediscover a language for feelings, a way of reconnecting herself to her own feelings. I could sense within her a very angry, hurt and violent little girl who was never allowed a voice. My client was terrified of her 'little girl'.[7] Together we worked to provide a safe framework for her 'little girl' to merge into consciousness with her adult self – an example would be to feel her anger but not to do anything about it such as express it to others. Then she could safely bring it to the counselling session to work on it with me. She sensed rightly, as I was careful to reassure her, that letting her angry 'little girl' out too quickly and without the consent, maturity and awareness of her adult self, could be extremely dangerous. Paradoxically, the more she was able to experience her angry, bad feelings, the less she needed to act out her sense of being out of control through eating. As her other problems emerged, her obsession with food diminished.

A woman who feels out of control around her anger cannot reach her angry feelings, just like a woman who feels out of control around food cannot reach her body signals of hunger or fullness. Susie Orbach says in *Fat is a Feminist Issue* that the unconscious motivation for weight gain in many women is a flight from anger; the woman's fat is saying what she cannot say herself, an angry 'fuck you'.[8] A woman cannot take responsibility for anger which she experiences as out of control. It is described as 'something comes over me': an internal feeling becomes an alien thing which takes her over. She will quite rightly be fearful of her anger and the havoc it brings into her life. In flight from her anger, a woman denies herself access to its power and vitality. Ironically, the more a woman attempts to cut herself off from her anger, the more firmly is she bound in its grip.

I recently worked with a woman in her mid-thirties who described herself as having grown so fat that when she walked down the street with her mother in her town of origin, old friends and school-mates no longer recognised her. Worse, they would stare with disbelief upon recognising her. As a teenager she had been slim, attractive and popular, and she grieved for her lost teenage beauty. Otherwise she described her life in rosy terms: she had two children of 8 and 12 years, a husband who was a good provider, a nice house, mod-cons. 'Nothing to complain about,' she said. 'I have more than most.'

She described herself as always eating; she just couldn't stop eating. Her eating, she felt, was simply greed. When I asked her if she recognised her hunger and ate when she was hungry, she looked puzzled. She wasn't sure she really knew what it felt like to be hungry. Since hunger was not a factor, I asked what other feelings were perhaps being satisfied by her eating. She said she had noticed that she ate when she felt bored. She often felt fed up with life, although she was quick to add that she had no reason to feel that way.

It was noticeable that this woman did not feel entitled to her feelings, particularly her bad feelings. Her life, her home, her family were well matched to the cultural ideal – nice home, kids, faithful and providing husband – so what could possibly be wrong? Why was she actively engaged in eating when she wasn't hungry, in making herself feel huge and ugly and grotesque? Her world according to some external model was fine, therefore she could not allow herself to acknowledge that she, as a unique individual, felt things were not all right.

During the process of counselling she explored her boredom. In the early years of her marriage, her husband was attentive; the children came early and she was very busy. She liked being occupied. She particularly liked mental stimulation – ideas, books and conversation, interests which her husband did not share or seem to understand. Secretly, she thought he was not her intellectual equal. Ironically, as time went by and his business expanded, he spent less and less time at home, less time with her. As this meant improved financial provision, he could not hear her wish to spend more time with him. Her husband had traditional views about marriage and wanted her to stay at home and look after the children and the house; he would provide. A good husband was a good provider. Now that the children were in school, she wanted to get a part-time job, but he wouldn't hear of it. Nor would he countenance child-minders so that she could take night courses. A woman's place was in the home.

One homework assignment was to eat when she was hungry and stop when she was full. She returned saying that she had really felt hungry for toast and marmalade in the morning and had had a thick slice which she very much enjoyed. With that and a cup of tea she noticed that her hunger was satisfied. She had felt physically full.

Then she watched herself get up and cut two more generous slices of bread, toast them, spread them with marmalade and eat them, knowing that she was not hungry but unable to stop herself. She couldn't connect this eating with anything out of the ordinary or with any particular feeling. She felt all right. Nothing unusual had happened that morning or the day before. It was baffling, particularly as it happened over and over again.

Breakfast was a time shared with her husband and children. I suggested she give her fat a voice and let it speak to her husband. All hell broke loose! Her husband hated, loathed her fat. Her fat was furious with her husband. Her fat said, 'You can't control me like you do, Annie (her name). I don't have to be nice to you. I can make you suffer the way you make me suffer. I stop you getting your sexual needs satisfied, just the way you don't let me get my needs satisfied.' Annie realised and re-experienced as she was doing this Gestalt exercise how much she enjoyed eating those extra pieces of toast, thick with butter and marmalade, with her husband watching. She would eat them slowly and relish seeing him squirm. Her only power to express her anger lay in her eating, particularly at breakfast because he was with her then.

Annie's fat was her ally. It was holding her anger which she couldn't allow herself to feel, anger to which she was not entitled. Her fat expressed her anger towards her husband who wouldn't let her work or study and who was also not available to her as a companion. This unconscious anger had to be raised to the surface before Annie could begin to work on her real problem: her anger that her needs weren't being met. Then she could work on finding other solutions to her problem, such as using her capacity to confront or negotiate with her husband to get those needs met. Even more fundamental, she had to feel entitled to her needs in the first place. As long as Annie's fat was the only way she could express her angry feelings – and paradoxically hide them from herself – she could not afford to give it up or lose it. Her fat served too important a function.

A compulsive eater in flight from her anger will not actually know that she is angry. Hand in hand with noshing or bingeing, she may project her anger in a way which produces anger in others and at the same time proves that she is helpless, unable to cope or out of control. By projecting her anger, a woman can hide it from herself. She need not deal with her fears about what her anger will do to others or how they might retaliate. Instead she often feels the slighted victim of others' wrath and exasperation. Most important, she never has a chance to deal with the real issues underlying her anger; it is unowned and impotent and, like a boomerang, turned back upon herself.

I counselled a young woman, a single parent, who brought as part of her eating problem a pattern whereby friends – in this instance her flatmates – were always getting angry with her for no reason. She, in return, felt persecuted and unloved, and would eat uncontrollably to avoid those unhappy feelings. We explored carefully situation after situation in which this pattern of events unfolded. The current situation in her shared house had reached boiling-point. Her flatmates were furious with her and she feared that they would pressure her to leave, despite the fact that she had put a lot of effort, time and money into the house, and that she liked living there really. In considering what had led up to this situation, she said she felt that as the only single parent in the house she had a lot on her plate. She felt that she did too much housework and that the others did not pull their weight, that she was carrying far too much of the load.

Instead of voicing her growing irritation at house-meetings, she would either not bother to go or, if she went, turn up very late, leaving herself no time to raise the crucial issues. She was genuinely

not aware of her anger expressed through her actions – being absent, coming late – and only became aware of it as she allowed herself to perceive that her actions contained an angry message, unclear to herself, but evident to others. What exactly the problem was no one could decode and so it could not be worked on.

This situation left everyone (including my client) feeling ill-used and taken advantage of, thoroughly pissed off and impotent, and this was the underlying problem. Potent anger can be used to deal with and resolve a problem; impotent anger creates a kind of chaos in which everyone feels bad and the central issues, e.g. the distribution of work and responsibility in a communal housing arrangement are not tackled. In this instance my client was asked to leave. The situation had gone too far to be retrieved. My client's eating escalated. She described herself as feeling hopeless, helpless and out of control. What she could not allow herself to feel was her anger.

This pattern was manifested in our relationship too. I consider this, in a counselling situation, the proof of the pudding. I cannot be with my client in her interaction with others, nor would this be appropriate. I can glimpse the world through her eyes. I can help focus on the bits that do not fit – inner conflicts which are manifested through body language or jarring images. Equally important, I must remain awake and alive to the feelings which are kindled in me in the reality of our relationship.

In this instance, as my client grew in size, she began to miss appointments and forget to pay for sessions. She discovered that her absences and making me wait for money had several messages. One was that I couldn't really help. I hadn't made her fat disappear and that was the reason she was coming to see me, wasn't it? Once her anger was out in the open, she could work on her fantasies about the counselling relationship: I, like a good fairy, was to wave my magic wand and make things better.

Her anger with me for not making things better led to a deeper understanding of her relationship with her mother. Her mother had also been a single parent, a country girl who had got 'into trouble' and then devoted herself to rearing her child. She felt that her mother needed her to remain her chubby little girl in order to feel strong and needed. Ironically, her mother appeared strong to others, but my client sensed something fragile beneath her mother's strength, and feared that her mother could not withstand or survive her anger. She desperately needed her mother and wanted her love. The price for that love was to be unable to cope or to grow up. Her fat said to her mother, 'Look, I am still your baby. I still need you.' My client was faced with an unbearable conflict: she was convinced that being the strong, capable woman that she was made her inherently unlovable, and she was unable to express her rage and her fury openly to those who she felt loved her only when she was weak, because then she would lose their love which she so badly needed.

It is hard to see in the intelligent, charming woman my client was, the hungry, needy little girl behaving in the only way she knows how to secure some love. Irritating and provocative though her actions were, it became clear that my client was treating me as she did her mother (and, of course, others to whom she became close emotionally). By showing me she couldn't cope financially, time-wise or food-wise, she was actually showing me her needy love and asking for mine. My growing. irritation with her behaviour was exactly what she had described happening with her flatmates. Denied access to the creative potential of her own anger, she unconsciously wound others up and became the target of their anger. The hidden message had been decoded. I very gently fed back to her my perceptions, and she slowly but steadily reclaimed her anger and her enormous capacity to cope. Her relationships with others improved. Suddenly, remarkably, she discovered her hunger and not long afterwards her *fullness* – the feeling of being full up. She no longer needed her fat. Her body grew firmer and she felt more energetic. When she had felt persecuted and unable to cope, she had looked dishevelled and unloved. Now she began to let herself look attractive and be attractive. She even gave herself permission to have some fun, including having more time for herself and for her child too.

The mother–daughter relationship is often complex and difficult. The root to this problem lies with the many forces in our culture which subtly undermine women's sense of inner worth and self-confidence. Among the most pernicious of these forces are the image-maker's fantasy of desirable womanness, for most of us a never achievable 'ideal' which denies the rich and wonderful variety of our sex.[9] All too often women's painful, unhappy and unbearable feelings about themselves are replayed out unconsciously in the mother–daughter relationship. Unacceptable feelings such as envy, jealousy, competitiveness and hostility can only be expressed covertly.

Although she will not be consciously aware of it, a woman who does not feel separate from her mother may find her fat very useful. Being fat (especially if her mother isn't) enables a woman to feel different and thus separate from her mother. Using her fat she attempts to create a boundary which she does not feel in her inner world. Fat may also express hostility to her mother (particularly if her mother disapproves). The mother may be unconsciously competitive with her daughter, the 'mirror, mirror on the wall' syndrome. The mother, feeling insecure and unworthy herself, may demand that her daughter conform to others' expectations, that her daughter meet or fit some approved image of which slimness, fashion or sexual availability may be a central concern.[10]

Such expectations leave her daughter feeling trapped, wounded and furious. She is trapped because she deeply desires her mother's approval and love, but naturally she wants it to be for herself as the unique individual she is and not to be contingent upon the extent to which she lives out her mother's fantasies of what a daughter ought to be. She is wounded because she is certain that her mother does not like, does not know or perhaps is not even interested in the person she really is. She cannot give up the hope that one day her mother will actually see her and like her as she is, but at the same time is furious with her.

The solution lies in her fat. Her fat says, 'I will not be what you want me to be!' In all other ways she can be compliant and agreeable – all the unpleasant confrontation between her and her mother will centre around her fat. Daughter and mother can collude that if only her fat were to melt everything would be all right. One young woman in a moment of great clarity expressed her dilemma thus: 'If I lose weight, then mother wins!' Here we see one classic no-win situation of the compulsive eater. Change can only occur when the rules of the game are altered. One way of doing that is for the woman to allow her angry, painful and desperate feelings (that she cannot now and will never get from her mother what she always wanted and needed) to surface to be re-experienced and reintegrated in the counselling situation.

The completion of this process will relieve the woman of her unconscious need for her fat. Fat is her military might, no longer necessary once the battle has ended. At this point, however, the client may suddenly and frighteningly realise that she doesn't know what she is, that her psyche has been so long occupied by a struggle not to be engulfed by the mother that it has never tackled the pressing problem of a positive personal identity. (Addressing the truly monumental task of being one's own self, Rabbi Zussya of

Hannipal once said, 'In the coming life they will not ask me "Why were you not Moses?", but "Why were you not Zussya?"')

If the counsellor is a woman, the client may have to struggle to determine whether she is losing weight to please the counsellor or to please herself. It is absolutely imperative that the counsellor be clear about her own investment in the client's size and shape. Using the Rogerian model,[11] I find that to the extent that I can accept and delight in a woman as she is, largely to that extent will she begin to accept and take pleasure in herself. Entering a very new terrain, the client may experience moments of real terror and be unable to resist lashing out at the counsellor with her unacceptable bad, angry and hostile feelings. This is, in fact, a big step forward and a great act of trust in a woman who has never succeeded in expressing her anger to her own mother. The counsellor must both acknowledge the feelings expressed and manage to survive them. If the counsellor can continue in the face of her client's anger to genuinely like, care for and be concerned about her, it facilitates in the woman a growing sense of being real, whole and worthwhile.

Winnicott suggests that early thwarting or retarding of the aggressive impulse in a child will lead to loss of the capacity to love. Before the child sees itself as a separate individual, its aggressive activity is ruthless, without concern for the object of its excited attack. Our connection to the object world (the world of 'not me') is via our love and our hatred. If the loved one (i.e. mother) can survive the child's attack, it helps the child to sort out the fact from the fantasy of her hatred – that others can survive her hatred and she can survive the hatred of others. She can also feel remorse and concern for the other. Moreover, the child can begin to tolerate ambivalence, the uncomfortable truth that we can both like and dislike another, both like and dislike ourselves. My experience is that the compulsive eater has enormous difficulty in tolerating ambivalence.[12] Everything that is wrong in her life, all her bad feelings get deposited on to her fat and her eating, all the good feelings on to the fantasised '*mañana*', when she will be slim and gorgeous and everything will go her way.

A healthy capacity to feel and use her anger speaks for a healthy capacity to distinguish self from other and to protect self from the intrusion of others when the need arises. The compulsive eater symbolically 'stuffs her anger down her throat' with food she neither needs nor wants. She does not feel herself to be a whole and separate person. The boundary of self and other is blurred.

Woman's traditional role as staff, support and servicer of others' needs does not include getting her own needs met. As giver to others at the expense of her own unmet needs, a woman may well resent some of those demands upon her, but she will have no way to protect herself, she cannot say 'no'. Saying 'no' to another may well be saying 'yes' to one's self, and for many women this is a new and frightening experience. Many a compulsive eater will experience her own needs as selfish or greedy, whether those needs are for privacy, time to herself or food.

Anger may be denied because of the discrepancy between what a woman thinks she ought to be or feel and the shame or guilt which may arise when she faces her real feelings. I was told by a woman who was in despair about her eating and her weight that she couldn't practise eating when she was hungry because she had to wait for her husband's unpredictable arrival to prepare and share a meal with him. She had never connected her fat with the fact that she had no permission to eat when she was hungry. Instead she would nosh and nibble away her time until he arrived, denying her hunger and her resentment at having to wait to feed and eat with him. Her awareness was that she was fulfilling her caring and nurturing womanly role.

Lurking behind my client's binges were angry feelings which slowly began to surface. She never thought to ask why and was very surprised to discover her anger (and under that a sense of hurt) that her husband never took her out to dinner any more. He had, indeed, even stopped without explanation taking her out to his firm's yearly dinner-dance shindig which she had looked forward to in the past. She felt this had something to do with her 'no longer being a size 12'. She discovered that she was hungry for her husband's waning tenderness and affection.

She recalled feeling starved of affection and that even her food needs as a child did not come very high on the list. Visions returned of her own mother feeding her father first and best. Next came the children, and when times were hard, her mother would make do picking at the leftovers. My client feared becoming fat and frumpy like her mother, who for all her good efforts was scorned by father and the children as well. Following a punishing cycle of deprivation, my client was deprived of her food when hungry and denied access to her feelings of anger.

The task of working through this problem was slow and difficult. It extended into many areas of her life. Accustomed to feeling unworthy, second-best, even used and abused, she felt too uncomfortable about her anger to risk taking it out of our sessions into the world where it might serve to change her environment for the better. Angry, she did not feel like a 'nice' person. For some time it was easier for her to 'eat her heart out', to feel disgusted by her eating and her fat, than to face her anger and the possibilities of change.

My client had simply no framework of entitlement, no model of womanhood which included getting her own needs met as well as caring for her mate's. Her first big step had been to seek help. The second was to find a way to put her eating needs first. Work on her compulsive eating required her to eat when she was hungry, not when he was hungry. The breakthrough came when she realised with a start that she could eat and her husband could eat too – that there really was enough food to go around. The third big step was to allow herself to be painfully aware of her own difficult feelings, her anger and the hurt that lay beneath it. She realised that she could care about her husband and still be furious with him. This gave her the strength to reach out to her husband in her neediness and to confront him with her anger and her sadness.

Compulsive eaters share a very fuzzy sense of their own boundaries, both in terms of body-size and the separation of self and other. 'Yes' and 'no' lie very much on the divide between self and other. The compulsive eater often projects her anger, her fear of retaliation or her sense of vulnerablility on to others in a fantasy (never put to the test) of what their reaction might be if she were to say 'no'. Often the inability to say 'no' forces a woman unconsciously to push others away. She feels unable to take responsibility for looking after and protecting her person, her property or her time. In the extreme, this can lead to increasing isolation and loneliness. Naturally, the compulsive eater will blame her fat for this dilemma. How odd that never once have I heard a woman thank her fat for the good service it performs, as bodyguard, shield and protector from others. With surprising regularity, a woman's fat tells her in the 'Fat/Thin Fantasy' how it helps her to say 'no' in a host of difficult social situations which frighten her, anger her or leave her feeling vulnerable and exposed.[13]

A woman who says 'yes' to requests when she really means 'no', whose own most basic needs for privacy, time or space go unheeded, will feel taken advantage of by others. Her compulsive eating will partially numb her bad feelings, but compulsive eating is not a total anaesthetic. Anger sat on in this way tends to be explosive. It will erupt, often at some minor incident such as a child spilling milk or at a thoughtless remark by a friend or lover. Denying her own needs and her consequent rage at not having those needs met, the woman surveys the resulting chaos in her relationships, completely baffled and often horrified at the consequences of her volcanic temper. The woman genuinely doesn't know what comes over her, and nor does anyone else! Such anger is clearly impotent. It never reaches its target. Like a boomerang, it is thrown out with great force and returns to batter the woman who threw it. The compulsive eater's low sense of self-worth is confirmed. She is out of control of her eating and her rage, out of touch with her hunger and her anger.

It is interesting to note that it has long been fashionable and feminine for women to be out of control. The notion that a woman needs a mate who is bigger, stronger, smarter – a real man who will keep her reigned in and hold the little flibbertigibbet to a sensible course of action – is not totally unrelated to the diet sheet. The diet sheet offers an external control or formula with no regard to the woman's bodily needs and inner regulators, her hunger and her fullness. Feminism has made inroads on this sexual caricature, but the dumb blonde, for example, is in no way a thing of the past. How many women affect a child-like lisp or manner in order to hide what is felt to be unacceptable, a strong, intelligent, determined and coherent personality?

The dilemma of the compulsive eater is that she is unable to own, discover or to take responsibility for her own anger. Whether her anger reflects difficulty in separating from people she is emotionally attached to, a need to be out of control, a lack of boundaries, or is used as a defence against vulnerability, her anger will inevitably be impotent. Impotent anger is destructive. It misses its target. Impotent anger is not available to its owner as part of her emotional equipment as a self-determining, responsible adult in relationship to others.

Potent anger is aggressive energy channelled into an effort to make something right which can be made right, e.g. in protest against injustice, in self-defence, in negotiating one's needs. Impotent anger is all too often energy channelled into an effort to make something right which can never be made right. It is a symptom of a deeper conflict of which the woman is not consciously aware, which must surface if it is to be resolved. Impotent anger is not based in present time. It contains within it a coded message. In order to decipher this message, we must track it to its source.

The first stage in building a bridge from impotent to potent anger

for the compulsive eater is to uncover the hidden link between her
eating pattern and her anger. The client is encouraged to watch her
repetitive pattern emerge. One significant difference between
impotent and potent anger is that the former is not experienced as a
flexible tool available when required; rather, it has a repetitive,
almost predictable pattern which the woman can see but whose
significance she cannot understand. It is important to stress, 'watch
the repetitive pattern emerge', and not to try to change it at this
stage. The second stage is to track the repetitive pattern back in
time to her earliest family experiences with anger. We consider how
her parents expressed (or didn't express) anger towards each other,
towards her and towards other siblings. We also look at her
response to their anger and theirs to hers. The third stage is to
uncover the angry but coded message held in her fat in order to
permit her to re-experience the painful conflict which has long been
avoided. The hidden message, e.g. the woman whose fat said to her
mother, 'I will not be what you want me to be,' provides the clue to
how a woman's impotent anger stored in her fat is serving her.

Once a woman is aware of how her eating masks anger and of the
angry statement contained in her fat, she stands on the threshold of
change. She may now allow herself to re-experience terribly painful
and angry feelings and grieve for early losses, so that she can begin
to live more fully in present time. Metaphorically speaking, many
women are starving but they cannot eat and enjoy the feast that lies
before them in present time because they are so hungry for the food
they didn't get as children. Now a woman may experiment with and
learn new and more functional ways of expressing her anger than
simply to numb it, blast it or stuff it down her throat. Awareness
brings choice, but we must remember that change is enormously
difficult. A woman needs both time and tremendous support at this
stage in the counselling process to integrate and consolidate her new
concept of self and her inner processes, and to find ways of taking
her anger with her creatively into the world.

Notes

1. I have used the concept of aggression being rooted in activity
   and the idea of the 'me' and the 'not me' developed by D. W.
   Winnicott, child psychoanalyst, in his paper 'Aggression in
   Relation to Emotional Development (1950–55)', *Through
   Paediatrics to Psycho-Analysis,* The Hogarth Press, London,
   1975. For further reading on the connection between aggression

and the capacity to love see note 12 below.

2. *Webster's Third New International Dictionary* (Unabridged) part definition:

> 'anger' (derives from the Old Norse *'angr'* meaning grief or sorrow) as 'extreme displeasure'; 'aggression' (derived from Latin root *'ag gradi'*, *'ag'* meaning assimilate, and *'gradi'* walk or step) as healthy self-assertiveness, or a drive to accomplishment or to mastery, esp. of skills.

3. I recommend Robin Skynner and John Cleese's *Families and How to Survive Them*, Methuen, London, 1983, for an interesting statement on the usefulness of our emotions and particularly of the emotion called anger.

4. Orbach, S., *Fat is a Feminist Issue*, Paddington Press, New York and London, 1978.

5. Bowlby, J., *The Making and Breaking of Affectional Bonds*, Tavistock Publications, London, 1979.

6. Marilyn Lawrence says the same thing about anorexia in *The Anorexic Experience*, The Women's Press, London, 1984, p. 21.

7. This concept of the 'little girl' I owe to Luise Eichenbaum and Susie Orbach's *Outside In – Inside out: Women's Psychology: A Feminist Psychoanalytic Approach*, Penguin, Harmondsworth, 1982. 'Inside each mother lives a hungry, needy, deprived and angry little girl' (p. 38). As women, we learn from our mothers (and unconsciously teach our daughters) to split off our wants and needs, to always be there for others whilst our own needs are unmet. Our 'little girl' is the needy, demanding, banished bit of ourselves which must never be heard or satisfied.

8. Orbach, S., *op. cit.,*pp. 56–7.

9. The media image of the 'ideal woman' I found well presented in: Kim Chernin's *Womansize: The Tyranny of Slenderness*, Harper & Row, New York, 1981; The Women's Press, London, 1983; and Rosalind Coward's *Female Desire* Paladin, London, 1984.

10. I should like to recommend Chapters 1 and 2 of Luise Eichenbaum and Susie Orbach's *Outside In – Inside Out*.

11. For a fuller discussion of the counsellor's role as facilitator, see Rogers, C.R., *On Becoming a Person*, Constable, London, 1967, Chapters 2 and 3, pp. 31–59.

12. These ideas are presented in two of D.W. Winnicott's papers: 'The Development of the Capacity for Concern' (1963) and

'Psycho-analysis and the Sense of Guilt' (1958), in *The Maturational Process and the Facilitating Environment*, The Hogarth Press, London, 1965.
13. Orbach, S., *op. cit.*, pp. 139–40.

3
Boundaries: One-Way Mirror to the Self
Mira Dana

In this chapter I would like to discuss the concept of boundaries and the expression of the self in women who have eating problems – anorexia, bulimia and compulsive eating. I will use the idea of 'mirroring' as a developmental process which plays a part in the acquisition of a sense of self and of boundaries in early life. I will relate this to the important role the actual mirror plays in women's lives. I will try to explain how a woman gets to a point where it is only through other people's view of herself, and what other people want and need of her, that she can see herself and her own needs. This is the one-way mirror.

The concept of boundaries is abstract and difficult to grasp. I would like first to clarify it and then to relate it to women with eating problems. It relates both at the level of food and eating and at the level of body-image and body-size.

Food and eating

Boundaries can refer to a woman's relationship to food and eating. It can include the knowledge of what to eat, when and how much. It implies the 'self' and is related to internal control.

Body-image and body-size

A woman's body can be seen as a boundary. Women make statements with their bodies. Being a certain body-size means something very important in a woman's inner world. It expresses for her messages she is unable to express through words. I will discuss some of the different messages it delivers and expresses in indirect ways for women with different eating and body-size problems.

This chapter may appear unduly categorical. This is because I have imposed clear-cut categories on a reality which is unclear, uncategorical and intermingled. Even though I know very well that compulsive eaters are not necessarily overweight and bulimic women are in some instances very fat or very thin, for the sake of theory and comparison (not the complex reality) I have imposed the 'majority' on the rest. Thus I relate to compulsive eaters as overweight, bulimics as 'ordinary' (neither particularly over- or underweight) and anorexics as very thin. I am very much aware of the ways in which these weight categories control women. I use them here simply as a convenient shorthand.

The two levels of eating and body-size which I have mentioned are closely linked. Having boundaries is about knowing what one's body needs, what is good and pleasurable and what is not liked or unpleasant. It is also about finding ways to get and take in the good, nourishing and pleasurable as well as rejecting the unpleasant and disliked. Both of these aspects of boundaries are obviously very relevant to eating problems and taking in nourishment or not taking it in.

A metaphor may be useful in understanding the concept of boundaries. A boundary is the line around the person which defines her inside and outside and differentiates between them. If we look at it as a garden where the person lives with her feelings, thoughts, emotions, desires and needs, we can imagine a fence round the garden. Some people will have wide gaps in their fence, letting anyone in and anything out without questioning, 'Do I want this specific person/event/experience to come in at this moment?' Others will have their fence tightly surrounding them so that there is no room even for themselves to move about in. They will say a rigid 'no' to any experience, and any interaction feels like an intrusion, an imposition, because the space is so tight. Others again will leave space enough for themselves to walk around in, have an opening wide enough for people to come in, but only under certain circumstances. We all have different boundaries and ways of using them.

If we take this idea further and look at the relationships between people and our relations to ourselves, we can see the implications of the ways in which we use time and space, especially the ways in which we allow other people to enter our space and time. Take the example of home. Some of us keep an 'open house'; friends are always dropping in without notice. Perhaps we are reading a book when the doorbell rings. We cannot say 'I'm busy', no matter who is at the door. We know we would rather read than talk to the visitor, but we cannot say so. Sometimes it is difficult even to acknowledge to ourselves what we would prefer to do. Others of us are totally preoccupied with our families, spending all our time in activities related to them. We send the children to school, clean and cook and then, when our husband returns from work, we feel we need to look fresh and feel lively as though we have not worked all day. In short, we have no time at all for ourselves. No time to read, write, think or do anything for ourselves. We don't even feel we need or deserve any time. So when we do have free time we don't know what to do with it and even on occasion feel guilty about having it.

The concept of boundaries is related to our knowledge of what feels good, what we want, need or like, and our ability to say 'yes' or 'no' to things. This knowledge and ability obviously changes from person to person, according to the kind of relationship we have with them, the level of intimacy and familiarity; it is a flexible thing.

As women, especially as mothers (we are all socialised into roles as potential mothers), most of our time and space is devoted to other people and structured by events which stem from caring for other people. If we take, for example, a mother in a family, she will get up in time to get the children off to school and her time during the day will be arranged around not only their activities, but also those of her husband. Her time and space are *externally* controlled and structured. She doesn't feel that there is a boundary round her space which can exclude her family. She will actually feel guilty if she does take time for herself.

The psychoanalyst D. W. Winnicott offers us a theoretical account of these ideas about boundaries.[1] In defining boundaries, he says that we can only begin to talk about self-control or internal boundaries when we have a sense of 'I' and 'me' and what he calls 'an integrated self', which makes sense of the terms 'inner reality' (me) and 'shared reality' (us, we). The *fundamental boundary* is that which separates the 'me' from the 'not me'; it corresponds to the skin of the body. The *fundamental* space is the place within this boundary, inside the body, where the self and the inner psychic reality begin to be and grow to become mature.

Winnicott claims that it is only when we establish a sense of self that we can draw on the understanding of a boundary differentiating between the 'me' and the 'not me'. This means that there is a boundary which encompasses a space, a self, which can fluctuate according to the events, people and interactions the person engages in. Others, like Fritz Perls,[2] will claim that only when and where the self meets the 'foreign' does the ego come into existence, start to function and determine the boundary between the personal and the impersonal. The boundary is the point of contact between them. The difference seems to be that Winnicott believes that the self exists and develops and that the baby organises around it, both according to its own level of development and to the events and people with which it comes into contact. Perls, on the other hand, claims that it is only through contact with an 'other' that the ego and the boundaries are defined. Winnicott goes on with his description of how the sense of 'self' and boundaries is slowly developed; it is a process of maturation. To begin with, the baby does not feel herself to be separate from the environment. There is no difference between the 'me' and the 'not me'. The mother in particular is merged with the baby. Her actions, heartbeat, breath and warmth are felt as no different from the baby's. Next, there are moments of 'integration' in which the baby relates to specific objects which are not yet separated out from the 'me'. The first 'I am' moment, when the baby recognises her separateness, contains an attack and carries aggressive feelings towards the mother. It is something like 'I love you, I eat you'. This brings up a great deal of anxiety, because if the baby consumes the mother, she will lose her. Thus, at this stage, love is accompanied by the fantasy of eating up or consuming the object of love, the mother, and the beginning of integration involves both the recognition of this attack and the consequent anxiety about losing the mother.

These two points are very relevant to our understanding of women who later develop eating problems. It is as though through eating actual food women are trying to consume the loved object, the mother, to take in her care. Overeating is therefore an attempt to satisfy a need and a longing for mother's care which should have been satisfied in the earliest stages of life.

Eating food becomes a means to avoid experiencing the anxiety that accompanies the wish to consume the loved object and the fear of the consequences (destroying the mother) as well as the anxiety about losing the object (being abandoned by the mother and consequently being destroyed oneself).

According to Winnicott, if development continues in a 'healthy' way, 'As the "me" becomes separated from the "not me", the mother's care becomes internalised and independence is possible.'

In the case of women with eating problems, we often see instances where this process did not happen in a straightforward way.

The reason for this is to be found within the mother/daughter relationship. If we look at this relationship we can see that the situation for women is much more complicated than the already complex situation described above.

These complications are caused in part by the over-identification of the mother with her baby daughter. With a son, because he is different from her, the mother is more likely to understand that she will have to get to know him, to find out who he is and what he wants and needs. With a girl who is 'the same' as her, she assumes she knows what the baby wants, needs and likes because of their similarity. The result is that the little girl does not have a sense of having her own real needs met by her mother.

From Eichenbaum and Orbach's description in *Outside In – Inside Out*,[3] we learn that the experience of the initial relating with her mother means that the girl is left with feelings of deprivation, unworthiness and rejection. Attempts at separation and individuation are frightening; the mother is still the focal point. The mother's own experience is of not having her needs met. She anticipates that her daughter will suffer the same fate and, unconsciously, she teaches her daughter not to expect too much. She is severely inhibited in her ability to meet the daughter's real needs. Because of this, the 'needy little girl' part of the daughter's ego has to be split off. It is not attended to and continues to be deprived of the nourishment and contact that it needs for maturation. As a consequence, the boundary that should have been constructed between the woman and the outside world, between the 'me' and the 'not me', is constructed internally instead, between herself and her needy, dependent, weak part.

These are in fact false boundaries. They come not from an integrated ego structure but rather from separating one part of herself from another part and keeping the little girl inside shut away from the outside world. This part then becomes unacceptable to her: bad, unacknowledged, hidden. This creates a strange and often very painful interplay between the woman and the people she relates with. She may invest a lot of energy in disowning a part of herself, making it a 'not me', and at the same time she may be confused about what is 'me'. It is almost as if she is open to the outside and closed off somewhere inside. Again, in a symbolic way, the energy that is supposed to be put into creating a differentiating line between 'me' and 'not me' is put instead into the internal differentiation between herself and that part of her which cannot be acknowledged.

She will be able to 'know' what other people want, but not what she herself wants. She will give to other people what she dares not experience as needing or wanting herself. She will let people and experiences in without any notion of what is good for *her* but rather according to what she imagines they would like or want. She will take care of others in the way she would have liked to have been cared for herself. In short, she says 'no' to herself and, more often than not, 'yes' to other people.

Women with eating problems are all directly saying 'no' to that needy part of themselves, but they deal with the consequences of this in different ways, ways which can be understood through their eating patterns and body-size. The anorexic woman is saying 'no' to her neediness and the 'no' becomes an expression of her 'self' . Her boundary is very tightly closed, her body is very small. The compulsive eater will also say 'no', but will try indirectly to feed herself with excessive amounts of food. The bulimic is saying 'no', but she has a sense of something missing. She will express her ambivalence through overeating and, immediately afterwards, rejecting the food. When faced with the issue of her own needs, she will say, 'yes . . . but . . .', both to food and to people.

As well as a part of her being 'split off', the daughter's sense of herself is fused with her sense of her mother. She does not know who she is; she is confused as to where she begins and her mother ends. She is unable to separate herself from her mother as there still exists the hope that one day that promised nourishment and care will become available to her.

I have made the connection between the concept of boundaries and that of mirroring in order to lead me to a description of woman's actual relationship with her mirror. One of the ways in which a baby learns who she is, what her identity, wants and needs are, is through the reflection of the mother. Our development of a sense of self, our understanding of where we begin and end, of what is 'me' and what is 'not me' is related to the way our mothers reflect or mirror us, our actions and expressions.

Obviously this is not the only process operating in the development of a sense of self and boundaries, but I have chosen to explore this one because of the very peculiar relationship we have with our mirrors in later years and the way in which we look for an identity in the mirror which reflects our external body – the boundary of our physical existence.

Winnicott describes this process of mirroring as one of the bases from which the baby learns who she is and how she acquires the ability to communicate and exchange with others.. In the very beginning, when mother and baby are identified together, they look into each other's eyes and the mother reflects back to the baby what she sees. Looking into her mother's eyes, the baby sees herself there. This process has a dual significance. It is both part of the way in which the individual learns about herself and also part of the discovery of meaning in the world of seen things. If the process does not take place, Winnicott says, the individual grows up puzzled about mirrors and what the mirror has to offer. If the mother's face is unresponsive, then the mirror becomes something to be looked at rather than looked into. He quotes one of his patients as saying, 'Wouldn't it be awful if the child looked into the mirror and saw nothing?'

This reflecting back of the self by the mother in the beginning later becomes internalised and part of the self. In later relationships, reflecting back continues to be an important part of the interplay of communication, with the use of eyes, voice and body to express feelings and attitudes.

Alice Miller, in *The Drama of the Gifted Child*,[4] describes the way in which the mother mirrors the child in order to give her a sense of who she is. She also describes the problems which arise when this process goes wrong. This, as I will discuss later, is very relevant to women with eating and body-size problems. She writes, 'Every child has a legitimate need to be noticed, understood, taken seriously and respected by her mother. In the first weeks and months of life, the baby needs to have its mother at its disposal, must be able to use her and be mirrored by her: mother gazes at the baby in her arms, and the baby gazes at her mother's face and finds herself therein, provided that the mother is really looking at the unique, small, helpless being and not projecting her own needs on to the child, nor her own expectations, fears and hopes for the child. In that case the child would not find herself in her mother's face, but rather the mother's own predicaments. This child would remain without a mirror and for the rest of her life would be seeking this mirror in vain.'

For the baby, the mother is supposed to be there to mirror a 'unique, helpless being', and not to project her own needs on to the child. This, however, is sometimes no easy matter. When the mother looks at her girl baby, what she may actually see is an extension of herself; the needy little girl part of herself which she

It says if you do the ironing for 4 hours you can burn off the calories in 2 pieces of chocolate

keeps hidden from herself and others and which therefore causes her a great deal of pain. She may also be unable to look at her girl baby with respect, because of her own awareness that she is part of a society which regards women as second-class. For these reasons, the mother may be unable to mirror her girl baby and provide her with a sense of who she is. The continual searching for a mirror might in consequence be a predominant feature of the child's later life. This searching for a mirror manifests itself at two levels. It is looking for approval and acceptance from other people, looking for other people to mirror her, define her, tell her who she is and create boundaries for her. At the level of the actual mirror, she may continue to try to define herself in terms of her reflection. Her body will become the focus of her search for her identity, both because in our society her body represents her commodity and because it is what is reflected in the actual mirror. Most women with eating problems have a peculiar relationship with their mirrors which is connected to the way they experience their bodies. Anorexic women expecially have a distorted image of their bodies and see themselves as much bigger than they really are. They might spend hours in front of the mirror, trying to see how fat they are, pinching themselves all over to feel that imaginary fat.

For compulsive eaters, their body-image will fluctuate according to both how they feel and how much they eat. After a big meal, suddenly, within half an hour, a woman may feel herself much bigger than she usually perceives herself to be when looking in the mirror. Similarly, if she feels anxious or upset or angry about something which has happened to her, again, when looking in the mirror this may be expressed within her through feeling fat. For example, a woman whose brother visits her after a long period of separation, argues with him and he insults her about an issue which is very close to her heart. She feels very uncomfortable after he leaves. She has been invited to a party and on getting dressed in front of the mirror she feels enormous, huge, fatter than she has experienced herself for a long time. (On the other hand, women who are considered to be very fat will often perceive themselves in a distorted way: as fat, but less than their actual size.) Some women who eat compulsively will spend hours watching themselves in the mirror but only with the intention of finding out whether they are fatter or thinner. There is no other consideration. But many will avoid this agonising experience altogether. They will develop the opposite obsession and avoid mirrors at any cost. Refusing to have full-length mirrors in the house, they will nonetheless hope that one day, when they are thin, they will be able to have the expected affair with their mirror.

Alice Miller[5] suggests that this process will also be experienced internally. The woman will treat her feelings with ridicule and irony and will try to persuade herself that they do not really exist; she will belittle them and either not become aware of them at all or only do so after several days, when they have already passed. She will be forced to look for distractions when she is moved, upset or sad. In most situations she will try to see herself as other people see her, constantly asking herself what impression she is making and how she ought to be reacting or what feelings she ought to have. On the level of eating, food and the obsession with it becomes the distraction from unpleasant feelings. Eating is not in response to an internal demand but rather it is used as a tool to push feelings aside.

Alice Miller continues, 'I have to despise everything in myself that is not wonderful, good and clever. Thus I perpetuate interpsychically the loneliness of childhood: I despise weakness, impotence, uncertainty – in short, the child in myself and in others.'

Because there is such intense energy invested in pushing away these despised qualities, in subduing the needy, dependent, weak child inside, the issues of neediness and dependency become a central focus of her attention. The obsessional preoccupation with how to keep these needs locked away brings about a sense of deprivation, a sense of 'something missing'. The stronger the attempt to push these feelings aside, the stronger the feeling of deprivation and the sense that if she allowed herself even the slightest feeling of neediness, the dam would open up and everyone around her would be overwhelmed by the flood.

Miller writes again about the experiences of childhood: 'There are children who have not been free to experience the very earliest feelings such as discontent, anger, rage, pain, even hunger and, of course, enjoyment of their own bodies. Discontent and anger aroused such uncertainty in their mothers about her role, pain had made her anxious. Her children's enjoyment of their own bodies sometimes aroused her envy, sometimes her shame about "what other people would think". Thus a child under those circumstances may learn very early what she is not allowed to feel lest she runs the risk of losing her mother's love.'

This creates a sense of shame around her body and bodily needs on the one hand, and, on the other hand, an inability to deal with her own most basic feelings in a direct way and feel entitled to them. For example, most women with eating problems deal with their anger indirectly, through their pattern of eating, perhaps eating to stuff down the anger or starving to purge themselves of these troublesome and unpleasant feelings.

Compulsive eating

As Susie Orbach describes in *Fat is a Feminist Issue*,[6] the woman who eats compulsively uses food in a way that indicates she has little internal knowledge of what she wants to eat, when she wants to eat it, where, how much, when to stop and so on. There will be little or no connection between her physical needs, her bodily demands and her food intake. Most of the time she will eat not out of hunger, and actually there are only very rare occasions when she can even detect physical hunger. She will usually eat according to emotional needs, or what is called 'mouth hunger' rather than 'stomach hunger'. She experiences a feeling , a bodily sensation, which is immediately translated into wanting to eat.

On those rare occasions when she does experience stomach hunger, she will not usually stop and ask herself what she would like to eat, what she fancies at this very moment, but rather she will eat whatever is to hand or else what is dictated by her diet sheet or calorie counter.

The initial fusion between her and her mother meant that mother knew best about what daughter wanted to eat, what was good for her, what was healthy, what was tasty. Hence the daughter did not have a chance to experience her own sense of tasty and untasty food, or else she was not allowed to eat according to her own sense of what was good. This means she finds it hard now to determine, recognise, know what she wants to eat at any given moment when physically hungry.

As she is cut off from the part of herself that knows what she wants or needs or desires, she experiences a lack of something, which she tries to satisfy by reaching out for food.

At the level of her body, she uses her fat to express for her statements which she cannot put into words. It serves her as a thick boundary, like a wall that keeps people's demands out and her own needs and feelings in. *Fat is a Feminist Issue* gives a good and elaborate explanation of the ways in which fat serves the compulsive eater as a boundary.

Bulimia

The bulimic woman usually sees herself as having two sides or aspects. One is competent and successful in the world, organised and 'good'. Underneath this, she experiences herself as messy, bad, unacceptable – the part of her which is encapsulated in the bulimia. The part of her self which appears 'normal' is the part she presents to the world. This usually corresponds to her 'normal' appearance: not too fat, not too thin. The other part of herself, the hidden part, is a terrible secret she must not reveal to others. This is represented by the pattern of eating and vomiting. This pattern of eating is a reflection of deeper feelings of having an internal part that is messy, unacceptable and bad. This experience of two parts of herself creates a situation whereby the bulimic woman feels a fraud. She feels that the 'normal' side of her is a façade, it is what she pretends to be in front of other people. If those people knew what she did alone and in secret they would not want to know her, she feels. She believes they would be as disgusted and rejecting of that part of her as she is. Her outside self – her façade – is the good girl who wants to appease everyone, to be attractive, both physically and in her behaviour. Her way of being attractive and liked is by being good, caring, giving – repressing the anger, aggression and other feelings which she considers to be messy and negative. These feelings she attaches to the other, hidden side of herself.

We can think of her façade, the image she presents to the world, as her boundary. This façade has to be a comfortable one, appeasing, giving, never saying no. This means the boundary has to be a very permeable one, otherwise people will not like her. She must be nice and not demand or ask for too much. Her dilemma, however, is that the 'self' is her part inside which is secretive, messy, the bit of her which no one is allowed to get near or even to know of. In this sense, the 'gate' to that area of herself must be tightly closed and very well guarded. Yet her boundaries, as I have said, are very permeable, so at a certain point, what is coming in has to be thrown out, rejected, pushed away. Hence, whatever it is that comes in – be it food, care, attention, ideas – is rejected immediately after it is taken in. For example, if someone says to her, 'I really like you, you are such an amazing person', she listens and thinks, 'Ah, that's nice to hear'. A moment later she thinks, 'She is just saying that. I am sure she doesn't really mean it and she must have some reason for saying it.' 'Yes, maybe that's how it seems on the outside. If only she knew what I'm really like inside, she would be disgusted.' Another way in which this ambivalence might be expressed is through her way of speaking. She might make a statement, then at the end of the sentence, negate it, contradict it or doubt it. One bulimic women I met used to end every sentence with the word 'but' and immediately contradict what she had just said. Again, she is expressing something and rejecting it immediately afterwards.

In terms of food, the bulimic woman does not stop to think what she wants to eat, what kind of food she is hungry for, whether she is hungry at all, how much she should eat. She just consumes huge amounts of food and vomits it out immediately after. She has 'binge food', which is the fattening food she eats when she knows she is going to throw up, and 'good' food, which is the low-calorie food she eats otherwise. There is no attempt on her part to listen to internal cues about eating. She feels she is taken over by some force bigger than herself which draws her to eating and vomiting.

Anorexia

The anorexic woman tries to determine her 'self', her identity, who she is, through saying 'no' to food. This refusal of food symbolises a much larger statement she is making which is the only way she found to say 'no' to what mother represents for her. It is through this 'no' to mother, her food and her own needs that she defines herself. What this means in terms of what I have been discussing up till now is that, for the anorexic woman, the boundary creates the self rather than the other way round. She first says 'no', and that 'no' has to be very firm and rigid, and that creates for her a sense of who she is, even though it is a self that excludes a large part of her – all her needs and her wants. It provides her with an identity which is strong, rigid and secure as long as it keeps within its boundary of refusal. Even though her sense of self is invested in complete self-denial, it gives her a feeling of pride and superiority, of being beyond mundane feelings, messy needs and silly wishes. She can live without. She determines her existence through starvation on all levels, she is above any hunger.

The anorexic woman has totally abolished the needy part of her. She pretends it does not exist; she does not need people, she does not need relationships, she does not need other people to reflect who she is as she hardly wants anything to do with other people. She does not need even food. (Of course, in reality, this is not so, as underneath she is very confused about her identity as well as very desperate for other people's warmth and attention – and constantly preoccupied and obsessed with food too.)

The anorexic woman is the one amongst the three who has the longest and most tortuous affair with her actual mirror. Her mirror is cruel to her. It reflects to her the person she is so intensely trying to hide from herself and from others. It reflects her as a human being, a woman, the one she is forever running away from. She is trying in every way she can to reduce this tormenting figure in the mirror to a size she can cope with, a size that says what she pretends in her head – 'I am a person who needs nothing, who is emaciated.' Yet the figure in the mirror stays the same. As skinny as she may get, her mirror still says to her, 'You are fat', with a cruel smile. Some people claim her mirror is a liar, because it reflects to her a fat woman when in reality she is so skinny. But in some strange way this mirror is the most truthful thing she has, even though she may want to smash it every day anew. It is truthful because it actually reflects to her the internal figure she is viciously trying to kill. In the same symbolic way she tries to reduce her body to skin and bone in order to reduce her inner human self to non-existence, and the mirror refuses to agree with this harsh treatment of a part of her and hence does all it can to bring forth that figure.

In this chapter, I have looked at three categories of eating problems and made some connections with how each of them might relate to the issue of boundaries and expression of the self. I have tried to suggest how each will use the mirror and how this symbolises her eating and body-size problem. In short, most women with eating problems have problems around knowing what they really want and getting it, or even acknowledging what they don't want and rejecting it. This is reflected in the way they use food, which in turn reflects the way they are in the world.

For the compulsive eater, it will be in the way she says 'yes' to all food, even when she is not hungry and even to food she does not particularly want or like. This also holds true for her with people and experiences.

For the bulimic, it will be in the way she says 'yes, but' to all food, taking it all in without any selection and then throwing it out in the same way when it becomes poisonous to her. This is a reflection of the way she behaves with people and experiences too. In our work with bulimic women we have come across women who are very isolated, with no friends and no close relationships, who feel both unwilling and unable to create such relationships. At the other extreme is the bulimic woman who has many friends, many relationships, is much appreciated and well liked. At both of these extremes, the woman feels a sense of isolation and intense loneliness, a feeling of being a fraud and unreal. Even the woman who is at the centre of a network of friends still keeps their bulimia, secret life, apart from all relationships. The sense of isolation may for her be even more intense as the potential is there for her to have open relationships which would make her feel enriched and nourished. And yet the terror of exposing the secret and of being open and vulnerable is too great. This fear is sometimes reflected in her inability to tell anyone about her bulimia, which she is scared will revolt people and make them turn away from her.

For the anorexic it is the rigid 'no' that keeps food, people and needs at bay, away from the reality of her life.

Although the issues I have been discussing are basically theoretical, it may be helpful to summarise briefly the practical implications for working with women who present these problems.

Alice Miller[7] talks about how, in the therapeutic relationship, we must have the function of allowing clients to become aware and be in touch with feelings they have rejected throughout their lives in their attempts to become 'better people'. This means being that demand-less, need-less, body-less person their parents needed them to be. Therapists have to provide the space and the mirror which will reflect the whole person and not just her mind, or the 'good' part of her. By looking at the woman's relationship with her actual mirror, we can begin to see what function she will need us to serve.

The compulsive eater will need to learn to look at herself and see

things other than just how fat or thin she is. She will need to
understand that the 'fat' is a part of herself and not just some
unacceptable entity attached to her. She will need to change the
'heavy' negative connotations which she has relegated to the 'fat'
and to discover how she feels about herself apart from them.

The bulimic woman will need to learn to allow the hidden part of
herself to come more into the open. She has to allow the messy and
unacceptable feelings to be part of her life and not merely confined
to the bulimia. She needs to learn that she does not have to
continuously present an image of perfection which is nothing to do
with real life but rather with some fantasy of what 'good' people are
like.

For the anorexic woman, she needs her mirror to reflect the part
of her which is to do with her body, with the feeling part of herself.
This is the part she tries so desperately to kill inside herself by
saying 'no' to her bodily needs and her needy, dependent feelings.

Notes

1. Davis, M. and Wallbridge, D., *Boundary and Space: An Introduction to the Work of D. W. Winnicott*, Penguin, Harmondsworth, 1981.
2. Perls, F. S., *Ego, Hunger and Aggression*, Vintage, New York, 1969.
3. Eichenbaum, L. and Orbach, S., *Outside In – Inside Out: Women's Psychology: A Feminist Psychoanalytic Approach*, Penguin, Harmondsworth, 1982.
4. Miller, A. *The Drama of the Gifted Child*, Faber and Faber, London, 1979.
5. *ibid*.
6. Orbach, S., *Fat is a Feminist Issue*, Paddington Press, New York and London, 1978.
7. Miller, *op. cit*.

4
Anorexia and the Family*
Gill Edwards

> It turns out that that fly circling in the stuffy room was outside all
> the time – that fly, spray, room, observer, all were tricks played
> upon a more expansive reality, and that the trick player is itself
> *samsara*, the suffering consciousness.[1]

As you read this, thousands and thousands of young women (and
many men) are starving themselves, not out of religious or spiritual
convictions but because they know no other way to cope with life.
Despite their deep distress, and constant, interminable obsession
with food and body-weight, self-denial has become a way of life that
they feel unable to relinquish.

To become anorexic is to create and inhabit a nightmarish world
(like the fly's imaginary room) within which basic human needs
cannot and will not be met – an ascetic prison with ever-narrowing
boundaries. Only the vain hope of discovering a rainbow's end pot
of gold sustains the 'suffering consciousness'. This, the anorexic
world, is what Hilde Bruch[2] aptly termed 'the golden cage'.

If you have locked yourself into the golden cage, my heart goes
out to you in your painful, lonely struggle to find yourself. If, on the
other hand, self-starvation is mysterious and alien to you, I hope
that this chapter will help you to understand the roots of the
experience of being anorexic.

According to a psychological approach, if one has sufficient
information about someone's family background, culture, present
circumstances and way of seeing the world, even apparently bizarre

*This chapter is based on 'The Making of Anorexia', which was published in
Changes, Vol. 1, No. 2, 1983.

behaviour begins to make sense. So how do we 'make sense' of anorexia? What problems does anorexia represent an attempt to resolve? How does a child become potentially anorexic? What is the nature of the 'anorexic family'? And how may anorexia be understood in terms of Western society past and present?

A consensus is gradually forming as to what anorexia is 'really about – at least at the level of the individual, and perhaps her family. To summarise many views, anorexia is now widely understood as a desperate way of coping with the problems involved in becoming a self-respecting, autonomous person.[3]

Anorexia, then, is not an 'illness' which people 'get'. It is a state of being, a lifestyle, a way of coping. It represents an attempt to resolve certain life conflicts. It persists because, despite the enormous distress it causes to the young woman and those around her, it does serve several functions. It gives her a much-needed sense of control and effectiveness; it helps to maintain her fragile self-esteem (since both slimness and self-control are highly valued in our society); it facilitates social withdrawal (since relationships so often revolve around eating and drinking), thus enabling her to sidestep the issues of sexuality and intimacy; and the obsession with food and weight (which is partly a normal, healthy response to starvation) precludes thinking about more important, more difficult issues.

But how does a child grow up to be so lacking in self-respect and autonomy that she can only cope with adolescence by starving herself? Bruch[4] suggests that, in their early years, anorexic girls/women had mothers who were 'too good', who anticipated the child's needs, who used food as a reward or who responded to needs other than hunger by providing food. Thus, the child becomes confused about her bodily sensations and wary of trusting them; she may feel 'controlled' from the outside and later on be unable to make decisions for herself. She does not experience herself as an active participant in her own development, but as a helpless product of her parents and of other social influences – a puppet programmed to please others. This gives her the 'paralysing sense of ineffectiveness' which is so characteristic of anorexia.

Here lies our first clue as to why most anorexics are female: although all children are 'kept in line' by parents and teachers, girls in particular are brought up to be passive and submissive. Boys, on the other hand, are encouraged to be active, independent, assertive, even aggressive. ('Boys will be boys,' goes the old saying!) Those who later become anorexic seem to take this conformity to extremes. The parents of anorexics usually report a happy, trouble-free childhood; their daughter has always been good, helpful and considerate, never loses her temper, has done well at school and has done everything expected of her without complaint or rebellion. (Many parents would, I think, regard such excessive compliance as strange and even unhealthy, but the parents of anorexics seem to regard it as unproblematic.)

The young woman herself has often seen her 'trouble-free childhood' in a different light. Childhood for her has been a constant struggle to 'do the right thing', to guess what others want her to do (and even what they want her to want) and to be the perfect daughter. She has been so intent on pleasing others that she has not only lost contact with her own feelings but feels selfish and guilty at the very thought of considering her own desires.

In this respect, she might be identifying with her own mother. Mara Selvini Palazzoli[5] reports that the mothers in such families *tend* to be full-time housewives who withdrew from the outside world after marriage and 'refuse' to enjoy their spare time. They tend to be submissive, conservative and weight-conscious, and although they might rule in the home, they have low self-esteem. They are in fact 'model wives'. From such mothers, daughters learn a model of womanhood based upon self-sacrifice, submissiveness, dependence and consideration of others before self.

A woman whose life revolves only around her children rather than also around her own activities outside the home is likely to:

1. have difficulty in conceiving of herself as a separate person, or of her children as separate people;
2. expect a great deal of her children, since they are vicariously living her life for her;
3. be overanxious to anticipate and fulfil her children's needs;
4. feel enmeshed with her children's bodies;
5. *not* be autonomous herself.

Clearly, all of these factors could damage her children's *self-esteem* and *sense of autonomy*, and these are the crucial pre-anorexic issues. Girls have the additional problem of modelling themselves on their mothers; if they are taught that other people will be the centre of their lives (the 'wife–mother' role), they will find it difficult to feel self-sufficient and 'centred' in their own bodies.

So far, I have implied that these overprotective, conservative families merely 'produce' anorexia, i.e. are 'anorexogenic'; but some family therapists believe it is more appropriate to call the whole family 'anorexic', although only one member is starving herself. The family therapist Salvador Minuchin[6], in a statistical study of adolescent anorexia, noticed four factors which seemed to characterise the typical 'anorexic family':

1. enmeshment (i.e. the family members are poorly differentiated and 'lost' in the family system, there is great intensity in their interactions and any change in one family member reverberates throughout the family. As Minuchin puts it, there are 'no closed doors' in an anorexic family);
2. overprotectiveness;
3. rigidity (the family is unwilling to change);
4. avoidance of conflict.

These four factors fit in well with a psychosocial model of anorexia. First, to consider enmeshment: a child who grows up in a highly enmeshed family learns to subordinate herself and her autonomy to the needs of the family; her goals will be approval and love rather than knowledge or competence. And since her parents watch her every move, she will develop an obsessional concern for perfection (resulting in low self-esteem) and extreme self-consciousness (making it difficult for her to form relationships outside the family, thus creating increased dependency upon parental approval).

I say 'she' because this way of treating a child – restricting autonomy and identity, emphasising relationships rather than personal competence and achievement – is a typically patriarchal way of treating girls. Hilde Bruch[7] notes that more than two-thirds of her clients come from all-girl families, and one wonders whether these families have become more rigid, overprotective and enmeshed as a *result* of comprising daughters only (in response to sex stereotyping).[8]

But why should an adolescent become anorexic as a way of expressing and coping with her emotional crisis? One clue is to be found in Minuchin's observation that in the enmeshed anorexic family the girl's body does not seem to be her own: it 'seems to belong to the whole family'. (Hilde Bruch too writes of the 'fearful state of not feeling separated . . . from one's parents'.) A refusal to be 'fed' may then become a means of self-assertion, a way of establishing a boundary between self and others; simultaneously it expresses a split between mind and body (since bodily hunger is being ignored) and a lack of true autonomy. Anorexia can therefore be seen as both a *striving* for individual identity and autonomy and an acting-out of enforced *lack* of autonomy and the felt smallness of 'self' within the family. Paradoxically (and anorexia is full of paradoxes), in fighting her enmeshed identity, the girl becomes passive and helpless, and eventually her new identity as a 'sick' person increases her mother's concern and thus her own enmeshment. Her conflicts over autonomy therefore engage her in a typically neurotic 'vicious circle'.

The second characteristic of the anorexic family is said to be overprotectiveness. Therapists have noted that the mother of an anorexic tends to do 'too much' for her child, leaving her with a sense of incompetence and ineffectiveness, two classic components of anorexia. (In the case of one family I have seen, the mother was reluctant to leave her 18-year-old daughter alone for even a couple of hours and made all her phone calls for her. In another case, the mother of a 22-year-old anorexic woman asked me whether she was right to allow her daughter to go on holiday without her! It was naturally difficult for either of these young women, both of whom were isolated at home with their parents, to conceive of themselves as adults.)

Again, overprotectiveness may be related to the family stereotype: girls tend to be treated, almost from birth, as though they were frail, weak and helpless, while boys are expected to be more tough, sturdy and competent. In a strongly patriarchal family, then, girls *will* be enmeshed and overprotected, i.e. given an injunction not to grow up.

The third characteristic of such families, according to Minuchin, is rigidity, i.e. unwillingness to adapt and change. In such families, a teenager may be treated much as most 6-year-olds are treated. Often found in child-centred, conservative families, rigidity not only enforces the status quo but also produces a *fear* of growing up, and encourages infantile forms of self-assertion.

The fourth and final characteristic of anorexic families is said to be avoidance of conflict: any open expression of conflict is trivialised, remains unresolved or is simply proscribed. The family seems to need to preserve the myth that it is a hypernormal 'happy family' within which there is total harmony (except on trivial matters which may safely be ignored). Conflict and self-assertion provide a threat to the stability of the family system; the family, then, is more important than its individual members. In such a family, self-starvation may be seen as a form of 'silent protest', an internalised struggle for individual identity and autonomy.

Again, it is interesting that this family feature might be said to be typical of the patriarchal family. Girls in particular are dissuaded from being angry, assertive or aggressive, all of which might occur if open conflict were permitted. The avoidance of conflict reinforces passivity and makes it difficult to form a clear personal identity, thus creating a crisis during adolescence which may be 'resolved' by turning against the self. Overall, then, Minuchin's 'anorexic family' might represent a microcosm of patriarchal society.[9]

From this viewpoint, anorexia may be seen not so much as the result of pathogenic *families* but as an almost inevitable consequence of the clash between continuing patriarchy and our supposedly 'liberated', egalitarian *society*. In fact, what is perhaps most surprising about anorexia is that so many people in the 'vulnerable' group, educated young women, do *not* become anorexic. After all, adolescence for these young people is a veritable minefield. The

conflicting messages they must be receiving seem both powerful and irresolvable: 'You must be assertive and independent' and also 'You must be passive and feminine'; 'You must work hard for exams and do well' and also 'You mustn't outsmart any man'; 'You must have a career and be a high achiever' and also 'You must be a stay-at-home wife and mother'. What *are* we supposed to become? Nothing is simple for young women today. Once relatively straightforward issues such as having a child are now immensely complex. Who will care for the child? Will you continue to work? Will you work full-time or part-time? If not, when will you return to work? How will you feel about this? What role will your partner play in child care? And so it goes on. What about sexuality? Will you grow up as the 'good girl' who long remains a virgin? Will you act out the new stereotype of the sexually liberated, multi-orgasmic woman? Or will you discover your own unique sexuality? Similar problems arise in choosing a career, applying for jobs, selecting a life partner, negotiating roles with regard to housework and finances, and so on. Men's lives, by contrast, are still *relatively* simple: they still, on the whole, expect to have an uninterrupted career which can be combined, without difficulty, with marriage and a family; they do not grow up with the plethora of contradictory messages with which young women must juggle.

In my view, no one can fully understand anorexia without using a feminist perspective. It is quite possible to explore the psychology of anorexia *without* considering the wider social implications, but to ignore or trivialise the fact that up to 95 per cent of anorexics are female would be to fall into the trap which ensnares so many 'neurotic' women: to locate the source of all their problems within themselves, and thus to seek exclusively intrapersonal change. As Thomas Szasz[10] notes: 'Addiction, obesity, starvation (anorexia nervosa) are political problems, not psychiatric; each condenses and expresses a contest between the individual and some other person or persons in his [sic] environment over the control of the individual's body.' For women, socially identified with their bodies and stereotypically linked with food and the kitchen, this struggle for control is all too naturally expressed via eating disorders.

Many aspects of anorexia take on a new significance when one considers patriarchal role stereotypes. An anorexic young woman is *indirectly* powerful and manipulative via her weakness, helplessness and 'self-destructive' behaviour rather than being powerful via strength and direct commands. She is within the patriarchal stereotype of inert action, like the woman who is supposed to do nothing about her broken-down car other than sit on the bonnet, looking pretty and helpless, so that a knight in shining armour can come to her rescue. In anorexia, the young woman *experiences* herself as powerless and out of control (despite appearances to the contrary). The anorexic side of herself tends to be split off, so that she is caught in an interminable conflict between her desperate desire for food and the strictures of an inner 'ogre' (as one of my clients called it) which directs her towards self-denial,. This is what Marilyn Lawrence calls the 'control paradox'.[11] She is unable to integrate this powerful, controlling part of herself, and thus achieves power and control only in indirect or self-destructive ways. And isn't this what women generally are brought up to do?

Similarly, Luise Eichenbaum and Susie Orbach[12] have elaborated on the difficulties women have in coming to terms with our needs, our dependency and our longings. We are taught early on in life that our role will be to tend to *others*' needs and to subjugate our own. (If there is insufficient food in a family, it is invariably the mother who goes without; it is as if she *matters* less than the rest of the family.) No one responds to *our* needs, takes care of *us* – or not in the way that men are responded to and cared for. As a result, 'A woman's emotional world is strewn with neediness, both her own that she must so often repress, and that of others that she anticipates and responds to.'

The repression and denial of one's own needs is, of course, precisely what occurs in anorexia. (In bulimia, or compulsive eating, these needs occasionally break through and express themselves via a 'binge', provoking much guilt.) Thus we see again that the problems being faced (and also, paradoxically, being avoided) in anorexia are similar to the difficulties which most young women in our society must tackle.

Although there have been several feminist accounts of anorexia,[13] some writers on anorexia have almost ignored the fact that the vast majority of anorexics are female. However, some of these brief mentions *are* quite illuminating: Mara Selvini Palazzoli[14] writes of the 'contradictory roles and expectations made of young women' in today's society, and the 'ridicule and rejection of fat women'; Peter Dally[15] observes that the mothers of anorexics tend to be ambitious for their daughters, in the hope of compensating for their own frustrations; Salvador Minuchin[16] specifically mentions the patriarchal society, the female stereotype of passivity and frailty, and the 'irony' of the increasing prevalence of anorexia in the face of women's dawning emancipation. Several writers, then, link anorexia with high and yet contradictory parental/social expectations.

Hilde Bruch[17] suggests that today's increased *opportunities* for women may be experienced as excessive *demands*. We are all aware of the new 'Superwoman' stereotype: the woman who manages to combine a successful career, family and housework with several evening classes and writing the odd novel! The pre-anorexic youngster, usually from a relatively privileged family background (and/or possessed of unusual talents), grows up with the conflicting pressures to be passive-dependent and all-giving ('feminine') and yet also to be 'special', successful, a high achiever; her only solution to this irreconcilable conflict is to become anorexic. In this way she becomes both passive-dependent *and* assertive-independent; she both stands out as special *and* becomes small and invisible. The asceticism relieves her sense of guilt at being privileged and yet unable to meet the (excessive) demands, and is also an attempt to transcend her own humanity and female-ness by becoming an immortal pre-adolescent. It is such a neat solution, the answer to so many of her problems. Little wonder, then, that she will be reluctant to relinquish the anorexic lifestyle until the nightmarish obsession with food and interminable inner conflict become more than she can bear. Even when that stage has been reached, she must still face and resolve the original conflicts, and gain a self-respecting identity for herself. Until that happens she is likely to undergo a lengthy period of over- and undereating in a continuing endeavour to use food and body-weight to symbolise and resolve her emotional problems.

Anorexia is therefore far from incomprehensible. As long as one pays attention to the *experience* of being anorexic, and to the social context in which it occurs, anorexia may be readily understood as a complex, overdetermined response to the conflicts faced today by an intelligent young woman who was brought up in a traditional, patriarchal family. This perspective seems to explain why anorexia has reached almost epidemic proportions in modern, industrialised societies within the past decade or so.

But what of the more distant roots of anorexia? Did it occur hundreds of years ago, and if not, why not? Anorexia nervosa was first given its present name by Sir William Gull in 1873. However, we do not know how many of the once-numerous cases of 'consumption', 'neurasthenia' and other maladies may have been, in fact, disguised self-starvation. Thus, any theorising is largely speculative.

However, there is good reason to suppose, on theoretical grounds, that anorexia was rare or non-existent as long ago as the Middle Ages, because the structure of society was so different then.[18] Childhood, at that time, did not exist; and neither did the nuclear family as a social phenomenon. Children were seen as small adults and were never particularly close to, or dependent upon, their parents. Special clothes, toys, games and schools for children were not thought of. There was little sexual differentiation until the age of five: both girls and boys, for example, played with dolls. Many children were apprenticed away from home at the age of seven, and girls were often married at the age of ten or twelve (to a much older male). Given that children were afforded autonomy and respect (of a kind) from such an early age, self-starvation in an effort to achieve these goals would have been quite unnecessary.

At that time, since children were so independent from their parents, women too were relatively autonomous. Then the bourgeoisie developed, and with it came the child-centred 'nuclear family', in which mothers were required to supervise and care for their children constantly over many years. It was at that time that women's lives became devoted to catering for others' needs. In addition, children *and* women (our fate as women tends to be closely entwined with that of children) came to be seen as in need of protection; both were now equipped with special, non-functional clothing and were given specific tasks (housework and schoolwork respectively). Women were isolated in the home and children at school. Both were cut off from and seen as having little to offer the 'real world', i.e. men's world.

In this 'new society', children mix so little with adults that they can have only a hazy concept of what adulthood means. Thus adolescence, which does not 'exist' in some cultures, is widely acknowledged to be a turbulent, difficult period. For adolescent young *women*, as we have seen, the problems are greatly multiplied: they move from one oppressed group (children) into another (women). Today, we even have a 'psychology of women' and a 'psychology of children', as though both are different species from the normal human being, who is, apparently, an adult male! This is, sadly, not a joke; on the contrary, it is enshrined in our culture. Research has shown that while stereotypes of 'a normal healthy adult' and 'a normal healthy male' are identical (assertive, independent, rational, etc.) descriptions of 'a normal, healthy female' are quite different (passive, emotional, etc.). As Sheila MacLeod[19] has noted, for many women autonomy (adulthood) and femininity seem irreconcilable states of being. Little wonder, then, that for many young women the prospect of adulthood is confusing, frightening and even overwhelming.

The reason for this historical excursion is to emphasise that anorexia is culturally specific, i.e. it is closely linked with a society's current attitudes towards women and children. Just as it probably did not occur in our society in the Middle Ages, so it is not reported today in the underdeveloped countries. Its roots lie in industrialisation, in patriarchy and in the development of the bourgeoisie and the nuclear family.

On a more recent historical note, it could be argued that whereas sex used to be the common neurotic focus for guilt (notably in Freud's time), *food* has now become a major focus for (particularly women's) conflicts. (This is echoed in the media in, e.g., the advertisement of cream cakes as 'naughty but nice': why naughty?) Anorexic women are not the only ones who express their inner conflicts via their relationship with food; in fact, the percentage of women who feel totally at ease with food and their own body is probably quite small.

In conclusion, then, the fact that self-starvation has become the *raison d'être* for thousands of young women is an appalling comment on the pressures on female adolescents in our society. (There are, of course, a small proportion of male anorexics, and for them the basic underlying problems of identity, autonomy and self-esteem are similar, but anorexia is overwhelmingly a female problem.)

Kim Chernin[20] argues that anorexia is an expression of becoming a 'little girl' in order to please 'the patriarchy'. I would concur with Sheila MacLeod's criticism ('The Way of All Flesh', *Guardian*, 21 June 1983) that anorexia is more a form of rebellion, an opting-out, a protest. 'Normal' slimming may be due, at least in part, to patriarchal conformity; but anorexia, while encompassing *aspects* of conformity in its own paradoxical way, is essentially a (self-defeating) *striving* for autonomy, self-esteem and transcendence of the denigrated female body.

To those who become anorexic, the basic tasks of adolescence – to form a self-respecting identity, to achieve autonomy and to come to terms with intimacy and sexuality – present overwhelming and apparently irresolvable conflicts. For them, under the threat of total loss of self, the tragic art of asceticism becomes their desperate and only means of survival.

Notes

1. Anderson, W., *Open Secrets: A Western Guide to Tibetan Buddhism*, Penguin, Harmondsworth, 1980.
2. Bruch, H., *The Golden Cage: The Enigma of Anorexia Nervosa*, Open Books, London, 1978.
3. Edwards, G., 'Counselling for Clients with Anorexia Nervosa', *Current Issues in Clinical Psychology*, Vol. 1, Plenum Press, New York and London, 1983.
4. Bruch, *op. cit.*
5. Palazzoli, M. S., *Self-Starvation: From the Intrapsychic to the Interpersonal Approach to Anorexia Nervosa*, Human Context Books, London, 1974.
6. Minuchin, S., *Psychosomatic Families: Anorexia Nervosa in Context*, Harvard University Press, Cambridge, Mass., 1978.
7. Bruch, *op. cit.*
8. Edwards, G., 'Is There an Anorexic Family?', paper presented at the Symposium of the Anorexia Counselling Service, 1979.
9. *ibid.*
10. Szasz, T. S., *The Second Sin*, Routledge & Kegan Paul, London, 1974.
11. Lawrence, M., 'Anorexia Nervosa: The Control Paradox', *Women's Studies International Quarterly*, Vol. 2, 1979, pp. 93–101.
12. Eichenbaum, L., and Orbach, S., *What Do Women Want?*, Fontana, London, 1984.
13. See, e.g., Boskind-Lodahl, M., 'Cinderella's Step-sisters: A Feminist Perspective on Anorexia and Bulimia', *Signs 2*, Winter 1976; Orbach, S., *Fat is a Feminist Issue*, Paddington Press, New York and London, 1978; Lawrence, *op. cit.*; MacLeod, S., *The Art of Starvation*, Virago, London, 1981; Chernin, K., *Womansize: The Tyranny of Slenderness*, Harper & Row, New York, 1981; The Women's Press, London, 1983; Lawrence, M., *The Anorexic Experience*, The Women's Press, London, 1984.
14. Palazzoli, *op. cit.*
15. Dally, P., and Gomez, J., *Anorexia Nervosa*, Heinemann, London, 1979.
16. Minuchin, *op. cit.*
17. Bruch, *op. cit.*
18. See, e.g., Firestone, S., *The Dialectic of Sex*, Jonathan Cape, London, 1971.

19. MacLeod, *op. cit.*
20. Chernin, *op. cit.*

5
Anorexia and Adolescence
Wil Pennycook

Adult society neither expects nor accepts that children feel depressed. It is only recently that the existence of childhood depression has been acknowledged. Somehow, we want to continue to believe in the idyllic childhood experience, the fairy-tale world of princes and castles, a Beatrix Potter, bunny rabbit world. We deny to children the reality of their deeply felt emotions. We deny that their sadness is penetrating, and when we are forced to accept it, in extreme circumstances, we say that the child is ill. Magic and fantasy are encouraged in childhood, and then, in adolescence, they become restricted and defined by social expectations. And in the childhood belief in magic lies the seeds of the adult's belief in her own creativity; it is the essence of her creative life. If, at puberty, the magic and fantasy is destroyed, and the adolescent is required to 'be a big girl now', to take on all the responsibilities of being a woman (including the probability of bearing, and caring for children), then her belief in her own creativity may be seriously jeopardised. Her fantasy life takes on a different character; she becomes the subject of it, not the author.

And still she is denied her sadness; she is cheered up if she looks miserable; she is told to snap out of it if she mopes. Parents especially seem to find it difficult to come to terms with their offspring's depression; 'she has all her life ahead her, she shouldn't be depressed.' It seems that our society as a whole finds depression intolerable, and especially in its young. Girls, who reputedly talk about anything and everything, do not talk about emptiness and despair. The subject is taboo.

The anorexic takes on board these judgments. It is as though she is not only protecting herself against these painful feelings but also protecting her parents and society. In accepting the view that she should be perfect, she is not allowed the most human of feelings – despair, depression. It is the antithesis of what is beautiful, and it is a reminder of aloneness, separateness, vulnerability. That it would be inhuman, impossible, to feel happy all the time does not absolve it. Somehow, depression equates with self-indulgence and self-obsession; like greed, therefore, it cannot be admitted to and, like greed, again those who experience it are judged, and found guilty. They are ugly feelings and perhaps that is the most damning judgment of all, for only pure perfection is beautiful. The anorexic carries in her, for us all, that delusion of perfection, of the perfect woman who has no needs, who does what she is told, who loves when she is loved. What is offered to any young woman is a set of impossible, inhuman dilemmas, and it is the anorexic who, in her own way, finds a solution, which is at one and the same time a return to the 'ideal', creative world of childhood and a stand against the mould into which she, as a woman, has been set. Not only is she obsessed by her 'lost perfection' but she blames herself for its loss. She compels herself to search for it and to re-create it in order to be acceptable and approved of. She cannot either be herself or stop searching. And so her endless journey 'from mirror after mirror'[1] continues.

In many ways, this conversation with mirrors is part of process of growing up that most young people are involved in. The changes in the body that occur at puberty can disrupt the adolescent's view of herself considerably. The biological changes affect her concept of self, her body-image. Often she may spend hours in front of the mirror almost as though she were trying to stabilise her image by constantly inspecting it. Reassurance is found in the knowledge that she has not changed in any sudden, grotesque way. She may also talk to herself, either literally or in the form of writing thoughts down, keeping a journal. Certainly, there is a tremendous need to take a grasp of, to hold on to, something that is constant in this constantly changing time.

Adolescence is a disruptive process, not only because of the physical changes but also because, with them, comes a shift in social expectations. A girl has to leave behind the certainty and strength of her body, which was previously equal to and sometimes even superior to that of boys. She is expected to be passive, accepting, a young lady. She is expected to become interested in how she looks, how she behaves. Coquettish and flirtatious behaviour, which may have been acceptable and even encouraged by others when she was a young girl, now takes on a new sexual connotation. When she was a child, she could feel autonomous – confident and secure about her body – but with the onset of puberty her body has become something over which she may feel she has no control.

'Not to have confidence in one's body is to lose confidence in oneself,' says Simone de Beauvoir.[2] This is echoed by Mara Selvini Palazzoli: 'Nor must we underestimate the traumatic shock of menstruation: the sudden flow of blood seems far more dramatic than the first ejaculation of seminal fluid. The menarch is a sudden, mysterious and humiliating bodily happening over which the poor girl has no control.'[3] It happens to us whether we like it or not!

The implications of this loss of control over her body are far reaching; the adolescent girl realises what she is becoming and what that means. She is becoming a woman and to be a woman means that 'she is exposed to lewd looks, subjected to menstruation, about to be penetrated in sexual embraces, to be invaded by the foetus, to be suckled by the child, etc.'[4]

The young girl has to face the tasks of adolescence without feeling confident about what is happening to her. Nor can she rely on solidarity from other women, celebrating her new found state, for many women are not proud of their womanhood and wish to deny it at all costs. It is ironic that just when she is most confused by her new feelings, attitudes and experiences, the adult world begins to make new, more exacting demands. These include accepting one's body and using it effectively, achieving more mature relationships with friends of one's own age and an amount of emotional independence from parents and other adults. The latter is perhaps the most important of these tasks, namely separating from those people with whom she has had the closest relationship.

This is naturally a worrying and frightening experience and many adjustments have to be made on both sides if the task is to be completed successfully, without damaging effects. The parents have to learn to be tolerant of the emerging identity in all its forms and to give it space to grow, providing security without suffocation. The adolescent has to learn to cope with her emotional ambivalences, her desire to be free and her need to be cherished. She experiences a strong need to be understood, to be seen for what she is and to be loved for it.

As adolescence progresses, the expectations become more demanding. One of the primary goals of adolescence is to decide what kind of woman the girl wants to be. In our education system girls are caught up in a complex web of double messages. Girls have to deal with the contradictory expectations of being successful but

BEFORE   AFTER

not so successful that it is challenging to men. Marilyn Lawrence
discusses the correlation between anorexia and education in depth
(see Chapter 14).[5] She argues that, for the girls, the message 'Do
well at school', has always carried after it, 'but not too well'. Success
in society is still defined by men, for men, as competitive,
goal-directed and materialistic. For women, anxiety about being
successful is based on a fear that they will be punished by men:
success and femininity are mutually exclusive goals.

An article in *Company* magazine[6] bears out the dilemmas facing a
successful woman. The chief one appears to be that the goal that
every girl is socialised for, motherhood and the family, appears to
remain outside her grasp.

> One of the unpalatable truths is that successful, well-educated,
> high-earning women are not hot property on the open marriage
> market. In all western countries the tendency still is for men to
> marry women who are younger than them, less well educated
> and who earn less.

Many of the successful working women expressed confusion
about the contradictory expectations that they experienced. On the
one hand, in order to succeed at work they had to exhibit qualities
such as initiative, drive and competitiveness, whereas at home, in
their private lives, these very qualities had to be hidden lest they
appear to be intimidating or unfeminine.

Adolescent girls are therefore still inheriting the either/or
situation that faced their mothers before them. In order to be

successful they must renounce the 'feminine' part of themselves, the part that is reflective and intuitive, that is emotional. To be successful in a man's world women must accept the male values of goal-directedness, drive and rationality, and the payment is the loss of a fundamental and essential part of their identities.

In Margaret Drabble's early novel, *A Summer Bird-Cage*,[7] her heroine Sarah Bennett, faces the problems of all educated young women in her struggle between career and marriage. The achievement of reconciling one with the other appears to be inconceivable. She can only find two answers to who or what she wants to be. One answer is to be married to a don and the other is to *be* a don. The notion of being a don whilst married to one is fanciful. The straight choice is marriage versus career. She chooses not to have a career because 'I'll tell you what's wrong with that. It's sex. You can't be a sexy don. It's all right for men, being learned and attractive, but for women, it's a mistake.'

Drabble also describes the struggle to be both feminine and autonomous, the struggle between the body and the spirit. In *The Garrick Year*,[8] whilst the heroine Emma Evans is obsessed with food, cooking for others and breast-feeding her child, rarely does she eat herself. She cannot cope with her body, which contains 'the rubbish'. She hates breast-feeding because her breasts are abnormally large. She hates 'the mess of union' and of pregnancy and giving birth. In fact, Emma Evans would really rather not have a female body at all, for it reminds her of her desires, her longings; she would prefer to be dry and dessicated. She does not want to be either controlled by or defined by her sexuality. Instead, she wants to deny it altogether. To be a woman is fraught with problems and apparently mutually exclusive expectations. In order to express her spirit, to be a real, autonomous person, she has to deny her body. If she allows herself to experience her femaleness and to express her sexuality, she may be overtaken by it and then she will lose her autonomy. Like Sarah Bennett, she cannot have both.

Thus, the combined effect of the physical and social changes is often psychologically devastating for the adolescent girl. The stability, control and consistency that she acquired in the early years may be shattered. According to Erik Erikson, the psychological problem of adolescence is that 'deep down you are a man (or a woman), that you will master your drives, that you will ever grow together again and be attractive, that you will know who you want to be, that you know what you look like to others, and that you know how to make the right decision without once and for all committing yourself to the wrong friend, sexual partner, leader or career.'[9]

For many girls, under-achievement is the norm, as is unhappiness and depression. In a group that I recently attended a woman described eloquently how in her adolescence and young womanhood, she was, for a large part of the time, lethargic and largely uninterested in what was happening around her. She wasn't excited by or enthusiastic about anything. She felt that her body was large and ungainly. While her elder sister played tennis and other sports with enjoyment, she withdrew, sitting in her room, feeling miserable. Her main fantasy, in her early teens, was that she would build herself a robot that looked like her and that would carry out all the tasks which she had to perform – going to school, being present at family activities – but that she, the real person, would be hidden inside it, curled up against the world, protected by her robotic counterpart. As she grew older, she 'forgot' about her fantasy but created a layer of flesh which performed the same function. The 'inside person' encapsulated all the feelings that she felt no longer able to express. It held power and strength, joy and enthusiasm, curiosity and excitement. As time went on, the 'inside' became more distanced from the 'outside'; she became less and less in touch with the other part of herself until all that she felt was the outside, empty shell.

However, after the birth of her first child, she grew back in touch with that inner part of herself and experienced strong, powerful feelings of sadness and loss. She began to admit, firstly to herself and then to others, that she was depressed. It was a depression that consisted of two strands. One was the sadness over the loss of a fundamental part of herself and the other was the earlier loss of childhood, having to give up childhood attachments and her childhood beliefs that she could be creative in and excited by the world. Somehow, it had been conveyed to her that she needn't expect too much because she would be disappointed and that, fundamentally, being an adult was hard work, full of responsibilities and not necessarily rewarding. She could put away all thoughts of being happy. In her robotic state she did not have to face up to her depression and its causes; they were neatly avoided. Yet, despite the difficulties, she did manage, like many, many women, to take on the challenge of relationships and children, and to have a career as well.

Anorexics, on the other hand, do not meet this challenge; they find the terms under which they have to grow up impossible to comply with. Anorexics seem to take on board fully the negative feelings about womanhood. Their experience is that in our culture, which is essentially patriarchal, women are condemned to being either wives and mothers or sex objects. If they are to be successful they must deny emotional and sexual desires. They must engage in a war waged daily against their own bodies, bodies with their evil and uncontrollable desires, symbolised by their insides of 'blood and milk and tears – a varied sea of grief'.[10]

Enormous conflict is created for women who believe that their feelings, their desires and their passions are at best unacceptable and at worst to be denied at all costs. But how can one be 'a woman' when it means accepting a definition which denies the passions and the conflicts? Conflict for women is an extremely problematic area. Women who openly express disagreement or hostility are regarded as being strident or, worse, castrators. Women are meant to be passive and accommodating. However, conflict is essential for growth. If it cannot be expressed and is internalised, it leads to insufferable states of depression, anorexia and 'madness'. They all serve, as did hysterical paralysis in Freud's Vienna, as an expression of female powerlessness and an unsuccessful attempt to reject and overcome this state.

Anorexics do not, cannot, accept that which biology prescribes for them: the body which contains the 'rubbish' and which is good for nothing except reception and conception. And yet, in refusing to be defined by their desires and sexuality, how do they go about making a life on their own terms?

A young anorexic, Clare, faces this problem daily. When she talks, she describes a problem which is mammoth in proportions. It is how to create a life that is truly her own: 'Becoming what we are requires existential courage to confront the experience of nothingness . . .'[11] Through her anorexia she is rejecting her 'fate'; she is not living up to other people's expectations of who she should be. She is attempting to re-create life for herself on her terms. This is an extraordinarily painful experience which involves rejecting her need for and dependence on anyone and anything, as well as her desire and her appetite. She has to be psychically as well as physically pared to the bone – to deny her humanness in order, as she sees it, to become more human.

Clare lives with her mother and is the third and youngest child and the second daughter. Her father left the family after she was born. She has some contact with him. Her mother is quiet and very anxious, and Clare sees her as someone who is weak and fragile, who finds it difficult to cope with the demands of family life. She feels that she has always had to protect her mother from her demands – to hold them back from her. She became more and more withdrawn and finally anorexic in her early teens.

Initially, she admitted nothing, not even that she was hungry. Having got to that place of safety, she was frightened by anything that she wasn't in control of – the outside, family, friends, all allies were experienced as treacherous, no longer acting in her interests but in their own. Sheila MacLeod, in her novel *The Snow-White Soliloquies*,[12] describes the experience.

> I must be fed more, in order to go on living, in order to progress. I disagree with him inwardly and I know that the fear shows in my eyes. You see it is my belief that the food, coursing through my veins, will kill me. Doc pulls on the tubes and asks me if I can feel the difference. I tense myself as best I can against the sudden access of nourishment. It swells me. It swells in my veins and a pulse beats loud in my head. My whole body is swelling now – it reaches the corner of my box – and I feel faint. Stop it, Doc, stop it. He can't hear me call. Help me someone! Or does he just choose to ignore my protestations? If I go on growing, I'll become too large for my box. The glass will break. I'll be exposed and then I'll die.

Clare experienced the world as controlling and thoughtless, a fascist world. She was unable to challenge, to stand up for herself; she felt powerless. Her inability to challenge openly meant that a war raged inside her. Whilst she was denying that there was any problem, she was denying that there was any conflict.

However, as she became weaker, she became aware that she was physically unable to go on, 'hoist by her own petard'. All spontaneity was gone; she existed on willpower alone. That effort, having to determine every action, is ultimately very costly.

Our conversations revolve around her despair of ever finding her way – 'tell me how' – and her terror of being for ever entrapped by her 'only solution'. She takes nothing for granted, pushes herself unremittingly as though she is carrying some terrible burden (and perhaps she is). But with each point of relaxation in her will, each assertion that she is someone who can exercise choice, she becomes stronger. She has slowly become aware of the conflict inside her, of her anger and rage as well as, and instead of, her depression, and of her need to hold on to anorexia as well as her desire to be rid of it.

With these realisations has come the possibility for change. Somehow, the understanding that anorexia performs a function in her life allows her to acknowledge it. She is not being asked to relinquish it immediately, for that would mean that she would be left with an intolerable void – a psychic 'no-man's-land'. Anorexia provides her with a security that allows her, with patient exploration of her feelings, to grow stronger and, eventually, to leave it behind. Her work entails a separation from and a letting go of, which, like any other, involves a sense of loss, pain and terror, of constant return to and movement just that little bit further away, and then the heartfelt need to let go and the ability to endure the pangs of loss and the occasional desires to be back there.

Anna became anorexic when she left her home for the first time. A clever girl, she had won her place at university as had been expected. Her breakdown came very quickly – in fact, in her first year. In her mind she links the onset of anorexia with her rejection by her boyfriend, of whom she was very fond. She had wanted him

too much, she says. Their desires and needs became compatible no longer. She was left with the feelings that she had insatiable needs, a greedy appetite for love and affection, and that this had driven him away. And when he was gone, she was left feeling totally abandoned, unable to find comfort and solace with other friends or her family. It was in this state of feeling empty and absolutely alone that she became anorexic. She did not try to fill herself up in order to get rid of the empty feeling but rather the outside, her body, became a mirror of the inside, her feelings. Her actual thinness was the truthful reflection of how she was. However, in her thinness she felt more in control of herself, she felt more acceptable to herself. After years of taking in how a woman should be, what a desirable woman should look like, she began to feel that she was becoming one and was therefore acceptable. No longer would she feel her messy, conflicting emotions, or express them to anyone. To do so would mean rejection.

Why do Anna and Clare feel such a need to deny their feelings? Why do they feel that they are so unacceptable to the world? They both appear to be fleeing from relationships with people, for the quality of their reactions is one of extreme anxiety about, if not terror of, becoming involved with, becoming close to, other people or perhaps, more specifically, another person.

Certainly, as Anna explored her feelings, she came across the problem of closeness and distance over and over again. She wondered how she could love someone and still want to be away from them; how someone could love her and still love other people; how she could want to be close to someone at one time and not at another; how she could want to be known completely and yet still retain her privacy.

It seemed irresolvable. To be close meant to be so close, so intimate, that there was, there could be, no distance: she was at one with the other person. All distance was painful and, in fact, perceived as persecuting. To be absolutely close was the only place of safety; it was home. If she could not have that, then she would be cut off.

Food became a metaphor. As an anorexic she cut off from her hunger and her desire for food; she simply ate the same food at the same time every day. So too with her desire for closeness. She cut herself off from other people so that she didn't have to examine what she felt or what she wanted or *if* she wanted it. She removed herself from the responsibility for her own actions and the conflict of having to deal with her own, seemingly mutually exclusive, needs.

Often, conflict arises because that which has, at one time, been acceptable to the self, becomes unacceptable. This change and conflict may occur because one is no longer a child and has to put away childish behaviour. It may be, for instance, that sexual and erotic activities that were enjoyed, even encouraged, as a small child, have no place in adult life. This is part of growing up and no less painful for it. More problematic are the early feelings that the person has towards those who love and care for her. These are often much more difficult to give up, to let go of, and for most the vestiges of these childhood feelings remain. For the anorexic, those early feelings, both of love for and rage and anger against, are intolerable. She is guilty about the rage and anger she feels towards the person who is also passionately loved and she represses these negative feelings. One of the results is a constant attempt to create an acceptable, agreeable, lovable person who really doesn't feel bad and angry. However, these feelings are still there and this results in an internal damning and judging of the self.

The issues that I have described here – of ambivalence, of depression, of conflict, of creativity, of intimacy – are ones that are current problems for all women in our society. How can a woman be a truly autonomous person, and have and express her deeply felt needs and desires too. For the anorexic, to combine the two is impossible, for to be a woman is to be socially defined as dependent and not to be taken seriously. For the anorexic they are polarised: to have needs is to be weak, to be dependent; to be autonomous is to depend on no one, to want for nothing. To have needs somehow sullies her, flaws her. Intermingled with the feeling that having needs and desires is weak, is the problem of having them met and satisfied. Even if she could admit that she felt needy, how could she ask for whatever she needed to satisfy her? She is unable to believe that it is possible to be satisfied, which compounds, or creates, the problem of having needs in the first place.

The answer to autonomy and dependence lies somewhere in the balance or integration of the two and there will be, at times, apparent contradictions in behaviour or feelings. The anorexic is unable to manage the contradictions, the ambivalences, and her solution is to deny them. Her fear is that if they are admitted to, acknowledged, then she will be lost 'till human voices wake us, and we drown'.[13] However, the inability to integrate her opposing feelings means that she remains split, pushing away a vital part of herself, and so, ultimately, ironically, she is unable to be an autonomous human being.

Notes

1. Yeats, W. B., 'Before the world was made' in *Selected Poems*, Macmillan, London, 1962.
2. De Beauvoir, S., *The Second Sex*, Penguin, Harmondsworth, 1972.
3. Palazzoli, M. S., *Self Starvation: From the Intra-psychic to the Transpersonal Approach to Anorexia Nervosa*, Human Context Books, London, 1974.
4. *ibid*.
5. Lawrence, M., 'Education and Identity: The Social Origins of Anorexia', *Women's Studies International Forum*, Vol. 7, No. 4, (1984), pp. 201–11.
6. 'Life in No Man's Land', *Company*, October 1984.
7. Drabble, M., *A Summer Bird-Cage*, Weidenfeld & Nicolson, London, 1963.
8. Drabble, M., *The Garrick Year*, Weidenfeld & Nicolson, London, 1964.
9. Erikson, E., *Identity, Youth and Crisis*, W. W. Norton, & Co., New York and London, 1968.
10. Drabble, M., *The Garrick Year*, Weidenfeld & Nicolson, London, 1964.
11. Daly, M., *Beyond God the Father*, Beacon Press, Boston, 1973; The Women's Press, London, 1986.
12. MacLeod, S., *The Snow-White Soliloquies*, Sphere, London, 1972.
13. Eliot, T.S., 'The Love Song of J. Alfred Prufrock' in *Selected Poems*, Faber and Faber, London, 1961.

6
Compulsive Eating: Issues in the Therapy Relationship
Tamar Selby

In this paper, I am looking at issues which arise specifically with women who come to me as a specialist in compulsive-eating problems, women who are concerned with their own eating, believing it to be the only problem.

As in all therapeutic relationships, the compulsive eater brings her defences into the relationship with the therapist. These defensive patterns can make the therapist and client feel as though they are engaged in an endless battle. For the client, these defences are the only ones she has ever known since childhood. If she feels the therapist is trying to challenge her or prevent her from using them (mentioning her diet, her body or food), this will appear to the client as hostility or impatience, and she will hang on to them all the more strongly as her only weapons in the face of the hostile world. If this happens, and it does at almost all beginnings of therapy, the client is then not able to use the space she so needs if she is ever going to give up her defences and lead an easier life. She needs this space to enable her to reach her own true experiences, her real feelings and thoughts, so she can, perhaps for the first time, be her own self, become her own person, knowing her own story, painful as all this may be.

The experiences and behaviour I am going to describe are those which centre around the need to control, to coerce and to manipulate, together with the wish to be controlled and possessed – experiences and behaviour which are often disparagingly referred to, usually by men, as 'typically female'. Such behaviour is often unpleasant as far as other people are concerned, but it is far more so for the women who need to use it.

It is very important that the therapist allows the woman to try and involve her in this seemingly fruitless battle about control. It is the therapist's task to help the woman understand what it is about, how and why she has to hold on to it. The therapist will try to create the kind of environment for the client which will allow her to let go of her control. Perhaps the one or two or more hours a week she has with her therapist will be the only time she experiences life without it. This is a tremendous relief for her, and the starting point from which she can begin to change her life.

Compulsive eating is a defiant and compliant act at one and the same time.

The act of compulsive eating holds hidden as well as obvious meanings. 'I am out of control', 'I can't look after myself', 'I am a mess' and 'You should do something about me' – are, in compliance with a controlling environment, obvious pleas. But, 'I am the only person in control of myself, my body' and 'I control my environment by eating it' are, in defiance of a controlling environment, hidden meanings. These are some of a number of paradoxes which confront the therapist when working with women with eating problems. Othes include 'I eat so I can be here with you', 'I am yours', 'You should look after me', 'I need you' and 'I am dependent on you' on the one hand, but also, 'I eat so I am not yours', 'I don't need you', 'You can't get any closer to me', 'The food/fat protects me from you' and 'I am independent'. Then, 'If I don't overeat I will be too close to you', but, 'If I stop eating, I won't need to come to you any more'. And, 'I am here only because I am a compulsive eater', 'When I eat, you are responsible for me', but, 'When I eat I am independent. After all, I rely on food not on you' and 'When I stop eating I will be dependent only on you'. And, 'You love me only because I am fat', 'I am powerless and not in competition with you', 'You are powerful and beautiful', but, 'You also hate me because I am fat', 'I am a slob', 'I am needy, greedy', 'I am a big fat baby'.

A therapist has to be able to withstand and work alongside these paradoxes and contradictions. If she ignores her client getting fatter, the client will experience this as neglect on the part of the therapist. She will go on growing until the therapist notices it with alarm.

If, on the other hand, the therapist mentions or remarks on her client's body, this will be perceived as an attempt to put her on a diet, an attempt at coercion on the part of the therapist. She may be relieved by the therapist's care, but will rebel against the deprivation this kind of care contains. 'You want me to be thin so you will be successful at my expense.' This is an expression of anger and vengeance against a mother who was concerned with her own need for her daughter to be beautiful. Many such mothers actually have conflicting and paradoxical feelings about their daughter's looks. The daughter may be left with the mother's double wish – that she be beautiful and not-beautiful at the same time. Compulsive eating is a means of defying this double wish.

This means, of course, that whether or not the therapist notices or mentions anything about the client's body, the woman must go on overeating to defy her. It is because and in spite of the therapist that the woman overeats, because and in spite of the therapist that she gets fat. She feels as though she needs the therapist to take care of her, look after her body and regulate her food intake. If the therapist attempts to do this, the woman will respond by staying fat.

Therapists can sometimes feel as though their clients have them by the throat! The woman who is a compulsive eater tends to use her therapist in the same way she uses food. Like a cheesecake, the therapist's words are gobbled down, and yet she cannot really use them or make them her own. Nothing seems to sustain her. The therapy is swallowed, not tasted, and got rid of. The woman is left feeling empty again and once more demands something from the therapist. In this sense it creates an addiction to the therapist, similar to the addiction to food.

The woman who is a compulsive eater comes to therapy to solve her addiction to food. She wants to do it as quickly as possible so that she can get rid of her therapist in the same way as she dismisses the food she eats. But it is precisely because she re-creates the same kind of relationship as she has to food that she cannot just deal with her problem quickly and go. Instead of using therapy to understand her need for food, initially she becomes addicted to the therapist, and this addiction replaces her addiction to food. By 'addicted to' I do not mean 'dependent on'. She is engaged in an attempt at self-sufficiency which, like all such attempts, is doomed to fail. Self-sufficiency is a denial of other people. The woman who eats compulsively denies that she has a real need for emotional nourishment from other people. Instead, she attempts to manage without anyone and becomes 'hooked' on food. In a similar way, she might begin therapy by getting 'hooked' on the therapist. At this stage she does not yet understand that it is possible to have relationships which can meet her needs in a nourishing way. She asks her therapist to fulfil the same illusion which she gets from food: namely, to sustain her illusion and fantasy.

One client said to me, 'I felt very bad last night. I thought I would ring you up.' She did not ring me. She stormed the fridge instead. She took it absolutely for granted that I was available any time I popped into her head – like a Smartie. Then, without thinking (again, like eating thoughtlessly), she had it in mind to use me quickly and efficiently, like racing through the biscuit tin. Fleetingly, I pop into her head and out of it like a Mars Bar through her digestive system.

In her therapy, what the woman is most afraid of is dependency. What she achieves through eating and food is an illusion of independence. She mistakes self-sufficiency, self-reliance and control with true independence. She does not seem to need anybody, she can manage. She needs only food. She is, of course, a very dependent person, but she is able to maintain an air of independence which involves only herself and her food. She is so dependent on food that if she is asked to stop eating compulsively, she feels she may die. She can manage a diet, which provides her with a framework upon which she can rely for a time. If she breaks her diet with half a biscuit, the magic of this framework is gone. She feels as though she is losing herself. Chaos dominates her again and she is back with food as her rescuer as well as her persecutor. While she feels that food is the only thing she can take in, as soon as she puts anything in her mouth, she tries to get rid of it again, either by quite literally vomiting or by her self-punishment system of guilt, self-hatred, self-deprivation, diet, etc.

A compulsive eater who is so dependent can only allow herself to depend on something she can control. Unconsciously, she often has the illusion of controlling everything and everybody, while at the same time she has a sense of being herself totally out of control. This illusion of controlling the environment is mostly unconscious and unrecognised by her. The act of eating compulsively symbolises it and keeps her ignorant of her own unsuccessful attempts to control the environment. As soon as she experiences the slightest feelings of frustration, disappointment, fear or anger, the compulsive eater feels as though she is losing control of herself and her environment. It is mostly the 'outside' which she experiences as frustrating, disappointing and ungratifying. It is from the 'outside' that she seeks peace of mind. Her efforts to control her environment are symbolised by her eating. If she becomes angry with me, her therapist, she will hate me while chewing a stick of celery. To actually engage with me and to take something from me means to depend on me. She cannot afford that – after all, I am not around when the session ends. The issue of her need to control me and her therapy predominates for a very long time. When we achieve a real independence, we do not need to control the world. We are in the world, not in possession of it, nor possessed by it. The artificial division between us on the one hand and the world on the other loses its force.

A woman who eats compulsively feels most out of control when in great need of another person. Often, she will rush to overeat when someone walks out of the door. Similarly, when she is in a rage with another person, she can't afford to be angry – this would be to risk losing the other person – so she turns instead to food. She is hardly ever in touch with her fear of separation, dependence or rage; all those feelings are experienced as hunger and resolved by food.

Control is thus dependency in reverse. The experience of a woman who is a compulsive eater when she is just about to overeat is of complete chaos, of losing ground, of structurelessness. Momentarily she has lost herself, her world. I say momentarily because she will not allow these terrible frightening feelings for more than a few seconds. She will reach for food in order to gain some sense of balance. But it is precisely this 'cure' she stuffs in which keeps her away from the real contact she so longs for, from any possibility of reaching out. As she is so in need of the environment (i.e. food) to gain some sense of self, she comes to feel extremely inadequate and fragile. She feels empty, all her needs must be met, she must have control of what is not her. As soon as she manages to control the environment in order to have what she wants from it, it seems to turn bad.

A client of mine once begged me to see her on the very day on which I was going on holiday. In the session which took place that same day, she told me that she felt terrible because she had managed to get from me what she wanted. She felt that she was manipulative, and that I was a person who could be manipulated and changed; like the food she ate, which was always available yet made her feel ashamed and guilty. She had no self-respect, being so dependent on food, while at the same time she was unable and afraid to bring herself and her needs to another person.

Many of the women I work with started to eat compulsively at around puberty, the beginning of adolescence, around the time when they began to be aware of their wish for another person (a boy or a girl). Awareness of sexuality always involves awareness of someone else. This desire for the 'other' can make one feel totally out of control, almost the slave of the other, so to speak . Then, a woman can feel as dependent as she once did on her mother. Often in the history of women who become compulsive eaters, their mothers were experienced as frustrating, controlling or as simply not there. The old pain of this earlier relationship is rewakened.

Desiring boys or girls brings up the old problem of dependency on and separation from the mother. A girl who did not resolve these problems at the appropriate age will find herself in an impossible situation. She may turn to food as an outlet in order to make her feel fulfilled and to eradicate her desire for boys, but she will do her best not to be desired by them. As a result she will be led to feel inadequate, undesirable, unloved, insecure and unconfident. All her old feelings will be reawakened. It is not 'being fat' which makes her feel all this. Being fat reinforces it, makes it possible, apparent and felt. It is her state of utmost need which makes her feel inadequate and insecure. The fat merely obscures it.

A fat woman blames the fat for every misfortune that befalls her. The rest of her life and personality disappears. The task of therapy is to understand what the food/fat system covers so perfectly.

Women who eat compulsively are other people's possessions

Many of the women who attempt to deal with life by resorting to food are the daughters of mothers we might term 'narcissistic' to some degree. By this I mean mothers who experience a tremendous lack in themselves and who tend to see their daughters as their own extension or possession – a reflection of themselves. In fact probably as a reflection of everything they would have liked to be but never were. In order to be a good reflection for her mother, the daughter must be a perfectly good little girl. So her mother can take pride in her own self through her daughter. The daughter of such a mother will not develop as a separate person with her own sense of self. Her self is her mother's.

One of the most obvious ways for a mother to exert power and control over the child is through food. The daughter does not eat when she wants or as much as she wants. She eats what, when and as much as her mother thinks she needs or wants. Later on in life she will find it difficult to know what she wants, not only with regard to food but also in all other areas of life. She will always look up to her mother as her point of reference, whether choosing a job, a career or another person to share her life with. (As soon as she finds her or him, it will be her or his role to fulfil the same function as her mother did.) As soon as she finds a therapist, the same thing happens.

A woman told me she went shopping on Saturday. She went into a shop but could not decide what she wanted. She felt very anxious and lost. She wanted to run out, but then she called her mother to the rescue. She began to wonder what her mother would have chosen for her, found a dress her mother would have liked to see her in and bought it. I asked her if she herself liked the dress. She laughed. 'That's just it. Do you think I know myself what I like? I know what she likes . . . No, I suppose I didn't like the dress, but it was better than coming out empty-handed.'

The same woman had a dream two years later. In her dream, it was I who said to her, 'I always wanted you to wear pink.' She herself did not like pink and never wore it. A few days after this dream, she arrived at the session wearing a pink dress. I asked her if she liked the colour now. She said yes and from then on wore pink quite often.

When she told me her dream, she remembered that her mother always wanted her to wear pink but that she hated the colour and never wore it. In her dream, I wanted her to wear it. She did so and even liked it herself.

How are we to understand this? Was it that I, her therapist, wanted her to wear it and so she did because she wished to please me? Or did she need me to like pink so that she could like it herself and be able to wear it without feeling that she was complying with her mother? Or was it an attempt to keep the two of us together and inseparable? Or perhaps she felt she had to be compliant with me as she had been in the past with her mother. Whichever way we look at it, she was someone else's possession, whether she wore pink or not. She defied her mother by not wearing pink precisely because she was under mother's spell. Then she started to wear it because in her fantasy I liked it. Then she was under my spell.

Her life, like her body, belonged to someone else. Very often other colleagues and I hear women say they are scared to be thin because they won't be able to say 'no' to men who desire them. But further than that, many women say they would not know whether or not they desired the other person. 'I will find myself in this person's arms, not knowing why I am there.' It never occurs to these women to listen to their own desires or their own bodies. Of course not. After all, if her body is not her own, how on earth can she perceive a desire which is not hers?

Many mothers put their young daughters on diets. They express dissatisfaction with their daughters' appearance. They are unhappy if the child is too fat or too thin, dark or fair. A mother can't do much about her daughter's brown eyes, but can do a lot about her weight. The child soon senses the tremendous importance of food in their relationship and sooner or later will use it to comply with or to defy her mother. A daughter with such a controlling mother cannot really defy.

Girls who are put on a diet at a very early stage don't really understand what all the fuss is about. A woman told me how as a child she would sit around the table, not allowed to eat what the rest of the family were eating. She sat there, tormented, thinking to herself, 'But why does she want me to be thin?' The only answer she could come up with in her therapy was, 'For the glorification of herself in my father's eyes. I was her measure of success as a mother and a wife.' We can clearly see here how the insecurities of the mother about her own capacities to fulfil the roles demanded of her led her in turn to make such cruel demands on her daughter.

No wonder this woman struggled with me about my own success. If she became thin she would simply add to the list of high points in my career. This woman, as a young girl, would eat secretly but would always leave some clue which pointed to her crime. This showed her mother on the one hand that she was not in control of her daughter's body and her life, but on the other hand, how much she needed her mother to take responsibility for her.

When a woman with this kind of background comes to therapy, she soon expresses her helplessness and her wish to become the therapist's possession. (There is an important distinction between becoming possessed by someone and becoming dependent on her.) She will want her therapist to tell her what she should think, and what she should want to do and be. At the same time she will do her utmost to avoid dependency on the therapist.

If the therapist offers an interpretation, the client may take it as an attempt to manipulate and control her. She may overeat in order to regain control of herself and to control this powerful therapist. She will also use a binge to blame her therapist for her intrusion. Paradoxically, the act of taking control involves an uncontrollable act of compulsion.

If the therapist does not give the woman what she wants at once,

she will experience her as withholding. The therapist has something which she lacks. The therapist's silence will be regarded as the utmost cruelty and will send the client to the fridge to swallow her frustration and anger and to get what she feels she must have, then and there, without delay. In her therapy, she will do whatever she can to control her therapist and the session. She will demand answers, but reject interpretations if they do not suit her.

By demanding an answer and getting one the client feels as though she is taking away the therapist's magical power. She may feel as though she can empty her. Although she may do her best to manipulate and control the therapist, she is at the same time terrified and full of guilt when she can gain power in this way. If the therapist bends and bows to the client's every wish and whim, then she is really no different from a piece of cake!

Does she really want a therapist who will cure her as if by magic, while she stays passive and ineffective? The therapist would then become like the mother, who knew it all. The woman will feel as though she does not take any active part in shaping her own life. She will ask the therapist to do it for her, but then reject her through the only activity she really knows – her frantic chewing.

A binge is an event which is both passive and active at the same time. It comes upon her while she is out of control; it is rather like a dream. It is experienced as a happening that befalls her. It is as if part of her is observing this mad activity in the kitchen while the rest of her is shoving it all in.

This, in essence, is true; a compulsion is like a dream. It does come upon one like a powerful happening. The woman who stands in her kitchen and stuffs herself is totally lost in the midst of this overpowering force. Is she once again the little girl within her mother's power?

A client ate three or four times each night for many years. Sometimes she got up in the morning, walked into the kitchen and, to her amazement discovered the remains of a cheese sandwich or a bowl of cornflakes. She knew it must be her who had left these bits and pieces and yet, to her complete surprise, she remembered nothing of the events of the night before. After months of trying to find the meaning of these secret binges during the night, she came to realise what, in part, they were about. 'It all happens to me while I am asleep. I really have nothing to do with it. I don't even remember eating all this.'

After two years in therapy, I asked her if she felt ready to begin to take charge of her life, her body and her actions. She felt relieved and said, 'Yes, for quite a while already I have been saying to myself that I don't need this food any more. I don't want to wake up every night. Yes. I can and I will.' Next session she came in half laughing and told me, 'Since last session I have eaten much more than ever before, but I know what it means. I am saying to you that it is all your fault. You want me to stop eating. I don't like being told what to do.'

In fact it was *she* who had kept insisting that it was about time she stopped her night-time binges. She felt she did not need the food any more. She felt safe and relieved when I asked her whether she was prepared to take charge. She felt relieved partly because she felt I was taking care of her and partly, and more significantly, because she could now put all the blame on me for failing. I became prohibiting, controlling. 'I don't like being told what to do. I will show you.' Again, defiance on the one hand – 'You can't control me; I will eat when you can't see me' – and compliance on the other – 'I can't help it; you must take care of me; I don't even know I am eating, after all, I am still asleep.'

Another client told me at great length about her ailments and expected me to deal with them. I was to give her an explanation for her blocked nose, her backache, to give her a reason for her need to go to the toilet every few minutes during the night. She expected me to know and understand everything about her various illnesses yet my interpretations as a rule would be met with, 'Yes, it's possible, but it means nothing to me.' She actually rejected any understanding of them.

Some clients will try very hard to put their therapist into the position of the all-powerful expert, who understands everything. But as soon as the therapist accepts this invitation, she will be kicked back down as quickly as she has been elevated.

Although the woman who compulsively overeats feels herself to be worthless, with no self-respect and lacking any self-validation, she nonetheless tends to see everything as someone else's fault. It is the therapist's fault that she keeps on eating, it is the therapist's failure that drives her to the fridge, it is hardly anything to do with her at all.

One woman told me, 'I had quite a good day today, until I met a few people who irritated me so much I had to go and eat.' Another said, 'I ate three times the night after our last session, because of your comment at the end of it.' Another said, 'Guess what I did yesterday after the session? I took a plateful of food to bed with me and ate it all at once. This is what you did to me.'

She is possessed by the world and this world must provide all the time, non-stop. The world fails to do so and she feels so bad, so terribly frustrated that she must exert control over it with her teeth. This is an act of helplessness, but also of power.

Clients often describe how they have tried on a dress which did not fit them. 'I was fed up, I didn't give a damn. I ate like mad.' Or how they caught a glimpse of themselves in a shop window or a mirror. 'I felt so disgusted, I couldn't care less. I rushed to the kitchen.' They will tell me this, crying in despair. But looking at this statement more closely, I understand it as saying, 'I am disgusting, but it is my own doing. I don't care about anything or anybody. I am going to stuff my face.' In terrible desperation, it is true, but at least this is an act she will commit on herself by herself.

The compulsive eater feels that the world should change to accommodate her; she should not have to change at all. She would rather eat than assume any responsibility for her life. I have heard so many women say they don't want to be rid of their anger with their mothers or their fathers or whoever. They want to keep them responsible. I once said to a client, 'Your body is your responsibility, not mine.' She felt panic, and said, 'I am sure I will have a hell of a binge tonight.' Just before I said what I said, she had been telling me, over and over again, how she did not want to lose any weight, as though to tell me that all my efforts are in vain. But when I reminded her that, after all, it was her body and not mine, she felt abandoned and thought of a binge, which I would be responsible for.

One client told me that only now after many years had she realised that she was her husband's possession. She had to report to him every penny she spent and everywhere she went. Another had always used her father to handle her finances and her mother to deal with the rest of her life. Another found buying a flat a tremendously painful experience. For two years she waited for someone (a non-existent person) to take care of everything that was needed in the place. For the first time in her life, she possessed something of her own, but it felt to her as though the flat possessed her rather than the other way round. She was like an agent waiting for instructions. This woman was angry with me for not having miraculously made her thin. Another woman used to phone her mother in Germany every time she wanted to change the position of the furniture in her flat.

A client comes and shares with me some painful feelings or recounts some unpleasant events. She sobs in pain for a long time. From time to time she looks at me and tries to examine my reactions – the expressions on my face, the movement of my hands. If she feels she is getting some 'positive' feedback, she continues on the same track. My facial expressions and body movements are a confirmation of what she feels. If she fails to detect any reaction, she stops and tries another train of thought. It is not only because she wants to please me – although this is absolutely vital for her – but also because she truly does not know what she feels or if what she feels is 'really' what she feels. She needs validation for what she is going through. She looks for signs of what she 'should' feel, rather than following what she really feels. If at some point in the session I mention 'envy', she will come next week and be envious. If I mention 'anger', she will do the same with it. Many months pass with her trying to comply with what she thinks, I want from her. Eventually, she starts to find out for herself, regardless of what I want or don't want, what is really going on for her. Not only has she stopped trying to please me but she is also discovering, for the first time in her life, what *she* is about, rather than what I am about.

Many women who come from a controlling environment will either go on being in one all their lives, by exchanging fathers or mothers for husbands or lovers, or they will create a controlling environment for others. They may marry husbands whom they feel they can coerce or live with lovers whom they can control. They will also behave in a controlling manner with their own children. In therapy, maybe for the first time in their lives, women with these sorts of difficulties will be faced with the possibility of neither of these alternatives. It is a hard struggle for the woman and her therapist to get out of this pattern, but it is only when the client, through understanding, lets go of her need to control or be controlled that change can begin.

To illustrate what I mean, I should like to end this paper with some more examples.

A client had been in therapy with me for three years. She came three and sometimes four times a week. Her mother was, and still is, a very seductive and extremely controlling person. She is also very confused and confusing, and at times irrational. My client was 'chosen' by her mother to be the child to repair the mother's wounded sense of self. In order to achieve this, the mother exerted total control over her. My client never openly defied her mother, was always by her side, sweet and good-natured, helping her in the kitchen and around the house. She was never able to express any of her real needs and if she ever attempted to do so, she was crushed by her mother in a variety of ways. She began to eat a lot and was put on a diet as a very young child. She complied with her mother's need to be in control of her but also defied her by never being the thin and beautiful girl her mother wanted her to be. This woman, as a rule, used to miss at least one session a week without phoning me. She generally came late, sometimes very late, to the other sessions. No interpretation seemed to do the trick; she would still come late even when she understood why she was doing it. For several years it seemed that nothing would help her to change. One day, I was made to wait for her for over 20 minutes. She arrived, and I began the session by telling her that her late appearances were not going to be acceptable to me any more. I told her that I would not wait for more than two or three minutes, and if she came later than that I would not be there. She cried and felt terrible about it. She felt abused and insulted. Even I, the only person who accepted her entirely, was now prepared to leave her, to withdraw love and support.

For the next few sessions she arrived on the dot. Then one session she arrived late enough for me to keep my word. I was not there when she came. In the next session we got to the bottom of it. For the first time in the therapy she got in touch with the abuse and insult which she felt, but which she had so effectively pushed back on to me by making me wait for her. For all those years I was playing the part of the abused person rather than her. She could come and go as she pleased; I, by the nature of my work, had to sit and wait for her. For the first time in her life she could abuse someone else without feeling abused herself.

We both knew all of this all along and yet it did not stop her from continuing the same pattern. It was only when I decided not to take it any more that she experienced it for the first time herself.

All those years I was like a little girl waiting for the mother who did not take any notice of what she was feeling when she appeared or disappeared as she pleased. I was the abused child and my client was her own mother to me. It could have gone on like that for ever if I, the child, had not put a stop to it by defying her, openly and obviously, without fear of destroying her. I became the voice for this little girl who had never had a voice herself. The only use she, as an adult as well as a child, had ever had for her mouth was to fill it up with food.

For the first time in this crucial session, she was able to feel the terrible hurt, insult and abuse which her mother had poured on her all her life. Ever since then she has been able to come on time, or almost on time, and she calls me if she has to cancel a session. As never before, she is doing her best to come to sessions rather than to cancel them. She does not need to use this act of control over me and she no longer fears that I have control over her. She does not need to defy me in this particular way. She has found her mouth and a language with it. Of course, a real move did not occur overnight with one act. Her attempt to control and hide took other devious paths for quite a while afterwards, but I had to look harder for them. The first hole in the fence took its shape.

It is in her therapy that a women who feels so controlled by food, by everybody around her, comes to discover her own controlling behaviour. It always comes as a surprise to her.

A client used to go very silent with me when she felt I failed her in some way. Her memory of her mother is of a severe woman who used silence as a kind of punishment on her young girl. In the session she would suddenly become very quiet, her face taking on a defiant expression. I asked her a few times what she was thinking about. She ignored the question and continued to be heavily silent. We sat like this for quite a while until she said she was waiting for me to get her out of this tortured state of mind she got herself into.

Asking her what she was thinking or feeling was useless to her, and it was also a sign of my failure to do something about her. For a long time she used to fall into those deadening silences. She felt terrible in the prison she created for herself and could not break out of it. Often she would describe how terrible she felt when it happened and then we would try to understand the meaning of it rather than its purpose.

When, once again in a session she fell silent, I asked her if she knew what it was she was trying to make me feel while this silence was hovering heavily in the room. She glared at me with utter surprise. Why should she try to make me feel anything at all while she was so deeply buried in there? She was surprised to discover her wish to have an effect on me, be it good or bad, her wish to paralyse and imprison me, to make me utterly useless to her. She was surprised by her own wish and need to exert such control over a session. She did not like what she realised she was doing one bit. She genuinely could not believe that she who never had any effect on anything (in her experience only) would try so hard to have some.

Many months passed until she noticed that the silences had disappeared almost entirely. She then understood what they were partly about. She was doing to me what was done to her when as a young girl she had displeased her mother in some way. As a young girl she had stood there in front of her mother, not knowing what she had done to deserve this cruel and heavy silence, not knowing how to get her mother to speak to her again. She also realised that in the same way as it was not in her power to get her mother 'out of it', neither was it in mine if she chose to punish me for a crime I did not know I had committed. If I had tried to get her 'out of it', it would have meant I had done something wrong and now deserved to beg her forgiveness, which, needless to say, would not be granted to me as it had never been granted to her.

All I wanted to do and was able to do, was to create a space for her to gain some understanding of her behaviour. It was not for me to take responsibility for it. If I had assumed any responsibility, she would have felt overwhelmingly powerful. What she took as my failure was partly her refusal to take responsibility for her own actions, feelings or thoughts. Her terrible feelings were a manifestation of her inability and refusal to act. Of course, the silence also meant a tremendous rage and fury with me when she felt I had or when I genuinely had failed her. I had to hold her anger and fury for her for a long time until she was ready to experience those herself.

She tried to paralyse me and deafen herself so that we would not hear her rage, her hurt or her insult.

These examples illustrate the possible steps towards understanding and towards knowledge a client may take in her therapy. Of course, this is not to say that all will be well from now on once a move has occurred, or that therapist and client are now working together in a state of bliss until the therapy runs its full course. The defences that are confronted and understood don't vanish after an interpretation, albeit the right one. They take another form and appear in different disguises. It is the therapist's task to dig them out in order to have them understood again and again and again. If the client feels threatened or feels she is threatening the therapist with her experiences, she may need to hide the feelings which really she has revealed in and through her defences.

The therapist must be prepared and ready to allow everything the client brings to become part of the dialogue between them.

I hope I have not created the impression that there is a 'real person' behind the 'defences', and that all we have to do is to find what these are, get rid of them and then discover the 'true' and 'real' person. Defences are not like a locked door or a shut window, to be unlocked so that the person can get out. A woman who eats compulsively is just as real as she will be without her compelling need to eat. In her therapy she is not becoming 'real' or more 'real'; rather, she finds the security to be who she is in more ways than one, the only one she had at her disposal, her crazy eating.

In therapy, we are sitting with a woman who suffers a great deal precisely because of those 'defences', defences which she cannot give up and yet cannot completely give in to. Somebody once said to me, 'If only we realised that the indirect way we choose in order to avoid pain is just as painful as the pain we try so skilfully to avoid . . .'

But who can believe this at the beginning of therapy? And who knows the dilemma better than a woman who enters hell each time a peanut enters her mouth?

7
Bulimia: A Feminist Psychoanalytic Understanding
Carol Bloom

Julie is under a lot of pressure at work. She has a deadline; she's worried her work won't be good enough. Her boss keeps giving her more to do; she can't manage to say no. Her friend calls and has to cancel their plans; she starts thinking about the nuts on her co-worker's desk. She has already had six. Her body starts feeling too big. She leaves work very uneasy with the night ahead and starts feeling bad about herself and thinking self-attacking thoughts. She glances in the shop window and notices the curve of her hips. She is revolted and enraged; she knew she shouldn't have eaten those nuts. She starts to panic. She runs into the nearest deli and grabs the biggest cake. She dares not have the man think it's all for her, so she goes on to the next shop and buys a packet of biscuits and a quart of ice cream. Key in the door . . . safe at last . . . standing in the kitchen she stuffs the food in until her belly aches, making sure the ice cream has gone in last, knowing that it will make everything come up more easily. She is horrified by what she sees in the bathroom mirror. She looks obese and distorted. Panicked, frightened, disgusted and ashamed, she sticks three fingers harshly down her throat over and over again until she thinks most of it is out. She will do this two more times tonight. Exhausted and numb, holding her once again empty stomach, she falls into a troubled sleep.

Julie and the women who suffer from this problem are called bulimic or bulimarexic. This eating problem is characterised by women who alternately binge on large quantities of food and then purge themselves. The purges can take many forms, but the most

102

I just ruined EVERYTHING with 1 piece of chocolate

common are throwing up and using laxatives, fasting and sometimes drugs. While her anorexic sister may sometimes binge and purge, and a bulimic may sometimes starve, the bulimic woman's distinguishing feature is her frequent and regular cycle of bingeing and purging, often taking up many hours of her day. Unlike her sister who overeats compulsively, she cannot tolerate the food inside her and is terrifed of the resulting fat. She is, like most women with eating problems, obsessed with her food, and has a distorted and self-hating relationship to her body. Her body can be normal, under- or overweight. Her shame and disgust with her problem leads her to be very secretive. Her body often doesn't show her problem, and due to this, and to the lack of knowledge on the part of the medical and mental health practitioners, she can go unnoticed and remain very isolated.

She can cause harm to her oesophagus, to the lining of her stomach, strain her heart, break blood vessels in her eyes and face, lower her potassium level to a dangerous point, decay her teeth, and she has been known to die over the toilet bowl. Most of this damage, however, can be reversed when she stops the purging. She can emerge in any personality type. I have been seeing bulimic women in my practice for many years, but with the incidence of bulimia on the rise, a feminist understanding of it is essential since 95 per cent of people with bulimia are women. We must see this statistic and this dramatically painful and potentially harmful adaptation to life as a scathing criticism and a raging silent protest of what it means to be a woman today.

Woman's present position in life is economically, socially, politically and psychologically precarious. She is relegated to a subordinate and second-class status, with all of the psychological characteristics of being and feeling less than a full person. She is forced to feel unentitled, securing status through those more powerful. Her options for self-expression and fulfilment are severely stunted and her self-image and sense of self-worth are damaged. Within the restriction of who she is allowed to be, she is then told who she is supposed to be – which is someone who sees herself as a thing of pleasure and an object of beauty for others. Although this is an assault on her true need to be a whole person, she is caught, since if the core of her being is built around pleasing others, then to try and make her body into whatever is currently acceptable, i.e. thin, is highly seductive. She cannot be part of mainstream culture anyway, as it is still male and if she takes a further stand that goes against the norm, the limited position and access to power and acceptability allowed her as a woman is jeopardised.

But we do rebel. The urges to do so and claim our lives for ourselves are powerful, and more options are opening for some of us, but the tug is always there for all of us, and the message is pervasive and powerful, especially from the media, who exploit our vulnerability continuously. If we transform our bodies and change our shapes, we will be more highly valued. We can't help but buy it; we start feeling out of place in our own skins; our natural curves and fullness become alien to us, as if being a woman, in her varying shapes and sizes, isn't all right. We start seeing food not as life's most basic form of satisfaction and nurturance but as dangerous and the enemy. Then our healthy desires for food makes us feel out of control, and we go to things outside ourselves to secure that control and the promise of self-esteem. But we aren't successful; we can't live with the deprivation of dieting, yet we don't see eating as the one way to self-soothe that no one can take away from us, or that it is life-affirming, and so we feel bad about ourselves, inadequate and greedy. Once again we try, and the cycle sets in; the battle rages and our bodies become the terrain for achievement and worth as people. Our precarious position makes all this possible, but with a feminist analytical approach we have begun and continue to fight back, empower ourselves, rethink fundamentally what are incorrect assumptions and struggle against a culture that has us feeling that who we are is what we look like, an image not even of our own making. As a practitioner working with women, and especially women with eating problems, I feel a feminist analyst is essential to helping them. In discussing bulimia, one of the more desperate and anguishing ways a woman deals with this struggle, I would like to go back to Julie to give you a brief view of our work together in therapy.

Julie came to me because of the terrible obsession with food which occupied much of her psychic life, her vicious hatred for and distorted view of her body and its need for care, and her inability to eat in any way that resembled a satisfying and nurturing experience. This was most dramatically characterised by periods of extreme deprivation, where she might pick up little bits of food (anything more felt dangerous), which would give way to periods of violent bingeing and throwing up.

She was good at her work as a journalist, she was in a supportive and caring relationship and had a community of friends, but something was terribly wrong. She was deeply unhappy and frightened, and she had this dreadful secret that no one knew about in all its totality. It was as if she were leading two separate lives: one life in the world, where she was seen as competent, creative, very helpful and sensitive to others; and one life in her obsession, where she felt herself to be needy, inadequate, damaged and completely out of control.

The involvement, tenaciousness, power and importance of this symptom lies in the fact that it is functional and accomplished much for Julie in her attempts to reconcile the anguishes of her inner and outer past and present worlds. We can look at much of Julie's past to understand what shaped her development and current life's adaptations. I will mention a few of the salient influences and circumstances of her life.

Julie was born prematurely and lived for two months in an incubator, being fed by a dropper. She was the fourth child, born just one year after her sister Katie, who had been born with severe birth defects. Katie's physical problems took up a tremendous amount of the family's energy (especially the mother's). There was one crisis after another, the family was in and out of hospitals and doctors' offices, and Julie's mother was often away for days at a time. Julie's experience of her mother throughout her childhood was either that she wasn't there, or, when she was there, in an attempt to make up for her absence, she was overbearing and suffocating in her attentiveness. Julie missed and longed for her, but remembers feeling when her mother walked into the room that she had to move back to make room for her.

Julie's father's reaction to the family's crisis was to retreat. He was revolted by Katie's disability and removed himself continually from the family. Julie, therefore, had no one to turn to for adequate parenting.

Julie felt attached to Katie, and her earliest memories are laced with feelings of terrible guilt and worry about her, as well as revulsion and embarrassment because of her deformed body. But like her mother, Julie spent a lot of time caring for and being involved with her.

After Julie's mother and father divorced, her mother's emotional state deteriorated. She was often inappropriate in her responses and could not adequately meet Julie's needs for care and guidance. This made Julie's reality often feel quite shaky. A typical example of this is when Julie's mother encouraged her to dig a hole as big as she liked in the back garden; by the time a neighbour stopped her, it was almost over her head. Or when Julie was hungry, she would either find the cupboards bare or her mother would lay out a feast enough for 20. Food was often used as the medium for communication and connection between Julie and her mother. Her mother would, at times, disappear or forget to pick her up, leaving her waiting and worried for hours.

This alternating pattern of inappropriate responses in Julie's early life was to be reflected in her bulimia.

It is important to note that when Julie started kindergarten, and during other major transitions in her life, she would feel 'sick' and *need* to throw up. This often resulted in her spending the day at home with mother.

The stresses and demands of the need to feel successful and be accepted by the social world during puberty and in her early teens were upon her. She felt overwhelmed, incompetent and unattractive. Being good at home or smart in school wasn't enough, and with no place to turn for help in navigating these difficult times, Julie once again buried her needs and attempted, in the best ways she could, to respond to her anguishes and conflicts and to find a place for herself. She became involved with drinking and drugs. She did well in school in spite of this, but during her first year at college the one friend she had whom she loved and trusted died suddenly in an accident. From that day on Julie started taking drugs (downers and cannabis) daily and spent the rest of her college days in the haze of being high. Three years later she joined a support group and stopped taking drugs entirely. It is not surprising that her eating problems began around this time.

I would like to share how I understood Julie's life experiences translated into her present adaptations. From the first moments of Julie's life, and continuing through her development, she was severely deprived of adequate and continuous care. She had to bury, deny, defer and split off all her needs, wants and yearnings. Her fragile and developing psyche, needing protection from the anxiety and pain of unmet needs, had to bury the appropriately needy and hungry parts of the self. With the continuous experience of her needs either not being met or being inaccurately perceived and inappropriately responded to, Julie could not develop a sense of trust in the world around her or in her own feeling states, and without knowing or trusting what she felt, she could not adequately rely upon herself for comfort or inner-direction. Her inner and outer worlds felt fragile and dangerous, and the way little Julie experienced this was that something was terribly wrong and unlovable about her. This inability to trust her environment and to self-nurture and soothe satisfactorily was to wreak havoc throughout her life.

Current feminist theory has taught us that little girls have an inferiorised psychology, and that this gets reproduced in the mother–daughter relationship in the patriarchal nuclear family.[1] Julie, like all little girls, is relegated and directed for a life of denial of self in relation to others. Instead of meeting her own needs, her satisfaction must come from pleasing and caring for others. Because she does not feel entitled to her own needs and desires, when they do arise, they make her feel too needy, ashamed and greedy, and she meets them with disgust and rebuke. The drives or strivings for autonomy and separation are anguishing, conflictual and not successfully accomplished, and meet with much resistance and anxiety from those around her, and so much of her gets buried. Her gender requirements and her particular life experiences were fertile ground for the stunting of the shoots of her own growth as an autonomous and effective person.

Julie did not just feel bad and unhappy. She grew up feeling, like so many women, that something was terribly wrong with her, and

and *she* was bad and unlovable. And so, in her desperate need for love and approval, she took up the values around her. She felt driven to do well at school, take care of Katie, take care of Mummy, swallow her tears when Mummy forgot her, make up for the unhappiness in the marriage and be the good, normal daughter – the undemanding daughter Katie could never be. From the pain and emptiness of her own unmet needs, Julie knew exactly how to care for and meet the needs of others. Giving replaced receiving, for having would put her in touch with her terrifying hunger and feelings of insatiability. But as Julie described it and we could assume, she never felt satisfied or happy. Nothing she did was good enough. She had to be extraordinary, and if she was anything less she felt invisible; she would be swallowed up. She would not allow anyone to get close enough to know the real her; she feared they would find the door to all that she felt was unacceptable about herself.

The pain of losing her dear friend, the one person to whom she could reveal more of herself, was too much stress for her already damaged sense of self, and she had to bury herself further in the depths of drugs that would numb her.

Towards the end of her drug-taking, Julie became involved in a loving relationship and with help and encouragement joined a support group and embarked on the courageous and difficult path of becoming drug-free. For the first time in her life she had a support network and felt valued.

However, all was not well. Not only did this new life feel fragile, but it was fragile, both in its newness and because she felt fraudulent, unentitled, extremely controlled and inadequate, as if she were on very thin ice. Julie was terrified of being a responsible adult and felt incapable. It was not an easy world for a newly drug-free woman trying to make it in a male-dominated profession and society.

She started having trouble with her food. She got involved in a diet–binge cycle and started feeling out of control, a terrifying prospect for her. The diets got more stringent, rigid and compulsive, and as a consequence, the binges were more furious. She was becoming obsessed with her body and being thin. In a desperate attempt to keep her weight down, she started throwing up. Soon this behaviour became highly locked in, highly ritualised and much more than a weight-reduction measure. It became a way to cope, to survive, a way of life that she shared with no one. Given her psychological state, Julie was ripe for an obsession, and converging with the dictates and demands of the culture as to what is acceptable as a female, Julie was ripe for this obsession. The lure of dieting and changing her body-size was extremely seductive.

The lure of feeling good, the sense of control, the achievement, the success and the resulting promise of acceptability that come from dieting and feeling attractive (i.e. thin) is a powerful hook for women in our culture. Life problems and yearnings that are uncomfortable become food and body problems. This becomes the arena in which self-worth is measured. If only she could get skinny enough to transform herself, an idea attractive to Julie since she was so scared and overwhelmed by the needy little girl part, then perhaps she would be okay. It's as if the food and associated body states become magnets for good and bad feelings and perceived good and bad parts of herself. All that Julie feels is unacceptable, or that which she cannot tolerate and is deemed bad, is associated with food and feeling large. Feelings of comfort and safety and being in control are good and become associated with not eating and feeling smaller. Eating or not eating was her way to manage what felt unmanageable.

Our inner and outer worlds are not free of demands for help and soothing. We learn to meet those needs appropriately or inappropriately, successfully or unsuccessfully, depending on our early experience with being nurtured. Food is tied up here since our earliest needs for soothing are met with food and it is imbued with the quality of maternal care we received. For Julie this was problematic, and her later attempts were to reflect this. Her needs were either not met and she had to repress them, or they were met inappropriately and she couldn't 'digest' what she was given, she couldn't feel it to be helpful and had to throw it back up. Her binge–purge cycle, her reaching for and getting rid of, can be viewed as a repeat of this early and continuous experience. Her yearnings not met or met by loss and disappointment were compulsively being repeated in her current patterns of coping.

The conversion of feelings to obsession can be instantaneous and without conscious awareness. She takes up into her food and body what her psyche cannot tolerate. Looking more closely at Julie's bingeing and purging we can see this at work.

Any number of indigestible feelings could start the craving, and since she feels unable to live and help herself through the discomfort of the moment, it immediately gets converted into thinking about food or feeling that something is wrong with her body. This makes her even more obsessed with food, and she goes to the food for comfort, solace, connection and to bury the anger and fear, squash the pain of unmet needs, and for a few moments to be lost in the rapture of food. But she starts to panic and she can't sit with the food inside her. She doesn't see the food as good, doesn't accept her needs for nurturance and soothing, is terrified and doesn't know how to cope with that needy little girl's part. The food and all it represents feels too dangerous inside, and must be got rid of. She is now feeling fat, all this badness is showing, and she can't tolerate the exposure and humiliation of her unacceptableness. Her self-protective, rigid structure has been pierced, and she feels wild and out of control, and knowing she has a way out by throwing up, she goes with the binge and stuffs in huge quantities of food (always calculating, however, what will come up easiest). She finishes off the binge with huge amounts of water and forces herself over and over again to throw up until she is sure most of what was inside is out.

She is left with a feeling of tremendous relief, emptied out of the horrible discomfort and tension of all the conflicting feelings she has just swallowed. She has made sure that it will not show on her body. She could not bear this needy, inadequate, damaged, chaotic, devouring self to be dripping and hanging out of her body. While the fantasy is that she has just flushed that part of herself down the toilet, the positive attempts at self-soothing, the attempt to give to herself, by her own hands, and possibly even feed a hungry body is also washed away. She is once again left unnurtured, unnourished and yearning. On top of that, she feels bad about this shameful secret and the feelings start charging again. When she can't contain them any longer, she once again turns to the food for comfort, for numbing and for the sensation of being filled up. It is a way of taking some kind of action, but the panic takes over, the feelings of disgust and rage at herself rise. The empty boxes and packets are mortifying, she must get all this food out of her, then everything will be okay.

The powerful feelings of being able to get things back in order are coursing through her veins. It will be all over soon; tomorrow is a new day, and she falls asleep exhausted, wrapping her obsessive thoughts around her like a warm blanket, thinking about how she won't eat at all tomorrow to get rid of what might be left inside, or swallowing a handful of laxatives, desperately trying to keep out all the feelings and thoughts and unmet needs that sent her to the food in the first place.

Julie's body becomes her entire world. Even in the face of such hardship to her body and her anguish, Julie must do this, for she knows no other way. She has no way of dealing with her feelings so she absorbs everything back into her body to contain it. Instead of a life which can feel out of control, everything is transferred to a body that can be governed. The action of the bingeing and purging is her way of taking power, and she feels in control because she can make her body forcibly do something that will put things back into order, stabilise her and bring her great relief. The binge is the disaster, and the purge is the rescue operation; then she can feel powerful. If she creates the disaster in her body, it is contained as a food problem, and she can do something about it. If it's outside or has to do with other people or the world in which she lives, she doesn't feel equipped to, or trust that she can, cope. She has created this self-contained, self-perpetuating, rigid system that gives an illusion of control. Over time, and as a result of its reinforcing quality, this adaptive behaviour gets locked in and becomes highly ritualised. It takes up many hours a day of Julie's life, and due to her disgust and shame and secrecy about the problem, her already poor self-image becomes worse. Her sense of inadequacy increases and she withdraws. She isolates herself from the world emotionally, avoids contact, and the loneliness and emptiness she feels now can be filled up by her obsession and the binge–purge, which sometimes produces its own unique sense of excitement and aliveness. This was the state of Julie's world when she walked into my office.

Our work in therapy progressed along three main, interlaced tracks. The first was the slow, painful and courageous process of taking all that was being contained by the obsession and living and working it through with me in therapy. Julie came to understand that her symptom had to be respected and seen compassionately for the function it served in her attempts to carve out a space for what she experienced as unacceptable, as feared and as devouring about her, and what she felt to be irreconcilable or easily lost and swallowed up in her inner and outer worlds. Her symptom was not to be taken away, as some therapies might suggest. It expressed an important part of her, and without it, Julie would have suffered terrible loss. If prematurely removed, it would have left her highly susceptible to a new symptom.

We had to create room for the hungry, needy, deprived little Julie to emerge without revulsion or renouncement. She had to see that her wants and needs did not make her insatiable or greedy and were not invasions or proof of her inadequacies or damaged self. They were part of living and growing and had to be listened to and gratified appropriately.

She came to understand that her obsession (and the bingeing and purging) was an attempt to take care of herself but was as mismatched and insufficient as the responses in her early environment, and that that is why ultimately it was not the solution.

She had to make room in her internal world and relationships, rather than in her body, for taking in, tolerating and dealing with the rage, fears, challenges, limits, constrictions, joys and pleasures she was facing in her life. She had to explore what she could realistically expect of herself and the world around her. She came to see how the bingeing and purging ritual, which took up so much of her time, was a way not to feel the terror of her aloneness and separateness or the conflicts and disappointments and pressures she put on herself. Feelings of self-worth could come, not from her body, but from being active in the world. She had to make peace with what she could and could not control in life, and not assume that anything less than perfect was bad or an assault on her equilibrium and so, therefore, something she had to act upon. There is a lot in life that doesn't feel good; she had to learn to live through that without asking it into her body in order to have the illusion of control. This was certainly not an easy task for one so out of practice with experiencing her conflictual feelings.

The second track of her therapy was to help Julie learn to take food in according to bodily needs, and to take in and hold on to the pleasure and satisfaction that can come from self-nurturance, as well as to live comfortably in a body-size that was realistic for her. For a bulimic woman this is an excruciating task, for it might mean she has to accept a higher weight. Unconscious and conscious experiences of her different body states of fat or thin, food in or food out, had to be explored and decathected or divested of their emotional content. And she had to accept food and body for what they truly were and not as having the enormous and magical powers she gave to them.

Julie came to re-experience and work through her feelings about Katie's deformities, and she was able to let go of her guilt to see her normal and healthy body as something to which she was entitled. With new pathways created for self-expression and with healthier coping mechanisms and increased self-acceptance, Julie's relationship to food and her body changed dramatically.

My years of experience specialising in eating problems, and my feminist analysis and treatment model as laid out in *Fat is a Feminist Issue* allowed me to be extremely helpful in offering Julie a solution she could live with, for we can only imagine what it would have felt like if, at the end of this long struggle, she had the prospect of being on a diet for the rest of her life.[2]

The third track of her therapy had to do with the therapy relationship. In both working through the transference, and in exploring all her thoughts and feelings about our real and current relationship, Julie could have a very different experience from the one she had had with her mother. With the nurture of a caring, appropriate, consistent and reliable relationship with a woman whom she respected and valued, Julie's own possibilities of valuing herself as a woman could grow. I was a strong and capable person living and dealing with all the contradictions facing women today. I could handle and contain her anxiety, rage and despair without abandoning or rejecting her. I could affirm and support her yearnings and endeavours without being threatened or feeling betrayed. She could love or hate me without fear of losing or hurting me, and she had to learn how to take in that my care and acceptance for her were not dangerous or consuming. This helped Julie to see that the world outside her obsession was possible to live in, and she wouldn't have to fall apart like her mother or hide in her obsession.

I would like to close with something that occurred in a session a year and a half into therapy and about a month before the bingeing and purging subsided. Julie came in and pronounced quite energetically, 'I've got it! If I don't accept myself I'll starve or vomit myself to death. I kept thinking I have to become or make myself totally different in order to be okay. That's what you've been trying to tell me, right? I have to accept *this* body, *this* person. If I keep thinking that changing my body and getting rid of all my uncomfortable feelings would make me a good person, I could end up dead. I could never change enough not to be me. I wanted to be perfect, but perfect wasn't me.' She then blurted out, 'What is so bad about me, anyway?' The tears welled up in her eyes and the lump in my throat was substantial.

After the session I found myself longing, longing for a world where being a full woman taking pleasure in her body and her mind, and being an equal, active, creative participant in the world, is not an extraordinary achievement or a revolutionary act but her irrefutable birth-right!

Notes

1. See, e.g., Chodorow, N., *The Reproduction of Mothering: Psychoanalysis and the Sociology of Gender*, Berkeley, California 1978; Eichenbaum, L. and Orbach, S., *Understanding Women*, Penguin, London, 1985; and Orbach, S., and Eichenbaum, L., *What Do Women Want? Exploding the Myth of Dependency*, Michael Joseph, London, 1983.

2. Orbach, S., *Fat is a Feminist Issue*, Hamlyn, London, 1979; and *Fat is a Feminist Issue II*, Hamlyn, London, 1984. The essential concepts presented in *Fat is a Feminist Issue* are: a social and feminist analysis of women's complex relationship to our bodies and to food; an anti-deprivation, anti-dieting approach to feeding oneself, where food is accepted as soothing, life-giving and enjoyable. Bingeing and compulsive eating can stop only when food is experienced as bountiful and good; learning to sort out true physiological stomach hunger from other needs and internal experiences and to eventually use hunger as the guide for feeding oneself; discovering one's fat and thin self, and learning to find the 'true' authentic self in both. Our fat- or thin-feeling states don't then determine who we are or what we are entitled to.

8
Self-Help Groups: The Agony and the Ecstasy
Katina Noble

Six years ago I read a book that changed my life. The book was *Fat is a Feminist Issue* by Susie Orbach.[1] Its effect on me and thousands of other women was startling. Here was a book exonerating us of all the guilt and self-hatred and blame we'd carried for years. Its message made such sense: it showed us how and why dieting and compulsive eating were primarily a woman's problem. For the first time someone was looking at the issue within a social context, examining all the social pressures that forced women to be thin. It was so clear and so sensible. Society's obsession with thinness, i.e. adverts of lithe beauties on beaches, women's magazines full of lean, leggy models, had actually succeeded in making millions of women unhappy and dissatisfied with their bodies. How could women ever live up to the expectations of the media – on the one hand, you had to look like Meryl Streep, on the other hand, you were bombarded with pictures of delicious food, recipes and the image of the perfect wife and mother in the kitchen. To succeed, you had to spend hours preparing and cooking beautiful meals, but you had to resist them at all costs.

As well as this, Susie explained why diets didn't work for women – a completely revolutionary idea. 95 per cent of all women who diet put back most, all or more of the weight, so clearly something is wrong. Susie explained it very well. Diets were dealing with the symptom (being overweight) not the underlying problems.

For example, if you found you binged when you felt lonely (to fill a gap), even if you dieted and lost all the weight, once you felt lonely again, the bingeing would recur.

What you needed to do was to start to sort out your problems –

isolation, lack of friends, fear of intimacy or whatever – not put yourself on a diet. Dealing with loneliness could be extremely difficult and painful, but at least you would be tackling the issue, rather than seeing it all in terms of food.

Diets in fact exacerbated the problem. They made you more obsessed with food, because you had to count calories or weigh out a portion of fish. Also every diet was eventually followed by a binge: sooner or later, you would crack and then eat everything in sight. This was the common pattern and natural result of depriving yourself.

So the book was in fact encouraging us to give up diets and to stop internalising all the pain and guilt and secrecy – to blame not ourselves but the sick society we live in that treats women as decorative sex-objects rather than intelligent, powerful human beings.

Fat is a Feminist Issue so impressed me and was so relevant to me as a compulsive eater that I decided I wanted to 'spread the word', and I started setting up self-help groups for compulsive eaters, based on the ideas in the book.

Having set up self-help groups for a number of years now, I am constantly asked whether they actually work and what the success rate is. I almost feel with the word 'success' they expect me to reassure them of every woman's dramatic weight loss. And indeed it is hard for any dieter or ex-dieter to think of 'success' in other terms. For so many years we have all struggled towards the Weight Watchers' 'goal weight', jumped with joy when the scales showed we'd lost half a pound, been made to feel our problems would magically disappear if we were only eight stone two.

In the past, we have seen success as losing pounds; now, in the self-help group, we have to begin to look at success in a totally different way. Success, as I define it, manifests itself in many ways for the different sorts of women in the group. First, there are the rather thin, anxious compulsive eaters who have come to see they are not actually fat and that their problem is much more to do with how they feel about themselves and their self-image. Then there are those who, with the encouragement and support of the group, have learnt to accept themselves and even like themselves and their bodies as they are. Then there are those women who come to the realisation that the seven stone three they always yearned to be is totally unreasonable and unnatural for them. They had struggled to be a weight which was far too low for their body size and bone structure and therefore had to be constantly dieting to maintain it.

And lastly, there are women who actually do lose weight. These women were fat, but, having successfully worked through their compulsive eating and now only eating when physically hungry, find their body readjusts to what is right and comfortable and thinner.

What I want to do in this chapter is to try and give all those anxious women who asked me about success a clear and honest picture of the self-help group – its strengths and weaknesses – so they can understand more about how it works and what its limitations and achievements are.

Setting up a compulsive-eating group

If you decide to set up your own compulsive-eating group, be sure to make it very clear from the beginning that the group is going to be a self-help group with no leader. Women may easily look to you as leader/teacher/mother, because you have taken the initiative and courage to begin the group. This often happens and understandably so: women with eating problems feel particularly insecure and have often been used to a series of slimming teachers and doctors 'sorting them out'. However, it will help them and you much more to place power in their hands from the start, so everyone has equal responsibility. Talk about this at the beginning and structure the first session with other women taking responsibility in time-keeping. Impress upon the group the importance of a rotating leader/coordinator – someone who plans the session each week – and put that into practice as soon as you have set up the initial session(s). It will also help the balance and equality of the group if you keep strictly to time, and within reason give everyone the same amount of space. If the group still continues to look to you, make them aware of this and focus back to what your own needs are as an equal member of the group with similar problems.

Session 1

1. Introductions in the Circle In an initial session, where women are obviously nervous or apprehensive, it is a good idea to start in the safety of a circle. Everyone feels secure on their cushion or chair and everyone is able to see everyone else. Go around the circle, asking each woman to introduce herself and to give a brief history of her relationship with food. It is wise to give a time limit, three to four minutes, and to keep to the time allotted. Time-keeping is such an essential part of the group structure, it is best to implement this from the start, so that passing round the watch and giving everyone the same amount of time becomes a matter of course.

2. *Collectings* Now ask the group to get up, mill around and share with each other all the diets they have ever been on. Ask them to relate three diets and listen to their partner's three diets in return. Then, as quickly as possible, move around and collect as many diets from as many women as you can in four minutes. If you have been on more than three diets, tell different women the different diets. This game acts as an ice-breaker – the circle shifts to a shattered focus where women will feel easier talking. By mingling, there is movement and body contact and the game can ease tension and help relax the group.

After the four to five minutes, ask them to call out the diets they heard from everyone else. Write them all up on the blackboard and ask for explanations of any that you have never heard of before. Now ask the group to put up their hands if they've lost weight on a diet. And to put their hands up if they've put the weight back on after the diet. Write up the percentage on the board. We would expect most of the women to have put weight back on. Now ask them to tell you what feelings and emotions they associate with dieting and write those up as well. Discuss these feelings and diets generally.

I then reiterate what has just been said – that diets don't work, that they cause untold anxieties, depression, etc., and that the relief should be in the knowledge that they never have to go on a diet again. Now I ask them to play Collectings once more, this time collecting all their favourite foods. I urge them to be very specific about what kinds of foods they like – if they are chips, are they crisp or soggy, brown, crunchy, greasy? Again there is three to four minutes for collecting three foods from each person. Write all the foods on the blackboard and talk about their relationship to food, what food symbolises, etc.

I like to reassure them here that the group is going to help them enjoy food again without feeling guilty and that all these delicious foods are no longer forbidden, but available to them once again as they are to 'normal' eaters.

3. *Fat/Thin Party Fantasy*[2] Start with a short relaxation and then spend 15 minutes on the fantasy. At the end, when women are going to share their fantasy, choose to go around the circle one by one or to pair off if the group is larger than seven. If you do pair off, ask partners to listen and not to comment. Then allow a short feedback from the partner after six to seven minutes. Change over

and repeat. Finally ask the pairs to come back into the circle and feed back the most significant parts of the fantasy to the whole group.

Using pair work in the group can be very helpful, particularly when the group is rather large. It can be a good way to start a session – pairing off and spending five to seven minutes each on feedback from the week can save a lot of time and allow you to move on to other exercises and discussion topics more quickly.

Relate the fantasy in the present tense and then open the discussion up to talk about the positive aspects of fat and the scary aspects of thin, which is a vital on-going part of the work in the group.

Fat/Thin Fantasy. Imagine yourself at a party getting fatter and fatter and then thinner. It is extraordinary what strong images this fantasy brings to the surface and how clearly a fantasy can reveal the unconscious conflicts at work.

In one fat/thin fantasy I did with a group, when the woman got thinner, you actually couldn't see her any more. This really showed her how insignificant, powerless and invisible she felt or feared feeling as a thin woman.

Another woman got bigger and bigger and blew up like a Michelin Man. She was then so huge and bouncy and powerful, she jumped on a sofa at the party and bounced all the men on it right into the sofa, so that all that was left was their squashed and flat faces.

The fantasy helped her recognise her furious feelings against so many men she knew, but also made her see how strong and powerful her fat made her feel. It did have benefits, which she had never fully realised before.

Another woman hid in a corner at the party when she was fat, dressed in a huge crimplene tent-dress, talking only to one close friend. As soon as she lost weight and was thin, she was the life and soul of the party, dancing madly, surrounded by men, flirting and chatting. But although superficially this seemed fun, she realised that as a thin person nobody was talking to her for her; people merely treated her as a sex-object. She too felt very superficial and anxious, wondering which man would pounce first. She realised being thin wasn't quite the bed of roses she had expected and that at least as a fat woman the level of communication with her friend was intimate and meaningful.

All these women had conflicting messages about the meaning of fat and thin for them which the fantasy helped bring to the surface.

4. Tea-Break (optional)

5. Questions

6. Homework. Finally, it is important to carry on working on the problems between sessions.

Food Chart.[3] Fill it in for a day and bring it back the following week.

Hunger Awareness. Try to experience hunger during the week. If you can manage to, try to satisfy your hunger with something you really want. Note down what your body feels, when it is hungry and how you feel emotionally and physically about hunger. It is a good idea to keep a compulsive-eating notebook to note down any important issues that come up for you, e.g. how you're feeling just before a binge, what fears your hunger brings up, etc.

Session 2

1. A Warm-Up. It is a good idea to help raise the energy level or help relax the group with an initial warm-up exercise. If people are particularly tense, then some kind of relaxation is probably appropriate. For example: Being Moved or Trusting the Group[4] or Hand or Face Print

Hand or Face Print. Go around, eyes open, feeling everybody's hands/face. Be sensitive to the feel of the skin, how warm or cold the skin is, the shape of the nose or mouth, how bony the knuckles are and try to make an association between what you feel and the person. Break into two groups. The first group makes an inner circle facing outwards, eyes closed. The second group goes up to a person and puts their hands/face in her hands to feel and identify. When she guesses, move on so she has a new face/hands to touch.

If people are sluggish or tired, a high-energy game might be appropriate, such as Snake Pit or Jumping Jacks.

Snake Pit. Stand around a chalked circle on the floor, arms over shoulders. The circle is the snake pit. Try to push people into the snake pit (over the line). If you go over the line or touch the line, you are dead (out). As group gets smaller, draw a smaller chalk circle.

Jumping Jacks. In twos, stand closely together, one with legs together, the other with legs apart, hands around each other's neck or waist. Jump up and down and when someone shouts 'change', change partners. Jump higher and lower and try to keep a rhythm going.

These games and exercises are very easy to set up and generally woman are open to them, but you do need to be sensitive to the group, and if there are inhibitions, take it slowly and allow trust in the group to build up. To start with an exercise makes the structure clear and gives the session a sense of purpose and commitment. Also, as body-work is such a crucial part of what goes on in the group, it is important to include warm-ups, etc., which help the group become more familiar with each others' bodies and their own. It is important for a woman to be held and touched by others and know her body can be accepted and stroked and massaged in the group. This is the first vital step towards self-acceptance.

2. Pairs

Group pairs off and talks about their week: seven minutes each way and two minutes' discussion.

3. Feedback

Back in the circle, each woman talks about her food chart: seven to ten minutes each, allowing comments and questions from the whole group.

4. Supermarket Fantasy[5]

Feedback in pairs; seven minutes each way. Short discussion on food, your attitude to it, etc., for ten minutes.

5. How the Group will Function

Leave a good hour to discuss how the group will function in the future.
Ideal number: five to eight.
Time: 2½–3½ hours a week.

Important points

Punctuality

If women arrive late, the session becomes diffused and can easily fall into chat. It is important to start on time and for anyone who is going to be late to ring and warn the group. Some groups find a tea and chat session for half an hour before the group starts useful so that they can socialise from 7–7.30 and then begin punctually at 7.30.

Time-Keeping

Someone should always be time-keeper and make sure everyone gets their allotted time.

Structure and Plan

Each week someone from the group takes responsibility for planning the session. This might be discussed at the end of the previous session where something important has come up which needs to be explored in more detail the following week, e.g. our relationships with our mothers has come up in various exercises or discussion, so Pam decides to follow this through when planning the next session and to focus on the theme of mothers and daughters.

Line-Up

It is important to be aware of the line-up or form of the group and how we can alter it to sustain interest and energy, shatter the focus of attention, get more work done, etc. If the group remains in the circle at all times, this can become enervating or too informal or casual; everyone sitting back on their comfortable chairs can too easily lapse into chat.

Look at the form of a group. You can divide it into pairs, two groups, a milling group, two lines or one whole group. Each line-up can change the energy level, affect the intensity of communication between people and make the session more varied and therefore more interesting and effective.

Two women, D and J, talk to T about their experiences in a compulsive-eating group

D: The group was a new beginning. You could focus on the weekly meeting. I found it impossible on my own. It's very difficult with a group but not as difficult as on your own. The issues are so deep-rooted. Psychological issues are impossible to deal with on your own. You lose faith on your own. The group helps tő boost you, especially as self-image is the crucial issue.

J: Setting aside that time every week was important. The group made me realise my problem was not as bad as I thought; others had worse problems. There was a lot of encouragement from the group.

We had no outright leader, but each week someone organised the session.

D: My problem was I really wanted a leader in many ways, though I know it goes against what Susie is saying about self-help and taking control. I wanted someone, 'an expert', to reassure me, to say 'Oh, that's normal.'

J: A big problem initially was we were all there 'to get thin'. We'd judge a binge: 'Oh dear, a binge.'

T: So how could it work?

J: We did a lot of work on self-acceptance. We did a lot of exercises that picked out the good things. We concentrated initially on character rather than body and that helped our self-esteem. It was boosting to have positive feed-back from the group when our general self-confidence and self-esteem was so low. We didn't risk a lot in the early stages. But we did later in the group and found confrontation uncomfortable.

D: I freaked out just at the idea of confrontation. I was frightened of what might be said about me. I felt I was the only one there that bad things could be said about.

J: D has a 'total lack of confidence' and yet she contributed so much to the group. She thought so deeply, was so articulate, said things none of the rest of us would ever have thought of. She thought nobody would want to see her outside the group. She couldn't accept they might actually like her.

As the group became more confronting, the sessions were less enjoyable in one way, but there was definitely more work done. One woman continually criticising became destructive.

T: Did you have heavy sessions? Were a lot of tears shed?

J and D: Yes.

T: What techniques did you use to get in touch with those underlying feelings?

J: Fantasies, role play. There was one particularly powerful fantasy about going back to childhood, closing your eyes and imagining yourself as a little girl again, standing in front of the mirror and going back to how you as a little girl expected you to turn out, and were you the person that little girl expected you to be?

D: Lots of tears and anxieties came out of that. We used *In Our Own Hands* a lot. I found role play very cathartic. There was one situation in which I was playing a child. I became a very angry child, threw an enormous tantrum, as children do. I threw things, stamped, shouted, burst into tears.

T: How was that cathartic?

D: Well, it happened after a particular incident in my life that had angered and distressed me. Just to release all that was important. I felt in the situation that had angered and upset me like a child who'd had its favourite toy taken away. It seemed a very relevant role play to a real life situation. The situation was with a man whom I'd broken up with 18 months previously and I had never really accepted it. We met again, and I still felt very upset he'd ended the relationship. I wasn't feeling that much affection for him any more, but a childish rage at not having something, not having the choice.

T: *What else did that role play exercise do?*

D: It released anger.

T: *What else?*

D: I think 18 months before I would have persisted in thinking I was suffering from a broken heart. Even with all the reading, etc., and thinking deeply about it, I never came to understand the real feelings at work in the way I did doing that exercise in the group. That is one thing I've gained from enormously in the group.

T: *So what was the realisation? That it wasn't a broken heart?*

D: Understanding I felt like a child with its toy taken away. There were very important issues working here for me, powerlessness and choice. In that situation I had no power and no choice, very much like a child. All you could do would be to freak out all the adults by being uncontrollable.

T: *Was the group successful?*

J: Yes, very successful overall.

D: I have some reservations, and it came to an end before I wanted it to, but on the whole I feel very positive about it.

T: *What do you think is the power of self-help?*

D: Ultimately, it is you who helps yourself. It's difficult to come to terms with that. It is not necessarily the group that will help you. One has to do some tough thinking. Feelings brought up couldn't be easily dealt with on your own, but in the context of the group, it's possible.

J: The positive thing for me is that the group gives you time for yourself. You talk to the women in the group in a way you'd never talk to a friend, it's different. You start to recognise patterns. You'd feed back to the group about that and they'd be in tune with you enough to know what you were talking about.

T: *How have you changed?*

D: Change for me is in terms of self-knowledge. I know myself so much better. I thought I was a pretty perceptive person, but realise how self-deceiving I was. I was finding out so much but still I carried on compulsively eating. I started to find out the things triggering that within my emotional psyche.

J: Realising how much I thought about others' feelings rather than my own – men's, my children's. And the group has made me realise that food is actually no consolation. I have learned to treat myself in other ways. I'm still uneasy about food but much, much better.

T: How do you feel about your bodies?

J: One hundred per cent better.

D: Better, because I'm thinner, though still dissatisfied.

J: I no longer feel out of control with food. I still binge occasionally, but now feel it's not disastrous.

Problems that came up in D and J's Group

1. Getting Thin

For many women, coming to the self-help group is the last resort. They have been on every diet, suffered the humiliations of slimming clubs (where some women are even put in a pig pen if they've put on weight) and even gone as far as having their jaws wired or stomach stapled. They have all put the weight back on and now feel this is their only hope.

However, even if *Fat is a Feminist Issue* makes sense to you intellectually, it is very difficult to rid yourself of years of pressure and influence that told you getting thin was going to solve all your problems.

Acknowledging this desire early in the group is important. Then you are able to discuss what this means for the individual woman and help to remind her and each other that getting thin doesn't necessarily solve things. The important thing for a long-term solution to the problems is to look at the underlying feelings.

What needs to be reiterated is what I always say when I set up a group: that the group is not about getting thin. It is about breaking the addiction to food and learning to have a happier relationship with food and your body.

As long as women are there hoping to get thin, it won't work for them. All the anxieties and tensions at play go against the whole philosophy and approach of the group and undermine it.

The group needs to struggle to take the emphasis away from getting thin, to focus on the feelings and the eating and to reassure each other that this is the sensible approach and one which will lead to a more permanent solution.

It is also important to acknowledge women's bad feelings about their fat. What can happen is that a woman feels guilty because she secretly can't stop hating her fat and wants to get thin. This is perfectly understandable. She needs to try to learn to accept that the fat is there for a reason – not to love it or judge it, but simply acknowledge its existence.[6]

Wanting to get thin is perfectly understandable if you've dragged 14 stone around for years and find it hard to run for a bus. However, the reasons why you've got fat have to be explored first and the desire to be thin pushed from your mind. This is, without any doubt, a very hard thing to do.

As D and J said, they concentrated on self-image and their self-esteem and self-confidence to take the emphasis away from getting thin. They concentrated on Mirror Work[7] and games and exercises that made them start to feel better about themselves (see *In Our Own Hands*). 'I'm not getting any thinner. The group's not working for me,' says X. Expecting miracle diet-type results stirs up all the old tensions and anxieties that accompany dieting and make it impossible to find a calmer, more relaxed frame of mind to enable you to delve deeper into yourself.

These tensions act as a defence to probing more deeply and can make the rest of the group panic or feel unsure of the approach because X can't accept it. They can start to resent X and feel they are losing faith in the group. If X is still secretly trying to get thin, the group can often feel old competitive feelings stirred up: 'Look, she has lost weight already. It's not fair, look at me.'

In initial discussions about this desire for thinness, you could share how you see each other. Each person draws a picture of herself naked and a picture of how she'd like to be. Everyone comments on how they see her. To begin to realise others don't necessarily see you as fat or as fat as you think you are is a hopeful first step. They may see positive things you had never thought of.

The majority of women in the groups are not enormously overweight and very often the issue is far more about bad self-image, low self-esteem, etc.

2. Wanting a Leader[8]

Having been brought up to respect experts and specialists and to feel often unconfident of our own abilities, it is understandable that women, in particular, are frightened of the idea of taking something into their own hands. Doctors, psychiatrists and teachers have not helped to demystify the relationship between them and their 'patients' or 'pupils'. And similarly, in the dieting world, the hypnotist, diet doctor or slimming teacher is there to solve your problems for you. In fact, what they are doing is taking the power from you, leaving you passive, helpless, sometimes almost childlike in your desperation to be 'cured'.

This is the fatal role for too many women. We go to doctors who prescribe valium, psychiatrists who prescribe anti-depressants, diet doctors who prescribe slimming tablets and, helpless and hopeless, we find ourselves manipulated and controlled by men (mostly) who have no real understanding of our problems.

Being able to take the problem into your own hands is in itself a very positive move. It can give a woman a new-found confidence and morale boost just to know she is making efforts to help herself and, through her experience and knowledge, help others too. Let us not forget that as women we have been brought up to be the carers, the nurturers, to be in tune with other people's feelings and have gained enormous insight and perception from our conditioning.

My 'expertise' has come almost entirely from ten years' experience as a compulsive eater. That understanding, that identification with others, the knowledge learnt through the experience is unique. And it can give you enormous confidence to realise you have the ability to make changes and help yourself. Let's face it, the 'experts' aren't doing a very good job of it! And support, friendship and learning to listen to each other are far more valuable than a bottle of pills.

Clearly, there are times when a group feels it just isn't equipped to deal with someone, that her problems are overwhelming. An example of this was a woman in my group, J, who was bulimic. An took so many laxatives that she often fainted and had been in hospital with internal bleeding. The others were quite frightened by the seriousness of her problem, but didn't want to reject her.

It was important in this situation to talk it through. An exercise, Body Sculpture,[9] where the group arranged themselves and the others in a sculpture or tableau according to how they saw themselves in the group, revealed that J was seen as a woman crouching low in the middle, her head bowed, with everyone in a circle around her. This led to an easier discussion, in which the other women could acknowledge the difficulties. They felt they were carrying her and yet felt she did contribute a lot to the group. Eventually, she sought individual help, but still attended the self-help group for all its added support and friendship. This took enormous pressure off the group and her problem could be better dealt with.

3. Women's Role

The problems of food and compulsive eating are shared by women of all backgrounds – food becomes imbued with all kinds of symbolic meanings and seems magical and frightening at the same time whether you are working class, middle class or upper class. That this is a universal problem for women in our society is reflected in the compulsive-eating groups, which are generally made up of very different kinds of women – feminists, working-class women, middle-class women, married women, single women, career women and students. Of all the self-help groups at the Women's Therapy Centre, the compulsive-eating groups are the most mixed.

For many women, joining a compulsive-eating group is their first encounter with any 'feminist' ideas. But because problems with food are so common, they soon start to feel relieved and relaxed in the group. To bring the issue back to personal experience, then to open it up to see it in a wider social context often makes 'personal politics' clear and 'women's politics' suddenly have real meaning. For example, a woman might say: 'Yes, it does seem unfair that I have to cook all the meals, even though I'm working. I'm around food so much, that's why I'm obsessed. Why am I forced into the kitchen? Because I'm a woman and expected to be servant and cook. Yes, that's true. I'd never really thought about how unfair it was before, and of course men aren't obsessed with food like we are.'

Often, I have heard women agree wholeheartedly that their role as mother and wife was intolerable.

One woman in my group found her husband was very threatened by it. The group had helped her change her image; she really looked 10 years younger. She turned up to a 21st birthday party in a white boiler-suit and the family were appalled. They couldn't accept that she was doing it for herself. She had to be doing it to attract other men. She had pressure from her mother-in-law and pressure from her husband. She actually packed her bags one night. Eventually her husband stopped her coming. 'It's either me or the group,' he said.

The barrage of images from the media telling women to be thin when they have to provide, cook and touch food all day long creates an obsessive and totally unhealthy attitude to it. They realise television and advertising are to blame; they feel resentful of their husbands and children when they are indifferent to the food they've put so much feeling into. They start to become aware that they really are second-class citizens. And yet they still wince at the 'feminist' in *Fat is a Feminist Issue*. 'I can understand everything but not that feminism.' Feminism is still a dirty word (understandably, because women's power is very threatening to this society) and conjures up for many women the image of the man-eating virago.

What I always want to say (and I said this to a Weight Watcher on the *Man Alive* debate)[10] is that looking at women and food as a social issue is the feminist approach. To see women and their obsession with dieting within a social context reveals the pressure from society on us.

Feminism simply means looking at women and their position in society in a sensible and honest way. And women come to this kind of realisation in the self-help groups where they stop turning the obsession and pain in on themselves and start to realise they really aren't to blame, but society's pressures are. This is a relief and often the trigger for enormous rage at the injustice of it all. The issue makes personal politics real.

4. The Idea of the Unconscious

Most of the women who come to the groups find the ideas of only eating when they're hungry and giving up diets totally new and exciting and easy to relate to. These ideas are a revelation and make such sense to them. But something which is quite hard for most women to deal with is the idea of the unconscious and of unconscious forces at work in our eating behaviour. I find fantasies one of the most useful techniques in situations where some women are resistant to the underlying feelings and psychological issues.

A fantasy is a guided journey through the unconscious. In a fantasy, you close your eyes and relax, and someone talks you through a situation, e.g. a party or a meal at home. You try and imagine yourself there. What are you doing? Who are you talking to? What are you wearing? You abandon yourself to your imagination and feelings and see what images are conjured up. The fantasy can make you aware of your own unconscious without feeling too threatened by the situation. And one needs to make concrete as many issues as possible. To talk abstractly about the unconscious might seem totally irrelevant or silly. Once you've allowed fantasies to release unconscious feelings and experience it yourself, it can make a lot of sense.

Fantasies easily bring images and unconscious desires to the conscious mind. To make yourself comfortable and close your eyes (as you do in a fantasy) isn't too exposing; no one is looking at you and you can relax. Role-play, on the other hand, acting out situations, can be threatening and should only be introduced when there is a great deal of trust in the group.

5. Life after the Group

Recently I met two women who had been in a compulsive-eating group. They told me how much it had changed their lives, but how painful and difficult it had been to face everything coming up for them. Both of them had almost lost their husbands, who had found their growing strength and assertiveness very threatening. One of their husbands was quoted as saying, 'If I could only get my hands on that Susie Orbach', which I found funny and awful at the same time.

They seemed resigned now, looking back on everything, and I sensed they felt they should never have started 'to open this can of worms', and that the enormous pain had been for nothing, now they were no longer in the group, still married and very much compulsively eating.

I suppose the positive aspect was that they did acknowledge great changes in themselves and even if they weren't ready to deal with all their problems yet, maybe one day they would find the strength. That gave me some hope, though I found the situation they had both resigned themselves to very sad.

What had it brought up and why was it so difficult to change? Once women start exploring why they are compulsively eating, if they are married and in a very traditional role, they often find that they really aren't getting what they need from their husbands and their marriage. They give out so much: looking after everyone, cooking meals, etc. And what are they getting in return for themselves?

They often feel a hollow inside them, an emotional space that needs to be filled with love and caring and interesting work outside the home, but it is not, so they fill that space with food.

Of course, this isn't a problem exclusively for wives, but more often it is women with husbands and children who are in a far harder position to change their circumstances. What are their options? Being a single parent with three children, losing the security of their home, losing the financial support of their husband, possibly being alone or terribly lonely, taking their children away from the father. But at least in a group you can, in that kind of situation, be encouraged to face the feelings and problems directly rather than using food, and sometimes find the strength to make that break and feel good about it.

Understanding that you deaden feelings with food or push down your anger by eating is a positive step in the right direction. It can be possible to learn to be angry, to express your feelings and needs, and even if they aren't all then satisfied, you no longer have the problem of the food and the pain and neurosis that creates. It's an obsessive and self-destructive activity that distracts from the real problem. It is sometimes far easier to focus on something familiar like fat than address the real feelings.

But if you can learn to confront situations directly, even if you feel sick or angry or rejected, you hold the feeling rather than a stomach crammed with food.

These two women hadn't managed to solve all their problems, but at least they both said, 'We will never be the same again', and that was positive.

6. Breaking the Dieting Pattern

Many women, feeling a self-help group is the last resort, understand what *Fat is a Feminist Issue* is saying, believe in the theory and yet cannot quite find the confidence or belief to give up their old familiar ways.

Dieting has become a way of life for them, and has in its way been safe – a structure within which you function, being told what to do and what to eat. You don't have to take initiatives or make decisions, and you can focus on something safe – food.

In the past, for most compulsive eaters, being off a diet meant being on a binge. From supreme self-control to chaos and 10 packets of chocolate digestives.

Therefore, to stop dieting, even though you know it has never worked for you, is terrifying. It can mean being totally out of control of your food and your life.

Many women begin in self-help groups and still calorie count quietly or jump on the scales when no one is looking. This is common to begin with and the group leader and/or the rest of the group must try and reassure her that once she's experienced eating what she wants and experienced not being deprived, she will start to find her hunger and her own level. She may initially eat 10 bacon sandwiches a day (after so many years of deprivation), but that will soon ease when she realises she doesn't have to deprive herself any more.

I encourage 'scaleoholics' in the first session to try and weigh themselves twice that week rather than 20 times and to come back and relate how that felt.

Women shouldn't be made to feel guilty if they can't relinquish those various crutches to begin with. They need to build up trust in the group and in the whole approach and try to relax into the knowledge that they are following the sensible path.

However, if this continues too long, it can be very destructive for the group. 'I want to take all this and diet as well', or, 'I'll just get a little weight off first and then get down to it in the "right way".' Impossible. The whole approach is based on rejecting diets and all the guilt and anxiety that accompanies them. How can you start to relax and work on self-acceptance if lurking at the back of your mind is the ideal 'thin' you. It perpetuates a tense and anxious state of mind and makes it impossible to work on the problems.

Not only is it bad for the woman, but other women in the group can start to feel very uncomfortable in themselves. They can be thrust back into the competitive and resentful feelings they had as dieters. 'I'm working on my problems with food and trying to relax about my body, but X has lost five pounds!' Or it makes the group start to question the whole approach. If others can't embrace the philosophy and are still dieting, is it really worth pursuing? The 'dieters' have betrayed the group in a way by not supporting the other women. And yet the group doesn't want to reject the dieter, because she is in a way the most frightened and unhappy of them all, terrified at what is lying underneath. They find it hard to confront her and often want everything to be 'nice'. It's as though the group is cushioned by all their fat, so they're safe and warm and unthreatened.

I feel very strongly that if a dieter is going to undermine the group and prevent six or seven other women from helping themselves, that dieter should be encouraged to think about whether this is really the place for her and possibly be asked to leave. It may simply not be the right moment in her life to be in a group.

7. The Fear of Putting on Weight

For many women in the groups who stop depriving themselves and stop dieting, the initial weeks can be a mixture of elation and panic.

The elation comes from once again being able to eat all those forbidden foods you craved for so long, from feeling hungry again and satisfying it with what you really want. But, of course, the compulsive eating isn't going to disappear overnight, and there will be moments when you still binge or feel out of control. Many women do put on some weight at the beginning, because they have released themselves from a prison. The natural response in the past would have been panic, followed by a huge binge. Now one has to try to relax in the knowledge that a few pounds means little if you're on the road to sorting out your problems once and for all. The group needs to reassure each other that it is all right and this initial weight gain is quite common and doesn't necessarily continue.

What is important is to remind all those women in the group who are a little shaky about putting on weight that diets didn't work for them and that is why they've come to the group.

I've found in my experience that most women have managed to remain calm when they've put on weight initially. Many women haven't minded because they are getting so much support from the group and feel so much better in themselves.

8. Resistance

We have looked at the dieter in a group as the first example of a woman who is resistant to change. But there are all sorts of other kinds of women in self-help groups who are too frightened to let anything invade them. Some cannot do the fantasies, or rather won't allow themselves to relax and succumb to unconscious feelings. Fantasies can be hard, because after a busy day with your head full, it is difficult to empty it and allow your mind to concentrate and focus. However, women who 'just can't do them' often are too frightened to do them.

Compulsive eaters have protected themselves with a layer of fat, cushioned from the pains and worries of the world. Therefore it is sometimes very hard for them to open themselves to others, to expose themselves and to reveal their dark hidden secrets. Fat has kept them protected for so long. Also for many, secrets have been a part of their lives – creeping down to the kitchen in the middle of the night, ashamed at how many stale cornflakes they have eaten. It's often the tragic paradox of having a serious problem and yet not being able to acknowledge it, because it is too painful to face. One very large woman in a group of mine, protected by 16 stone, had come to the group knowing it was a compulsive-eating group, but never really admitted to having a problem. How could the group help her or how could she help herself. She was totally resistant to any change, and eventually the group dissolved because too many women weren't moving at all.

I feel it is only fair to the group that a woman is confronted in these situations. Because she is so resistant, the idea of confrontation can be frightening, but in the long run she will very possibly destroy the group and still get nothing out of it. Confrontation is very hard, especially in compulsive-eating groups, but often it is essential if the group is going to continue to flourish.

9. Confrontation

It is well known that compulsive-eating groups among all self-help groups find confrontation the most difficult. In other groups, emotions fly, tears are shed and anger is expressed. In these groups, this seems to happen far less often. As I've already said, compulsive eaters cushion and protect feelings with fat, they avoid conflicts by eating. This is their defence, and it is hard for them to face feelings directly, so confronting issues and personality clashes in the group can seem impossible or very traumatic. One woman said to me that she felt if she allowed herself to release all her anger, she would destroy everything around her or even kill. The fear of the power of her anger was overwhelming. Pushing anger down with food for many years can make you fear a volcano will erupt when you let it out. So compulsive eaters avoid it.

Starting to talk things through and expressing anxieties and resentments can be very positive. Also, if you don't confront issues, such as women dominating, taking and not giving, never speaking, being continually late, tensions will build up and undermine the feeling of trust and support so important in the group.

Sometimes exercises and role-play can help air feelings. They offer a safer and more structured way in which to look at problems. Using a game such as Group Sculptures to look at group dynamics can be an interesting and less threatening road to confronting problems and conflicts.

Conclusion

For all its problems, self-help is still a powerful and healing process that has helped thousands of women help themselves and change their lives for the better. Because of the power it gives each woman, the friendship and support, self-help has proved itself particularly useful for compulsive eaters and is now a growing movement in this country, which is very exciting. The more ways we can find of challenging traditional attitudes to women's 'sickness' the better. Long may they continue.

Notes

1. Orbach, S., *Fat is a Feminist Issue*, Paddington Press, New York and London, 1978.
2. *ibid.*, p. 139.
3. *ibid.*, p. 146.
4. See Ernst, S. and Goodison, L. *In Our Own Hands*, The Women's Press, London 1981.
5. Orbach, *op. cit.*, p. 143.
6. *ibid*, p. 91.
7. *ibid.*, p. 92.
8. See Compulsive Eating Leaflet, p. 25 (available from Mira Dana, The Women's Therapy Centre, 6 Manor Gardens, London, N7).
9. Ernst and Goodison, *op. cit.* p. 262.
10. The *Man Alive* debate, BBC 2, July 1982, Susie Orbach, Katina Noble and Clair Chapman (the Feminists) v. Weight Watchers.

9
Putting the Issue on the Boards
Clair Chapman

When *Fat is a Feminist Issue* came out, I can tell you I was ripe for it.

I remember looking at a picture of Twiggy when I was 14, realising I looked nothing like her and realising I was wrong, wrong, wrong. Where her straight lines hung as straight lines, mine got caught up over lumps and bumps everywhere. A slew of crash diets and excruciating binges took me through my American adolescence: through college I had the Stillmans and Atkins diets – two 'hi-protein' regimes that made your breath smell like a lion's. Very expensive for a college student, but satisfying: the pounds slithered off daily. Never mind that they went back on equally fast.

When I came to England in 1973 I knew, in the words of my mother, that I would have to be on a diet for the rest of my life. But surprise, surprise! Somehow the people I met in England didn't seem to be as obsessed about the whole business as Americans. People weren't dieting in such a fanatical way. It was possible to walk into a shop or to watch television without being bombarded by slimming aids. I knew that one day it would be time to start living my 'real' life and I'd go back to the States and go on a diet and get a proper job. I felt like I was living on borrowed time, that I was cheating somehow. I put off moving back, put it off and put it off, braving my mother's horrified expression when I got off the plane every summer. I stopped dieting. I relaxed. I drank whole milk (not skimmed), I ate real sugar (not Slimcea) and real bread (not Nimble). And I could nearly eat a chocolate bar without knowing how many calories were in it (350). And then I read *Fat is a Feminist Issue* by Susie Orbach.

Fat is a Feminist Issue said immoral and wicked things to me as a dieter and wonderful and liberating things to me as a woman. It said 'Stop dieting. Dieting doesn't work. Get hungry and listen to your body. And if you're not hungry, why are you eating? Are you lonely, frustrated, angry?'

I began to put this into practice. I remember coming into the kitchen having just read that I should eat exactly what I wanted and scanning the shelves trying to find it. I wanted something cool, crunchy, sweet and fruity – eventually I sliced a piece of melon and poured on crunchy granola. Perfect. I was so proud of myself. Naturally, since then I haven't always done it as perfectly. But these days when I find myself aimlessly buttering endless pieces of toast I no longer think, 'I'm – a – greedy – slob – I'm – going – on – a – diet – tomorrow', but rather 'Poor me. What's the matter?' And I don't consider myself a compulsive eater any longer. This article describes one of the most important facets in the process of my 'unbecoming' a compulsive eater: working with the theatre company Spare Tyre.

I began to think about starting Spare Tyre about a year after I'd read the book. I lay in bed one night thinking, 'Someone should write a play based on *Fat is a Feminist Issue*, I wish someone would,' and suddenly thought, 'I could write that play, I could.' And then there was the excitement the rest of that night: getting a company together, rehearsal space, money . . . I slept very little.

In June 1979, after speaking to Susie Orbach who was extremely supportive, I put an ad in the London magazine *Time Out*'s Theatreboard. It was very simply worded:

> Women interested in putting together a play based on Susie Orbach's *Fat is a Feminist Issue* please write to Clair, 100 Fortress Road, NW5.

I don't know what I expected. I was totally unprepared for the flood of letters I received – about 70 in all. Daily there were half a dozen more: 'I am an out-of-work, overweight actress'; 'I have just gained back all the weight I lost at Weight Watchers'; 'I am a 15 stone Spanish dancer.'

I had expected perhaps half a dozen letters and really didn't know what to do. Finally, someone suggested I hold auditions. So I compiled a letter, telling a bit about myself and some ideas I had for the project. I worked out a detailed time schedule on the day:

2–2.30 coffee and introductions
2.30–3.30 personal experiences
3.30–5 improvisations

Except for drinking the coffee, no one paid any attention at all to that schedule. We heard the story of the tiny woman who ate and vomited 20 packets of biscuits a day, the anorexic carpenter who'd been force-fed double portions of fish and chips at the Royal Free Hospital, the woman who'd been to diet doctors since the age of eight. And we laughed! So much pain, yet we laughed! Stories and stories. As if a dam had opened. Eventually we did some improvisations:

> Two friends meet after a year. One has gained a stone, one has lost a stone.
> A teenage girl has been put on a diet. Her mother finds a Mars Bar in her pocket.
> A woman goes into a dress shop. The overhelpful assistant keeps showing her the wrong size dress.

The audition was wonderful. So much talent! So much pain!

The group finally formed itself. Ultimately, I decided that more important than acting ability and eating angst was a potential commitment to actually making a play, that it was important to have women who were committed to the issue and committed to the play (i.e. would turn up to rehearsals).

We began meeting several times a week to talk about ideas. I found these meetings totally exhilarating: the lid had been taken off, anything was possible, oh the stories of the diets, the binges, the fasts, the pasts! We suddenly all donned fat glasses and everything in the world was seen in terms of a person's size and compulsive-eating problem, real or imagined: Margaret Thatcher, we fantasised, would be a far more humane prime minister were she not so obsessed with her appearance; and there were other such sadly misguided ideas.

We agonised over what to call the group. I had tentatively called it Heavy Women. This was rejected as being too, well, heavy, as were Heavy Ladies and Heavy Bevy. Femmes Fat-all was given the thumbs down by the accountant as being too risqué. Fat Lip was too cheeky. No one was very happy with Spare Tyre: it was felt to be the best of a mediocre lot; we were fed up with talking about it and anyway we had to get the stationery printed. We called our first play *Baring the Weight*.

For *Baring the Weight* I had devised a structure that the group was happy with. It basically revolved around five characters:

1. The Slimmer of the Year, Daphne. As my addiction to food and dieting lessened, I became addicted to slimming magazines with

their endless diets and stories (I was a miserable 17 stone, then I discovered . . .). One such story really struck me. There was the usual 'fat' picture – the smudgy, blurred grey and white woman in tent dress – and the usual 'after' picture – that self-satisfied thinnie in trousers. But this woman didn't look like that. There was a terrified look in her eyes as though at any moment she might look in the mirror and see every pound that she'd lost right back on again. I felt this woman would be one of the 95 per cent who put it back, and quickly. I also felt that she'd make a good character.

I'm slim! Goodbye to Piggy,
I'm slim! Just call me Twiggy!
Look at that! I don't jiggle anymore,
I'll walk into a new life when I walk through that door!

2. Daphne's best friend, Debbie. Debbie starts Daphne off on the big diet, then abandons it herself within several weeks. She is the eternal mother, incessantly feeding her husband and child. We felt that it was important to have this mother-figure represented with all the paradoxical demands on her: that she should spend hours preparing wonderful meals for her family, that she should look slim and gorgeous doing so.

3. Debbie's teenage daughter, Tracey. Tracey suffered the double blow of an anxious, overbearing mother and a sexy boy- and clothes-conscious best friend. When the withdrawal from the pressures occurred, it took the form of anorexia. We found this character difficult as no one in the company had experience of anorexia. Also, our medium was comedy, and we found it difficult to make her scenes funny.

I don't want it, I don't want it,
I don't want your food.
Stop feeding me, stop pleading with me,
I'm not in the mood.

I see me being tied to my bed,
Mum hovers round me, stands by my head.
Her face is big and round like a moon,
She's holding a plate and a spoon . . .

4. The fat American journalist, Joanne. We wanted to show a woman who needed her fat to give her weight and power in her work situation. We showed her satisfied in her work but unable to cope with a sexual life and constantly bombarded by maternal

phone calls from the US: 'How's your weight, sweetheart? How's
your love life?' She was the character we all identified with most.
She seemed to sum up the dilemmas we had as working women:
though we had jobs 'like men', society demanded that we be fragile
and coquettish and implied that without marriage we were invalid
human beings.

Why is it
Every time my mother rings me on the phone
I want a Mars Bar?
Is this the thing that Pavlov did with those dogs?

What is it
About my mother's 'Hello, Sweetheart!' makes me scream
I need a Mars Bar?
Mummy and chocolate, melted up there in the cogs.

5. The last character had no name. We called her The Jogger and
saw her as the eternal, obsessive dieter. I originally wanted her to
jog and exercise through the entire show, but this proved
impractical to say the least, so she had a series of commercial spots.
Announced by a slim and sexy media character, we saw The Jogger
go through a number of hideous tortures in the way of slimming
devices – a plastic track suit, a Wonder Wiggler – as she binged
frantically.

I'm gonna be:

Eight stone by my birthday,
In hot pants by July,
I'll start my fast tomorrow,
But today – I'll bake a pie . . .

The ending of the play was a problem. We had shown a reversal
in the play: Daphne starts to gain her weight back Joanne confronts
her mother and starts to lose. But how to bring these two together,
how to make them meet across the classes and talk. Impossible. We
finally set it in the context of Daphne giving up her title as Slimmer
of the Year and Joanne going to interview her. The class and weight
barriers go down, Debbie makes a lovely chocolate cake and the
women are able to talk. And, of course, sing:

Eat it – if you want to,
Eat what you really want.

Do you really want (are you hungry – are you hungry?)
Do you really want that piece of chocolate cake?
No –
What then?
I don't know –
Think hard!
Help!
Come on!
I know!
What!
I want a great big steak!

Eat it – if you want to,
Eat what you really want!

We have always done a great amount of eating in our shows.
People sit stunned and repulsed by what we manage to get down.
This is not gratuitous eating; it always has a point. Some of the
things we have eaten on stage:

> half a sponge cake with a cup of tea poured into it
> a Mars Bar
> six slices of Mother's Pride
> a bag of crisps
> a bag of Maltesers
> mouthfuls of whipping cream
> spoonfuls of Coffee Mate (really sherbet)
> an Aero Bar
> frozen Brussels sprouts
> a Swiss roll
> celery

These little binges always seem to precede a song and you spend
half the time trying to swallow and not spit all over the audience.
And as for 'eating what you want' in this context, we certainly do
not. And if I never see another Mars Bar in my life it will be too
soon.

Because of the vast amount of publicity Spare Tyre got, we
played to huge and varied audiences. The first two weeks we played
to slimmers and housewives in Croydon. It suddenly occurred to us
that this might be a very good way of introducing all sorts of women
to the concept of compulsive eating. So we held discussions after the
show (riotous, always – unbelievable experiences from all sorts of
women), and we would then take the names of women who wanted

to be involved in compulsive-eating groups – *Fat is a Feminist Issue* recommends that small groups of between five and eight women be set up to meet weekly and discuss their problems with food and body-image. So this was our pattern over the next year: we would perform, have a discussion and collect names for future groups.

Our next show, *How Do I Look?*, was actually set in a compulsive-eating group. We wanted to demystify this process and to show a very varied mixture of women meeting to discuss their problems about body-image and their lives as women in general. We portrayed Janice, obsessed by the size of her breasts, Rosie, whose husband would not help with the household chores, Candy, fat and fine about it, Sandra, a super secretary desperate to look slim, and Laura, the neurotic by-product of an overprivileged upbringing.

> Love it, love it – gotta love it,
> Love my flabby thighs and bum.
> Really love my every wrinkle
> And adore my sagging tum.
>
> Everyone around me from my mother to the magazines
> Tells me I'm not up to scratch, ties me in a knot.
> I should search inside myself and teach myself to love myself
> Learn to accept what I've got – yuck.

How Do I Look was well received but we had now been working for 18 months without outside financial support and people were beginning to feel very desperate. Personal and political tensions also had begun to appear. So the larger group disbanded and several months later a small group of three of us put together a show, *Woman's Complaint*, with the best bits of old material and some new material about women's health.

There was a real demand for this show. It was funny, accessible and musical, and we have performed it hundreds of times over the past three years, in incredibly varied venues – psychiatric day centres, mother and toddler groups, women's health conferences, and the American Embassy Wives Group, Holloway Prison. The latter was a difficult show for obvious reasons. 'Eat what you want, when you want to,' we said enthusiastically in discussion. 'Look,' the women said, 'if we get macaroni cheese at 4 o'clock for tea and we don't like it, that's our lot till 8 o'clock the next morning.' Not a situation dealt with in *Fat is a Feminist Issue*, sadly.

So Spare Tyre has been getting the issue on the boards for five years now. Although our last two shows have not been directly concerned with compulsive eating, fat and food still give the shows their contexts. *On the Shelf* showed a girl growing up fat and wrong in the US:

> That's the older one, standing in the corner,
> Stuffing in the chocolate cake, dreadful disgrace.
> Cindy's the pretty one, Sandie's the fat one.
> It's such a pity, she's got such a pretty face . . .

Just Desserts was the story of a woman whose husband leaves her abruptly: her instant reaction is to binge on chocolate gateau and Coffee Mate. She frantically does aerobics to slim down and get her man; she joins the secretaries in her office in a discussion of their diets:

> Did you ever stop to think, there's two different classes –
> No, not Hackney and the Ritz –
> I'm talking about those whose life is celery
> And those whose life is banana splits.

> Everywhere she looks there's Farrah and Brooke Shields,
> Aerobics make her want to cry,
> While her old man's fine at any size,
> Pigging out on apple pie.

The Invisible Woman showed how women are made to feel wrong and out of place in this society:

> I'm putting it off till I'm thinner,
> Home is a safe place for me.
> I'll stop being a mess and become a success
> But I'm putting it off – till I'm seven stone three.

But also it shows some hope:

> I'm a real big eater,
> I've got a huge appetite,
> I'm a great big eater,
> You won't push me out of sight.

We now start compulsive-eating groups through the Women's Therapy Centre. Their model has two initial sessions with a leader to start the group off; it functions as a self-help group and then there is a follow-up session with the leader three months later.

In these past five years of working with Spare Tyre I have learnt an enormous amount about myself. We sing songs and perform sketches – nearly all from our own personal experience – that we hope will make people laugh. In addition to the laughter there is something else, a kind of female murmur of self-recognition. 'That's me'; 'I do that'; 'Oh, *no!*' It makes for exhilarating work and work that is very close to home for us psychologically. After all, it is not only the issue but ourselves that we are putting on the boards.

10
Images and Eating Problems
Mary-Jayne Rust

For several years I have been working with women with eating problems, using guided fantasy and art therapy as a means of exploring body-image and a woman's relationship to food. The way in which I work involves using magazine images to build collages around the experience of being fat and thin. Because it makes direct use of the images that affect us I find this method particularly helpful in exploring the connection between personal and political issues for women with eating problems.

The group format I have been using consists of six weekly two-hour sessions for 6 to 10 women who define themselves as compulsive eaters. They have the following things in common:

eating when not physically hungry;
feeling out of control around food;
feeling awful about body-size and shape;
oscillating between eating too much and too little and between experiencing being fat and thin.

The women hear about the group through adverts in the local community or through word of mouth; thus they are mostly self-referred. The advertising takes the form of 'compulsive-eating group' or 'body-image and our relationship to food': the words dieting and slimming are not mentioned. The women who respond to these adverts are frustrated with trying to diet and are seeking some insight into their obsession with food and body-size.

For the first few weeks in the group we concentrate on the immediate problem of panic around food. Each woman is asked to monitor her eating patterns during the week to notice when she eats, whether she feels hungry at these times and what feelings are associated with before, during and after eating. Binge times are, of course, looked at especially carefully. Within the group each woman is given time to talk about how the week has been; in this way it is hoped that the underlying reasons for compulsive eating will emerge so that each woman can respond to her feelings in a more appropriate way. The focus on food and eating then gives way to that of body-image on which the last few weeks are concentrated.

The approach I use assumes that although compulsive eaters feel awful about their bodies and long to lose weight, there is some reason why they need their fat and why losing it feels frightening. It is these feelings that the women must contact in order to permanently choose their weight. We begin by using the guided fantasy from Susie Orbach's *Fat is a Feminist Issue*[1] which describes an imaginary evening at a party where the participant must imagine herself as fat, then as thin. In each instance she is asked to note in detail her surroundings, the people she is with, the clothes she is wearing, what she is doing and how she feels. When she is imagining herself as large she is asked to see if she can find any benefits from being this size; when thin she is asked what is scary about this situation.

For most women this fantasy highlights well the unconscious motivation to remain fat and the fear of losing weight. For example, Anne felt close to her women friends when fat and alienated from them when thin. She was able to keep men away by using her layer of fat to feel sexually unattractive but in her experience of being thin found that she automatically dressed in tight clothes and 'flaunted herself'. This made her feel very vulnerable and, to use her words, as if she had fallen into a trap of 'being a female stereotype'. Running back to the fat was the only way she could find of protecting herself, despite knowing that in other ways she was not comfortable with having a larger body.

When looking at her feelings in the group it is important for Anne to realise that if she loses weight she does not have to 'dress in tight clothes and flaunt herself'. With the insight that this makes her feel vulnerable towards men she can think of other ways to make herself feel safe if she wants to shed her fat, such as wearing the clothes that express who she is and what she wants. This will in turn affect her relationships with women: she can begin to see that becoming thin does not mean that she must lose her friends; she herself has attached this meaning to the weight in her fantasy.

However, for other women these insights are not so apparent. A typical example is Jill, who felt terrible at the party when fat and very good when thin. She could not contact any benefits from the largeness at all – the whole experience seemed depressing and stuck. Likewise she could find no difficulties in the thinness. She felt very lively, wearing the clothes she wanted to wear, and she also felt more able to interact with others, both men and women. For Jill it would be useful to explore the fear of getting what she wants; perhaps she imagines there would be no struggle once she has reached the weight she desires and that this is a death-like state. Or perhaps she fears being 'the perfect person'. Through exploration these insights can emerge and develop.

In the following week this exploration is carried further by using magazine images built into collages. Each woman is asked to create these pictures using the following themes:

how I feel when I feel fat;
how I feel when I feel thin;
how I would like to be.

We have a large pile of a wide variety of magazines in the centre of the room. I ask the women to put the above themes to the backs of their minds while leafing through the pages and pull out any images that trigger some reaction, be it love, hate, anger, sadness or confusion.

The images are then pieced together in whatever way feels appropriate, using the suggested themes as a guide. What then emerges is the creation of three different 'personalities': the fat person, the thin person and an image of the woman's potential. In many cases the thin person and the fantasy of 'how I would like to be' are so fused that only two pictures can be formed. This does not matter. The main task is to allow the separation of the fat and thin, as in the guided fantasy.

Each time a collage is made, new themes and images arise. No two are alike although obviously many similar themes emerge. Some women construct their pictures entirely from images of people; others use landscapes, animals, food, words or abstract colours and shapes to depict their experience.

For some the images follow on from the experience of the guided fantasy; for others completely new material is brought out. Whichever the case, these collages always cast a new light on the problem and can often evoke very powerful feelings; there needs to be a well-formed bond of trust amongst the women to allow these feelings to be explored in depth.

In the group each woman is invited to describe her pictures. I emphasise that the images are essentially private: it is her decision as to how much to reveal. As with the guided fantasy the exploration uncovers what is beneficial in the fatness and what is difficult in the thinness. All sorts of combinations of feelings arise attached to the two weights. Some women feel more powerful, independent and adult when fat and powerless, dependent and child-like when thin, while for others the reverse is true. Sometimes this feeling of strength is located in both states but has a different quality in each. Yet other women feel unable to locate any feeling of worth in either state. For example, Tina felt like a child when thin: she picked images of a schoolgirl and of very attractive-looking women. She described the girl as powerless. The attractive women she saw as 'fitting in with what men wanted women to be: falling into the trap of the female stereotype'. If she became thin and hence, in her eyes, an attractive woman, she felt she would have no right to assert herself since she was now the very stereotype that she was trying to fight against. In the fat picture she felt large and clumsy, out of control and again powerless. Tina was surprised by this discovery. When she felt fat she imagined that her thin self held change and effectiveness. With this insight she was able to separate the feeling of powerlessness from the weight; she could see that this was an issue for her to explore further and that losing weight would not affect it essentially, although she might then choose to lose the weight for other reasons.

After the first session of making and briefly describing the collages, they can be taken a step further using a method from Gestalt therapy. Whoever wishes to explore their images in this way has two cushions; on one cushion sits the fat woman and on the other sits the thin woman. The collages can be used as reference points. The client talks *as if* she were fat and *as if* she were thin, making the images come alive and the experience very immediate. Gradually, a dialogue begins between the two personalities, making clear the needs and desires of each.

The following examples show how this process takes place and how these experiences can differ from the guided fantasy in *Fat is a Feminist Issue*.[2]

Wendy

Wendy's experience of the guided fantasy was polarised as her fat self blocking out the world and her thin self letting things in. She described her experience of being fat at the party as follows: 'I want to block people out and hide in the eating. I am on my own pretending people aren't there. I am not participating in the party. I am in the background in a heavy, dark space of my own.' And she described her experience of being thin as follows: 'I am in the party dancing. I am lively and wearing dungarees. I am feeling very alive and having lots of fun. The music is loud and there's much activity. I am on Cloud 9; I am not feeling grounded . . . as if electric.'

I suggested to Wendy that she might feel pressurised when thin to live up to the life-and-soul-of-the-party woman she has fantasised. Perhaps one of the benefits of putting on weight was that she could be on her own, in a quiet and relaxed way, without needing to be so all-effusive.

A very different fantasy emerged, however, when she created her collages. She chose to become the fat person first and described herself as follows:

I feel very powerful; all the images are to do with power – the picture of the car head on, the back of the Volvo, the large settee, the tractor coming head on and the warrior standing there holding his spear and shield. He has a large belly and no one can get through. The images are about being grounded and heavy. I'm all right, I can manage, no one's going to get to hurt me. I am strong and capable. That warrior . . . no one's going to get through into my world because I just want to block it out. It's a defence. This is easier to cope with than being thin, because at least I'm strong and not letting the world in.

The tent . . . it's billowing and about to explode after stuffing. There's something very sexual about it. I can crawl inside there and hide.

The person underwater is submerged and dragged down . . . I am trying to get to the surface.

Wendy then sat on the other cushion and spoke as her thin self:

These images are to do with desperation. I am the little deprived monkey on the top-left – it reminds me of my mother and the way she looks. I am also the monkey being torn between my two parents. In a relationship I'm scared that if I show my sexuality I'll get torn apart.

Many of the other images are to do with feeling alone: the little zebra, the horse out in the cold and the person crouched over, drawing a circle around herself. The picture at the bottom is of a woman being accused by judges. They are saying, 'It's all your fault, you're all wrong.' That's the feeling I have when I'm vulnerable and wanting to eat everything. I'm no good . . . that's the feeling I try to run away from when I binge.

The woman on the horse is saying 'Come and get me' . . . she's thin and very sexual. If I become her I am very vulnerable to the men in the picture on the bottom-left. They are cold, hard and out for what they can get. I feel guilty for being sexual . . . It's wrong and dirty. I feel that I get what I ask for . . . I feel I'm in the wrong . . . that reminds me of my father shouting at my mother – he's a very powerful man who makes her and me feel wrong. He must be right.

The image of the person with their face crossed out is how I sometimes feel when I'm thin . . . I don't exist.

This experience was a great surprise to Wendy, who had come to the group to become thinner. She imagined, as in her guided fantasy, that thin was wonderful. The collage revealed that fat for her meant being able to cope, while thin was alone and desperate, child-like and vulnerable – but also sexual. Through sitting on each cushion in turn and enabling a dialogue to occur between the two experiences it was possible to discover what each side wanted.

As can be seen from Wendy's experience, there is a wealth of material to explore. I feel it is important to allow each woman to find her own way through the images; my function is to enable her to discover their meaning to the fullest degree and to separate this from the weight itself.

Several issues come out of Wendy's collage. First, having realised what fat and thin hold, how can she let go of the weight (if that is what she still wants to do) without losing her ability to cope and feel powerful? One approach would be to make herself feel big in other ways: for example, she can dress in clothes which make her feel large rather than making her body large. On a deeper level, she can discover which qualities of her own give her power. She might then see that in reality it makes no difference whether she is fat or thin.

Second, she must discover how she has come to link these qualities with fat and thin. On a personal level, it seems that the relationship between her father, her mother and herself needs to be explored; this became clear in her experience of being thin. On a wider scale, it is important for Wendy to see how her feelings are echoed throughout the experience of many women, thus taking it on to a political level. She can see that such links between thin, child-like and sexuality are fed to us through our social education.

The vast majority of women are less powerful than men in today's society; alongside this we are surrounded by images of thin women who are sexual and vulnerable to men through the very nature of their unequal relationship. With this insight Wendy can begin to piece together why she has made these links in her own fantasy.

Following on from this, the fear of her own sexuality seems important to look at. Does becoming more sexual *have* to attract violence and aggression? Perhaps there are other ways of being sexual without feeling like the woman on the horse.

There are many other paths to follow in Wendy's collage. The above are just a few main examples that I have picked out to illustrate the process involved in this exploration.

Nora

Not all collages are as clear-cut as Wendy's. The following example of Nora shows the use of more abstract imagery to depict thin as powerful and tight but frightening, and fat as vulnerable, open and comfortable. In Nora's words:

> The circle is the fat . . . I feel some kind of blockage . . . it's not like me. The right-hand picture is the world outside and how I feel about it; it's confusing and I'm trying to keep it away. Hurt goes with fat . . . it's a way of coping and hiding from what I feel I should be facing and what I want to face. The left-hand pale blob is a sweet, sugary, yucky feeling. The spikes on top are the cool, angular, confident, uncontrollably alone and not needy bits hidden in the pale part. The pale tips on the spikes are the warmth coming out. I'm cold inside and warm outside.
>
> The open mouths are the neediness and openness to others. I feel I can receive and give but I don't know when to stop and start. I don't know where I begin and end – I have no control. Like mother like daughter . . . she's fat and all the weak things I don't want to be. I want to know what I want.

Depicting thin, she continues:

> I am fragile . . . it's so precarious, like the glass. The power is uncontrollable. It's like the flashes of lightning on either side of the picture. What do I do with it? Where do I take it? How do I know when to start and stop? I feel glamorous . . . I'm wearing make-up and high heels but I don't feel right. I push everyone away. I feel shallow and disliked, concerned with looks. I feel

seductive but people are scared to touch me. I'm hard and tight-lipped. I'm cold outside and warm inside.

Nora began to realise that the feelings of not being able to start and stop and the lack of boundaries are in *both* fat and thin experiences, manifesting in a different form in each. She also realised that thin was a state that was very frightening for her, as well as containing things that she desperately wanted. It involved taking charge of her life, but without a strong sense of her own boundaries it could become wild and out of control, leading to possible destruction, like the lightning. Nora has managed to separate this issue to power from the weight and is slowly moving towards what she most wants to do with her life, at the same time looking at how this is frightening for her.

Her third picture is composed from much abstract imagery. She is still in the process of discovering much from it; she feels that it integrates many of the feelings previously separated in the fat and thin pictures. She describes it as follows:

> The fires and stars dotted over the many colours and shapes are my burning need to be creative, which lies inside all my different moods. The fires with bars on are more significant than the free ones – they are trapped in. The two pictures of a man and a woman are about my dependency. The central figure is relaxed and casual . . . that is how I would like to be.

Nora seems to have sucessfully taken her struggle away from the arena of fat and thin, and is seeing it in its more appropriate place: within her work and her relationships. She still has much exploration to do in the areas brought out by the collage work but this has helped her to identify the issues to look at.

Jackie

Jackie's collages show a similar theme of thin being powerful but dangerous and fat being nurturing and warm. In her words:

> I am obese, fat, overflowing and horrible, but also Pooh Bear. I'm warm, cuddly and everybody loves me. I'm always covered up and always looking at thin women. I feel trapped like the woman in the glass bottle. The Christmas picture is about my sister coming home and being very thin. Nobody told me that she was wasting away with cancer. She was accusing me of being fat

. . . saying that I was okay she was not. This makes me feel it's better to be bigger than thin.

She then describes her thin experience:

I am really scary, cold and aloof. I am very powerful. Those two women with their faces veiled look as if they are mourning. Thin is like death. I am very sexually attractive, and getting a lot of attention from men. I am very frightening, unapproachable and daunting, sophisticated wild and raunchy . . . I feel out of control and dangerous. The spikiness in the central picture is like a nightmare . . . dark and frightening. Things don't make sense. It's unreal and very scary.

When Jackie moved from one cushion to another she actually felt a change in temperature. She was very surprised to find the experience of being thin so frightening and so much linked to sexuality and death – an issue for her to explore further. As revealed in the above description, she discovered the connection between thin and her sister's death, making the loss of weight an understandably very frightening experience for her. It is therefore important for Jackie to realise that being thin does not equate with death in reality; she has made this link due to her personal experience. It is then important for her to find ways of protecting herself when losing weight. Through her third picture Jackie has been able to establish a self more separate from the weight and this has given her a new sense of confidence while exploring the more painful areas of the other two pictures.

In describing these collages of Wendy, Nora and Jackie I have tried to illustrate several ways in which such a technique can be particularly valuable within the context of compulsive eating. It can also be helpful for both bulimics and anorexics.

The use of the magazine images themselves seems so appropriate for such a problem tied to image. It is using the very material that so subtly pervades, persuades and influences women – and so provokes them. By tying the images to fat and thin, the compulsive eater can be free to experiment and explore *in her fantasy* the different images of women which both attract and repel her.

Each woman comes bringing her many desires and needs which must somehow be met. These desires and needs are frequently felt as being in conflict with one another, such as the needs to be dependent and independent. When such a conflict becomes felt, the weaker side becomes repressed, and this is often the side that does not fit in with the woman's ideological views. She then becomes bound by certain 'shoulds' and 'oughts', such as the woman with her own view of feminism feeling that she 'should' be independent or that she 'should' dress in a particular way. The 'shouldn'ts' then become repressed as images and with them many of the wants and needs that they enclose. There are many examples of such images. They are almost mythological in nature. A few of the more controversial are as follows:

the helpless woman saved by the knight in shining armour – she longs to be dependent and cared for;
the seductive woman in lace underwear – she longs to be erotic and eroticised;
the glamorous lady in high heels, make-up and slim-line clothes – she longs to be on a pedestal and admired;
the cool, sharp, intelligent business-woman – she longs to be independent and taken seriously;
the all-providing earth-mother – she longs to endlessly love and nurture all who come to her.

When in these wrappings, such needs and longings clash and appear unacceptable to many women. The function of this exercise, then, is for each woman to separate the fat and thin, unwrap the images and understand that the many feelings can be held in one place: that the 'cool, sharp, confident' feelings that the business woman holds *can* be contained with the 'loving and warm' feelings of the mother image. Furthermore, none of these feelings requires fatness or thinness in order to be expressed. The next task is for the woman to discover her own way of expressing these feelings in a way that is more acceptable to her.

I have attempted to show here that a common theme has run through this collage work: Nora, Jackie and Wendy all felt that to be thin in some way made them a different person. Only when the desires and needs are freed from the images can a woman begin to *own* her sexuality, her nurturing, her dependence, her power and her strength, so that she can discover and choose who she is.

Exposing these conflicts in a group situation allows each woman to see where the themes merge and differ. She can begin to see what belongs to her (i.e. personal) and what is of society (i.e. political), thus tracing back the conflict to its roots and hopefully freeing it.

As someone who works on a short-term basis, I feel it is important to acknowledge that the conflicts which are uncovered through this work can take some time to resolve. What *can* be achieved is that the painful struggle of women with food can be shifted. The out-of-control and panic feelings disappear and the struggle continues – in a more appropriate place.

Notes

1. Orbach, S., *Fat is a Feminist Issue*, Paddington Press, New York and London, 1978.
2. *ibid*.

11
'Going for the Burn' and 'Pumping Iron': What's Healthy About the Current Fitness Boom?
Jean Mitchell

During the 1980s, interest in health and physical fitness has turned into the cult of the body, a preoccupation that is both obsessive and destructive. One can almost hear the sharp intake of breath, the indignant denials as the healthy hordes peruse this statement: it is *good* to be fit and healthy and, using the terminology adopted by a popular women's magazine, full of zest. How dare anyone criticise the great god exercise!

The message that exercise equals fit equals good is all pervasive. In advertisements, young women clothed in the assorted paraphernalia associated with the fitness boom advertise just about every product you could think of. We read of the virtuous behaviour of 'beautiful' women who rise at 6.30, jog round the park for an hour, then cycle to work. As if that's not enough, in their lunch-hour they're swimming or limbering up at aerobics classes. The implication is that if we want to be like them (i.e. beautiful), we must stop being slothful, get off our backsides and run for our lives. Models photographed for fashion and beauty spreads display muscular bodies and adopt a glaring but sultry expression that says, 'I'm tough and powerful, but I sure am sexy'. Alternatively, they cavort in the strangest of places, smiling from ear to ear, or, worse still, laughing maniacally as if they had truly gone insane. I could be mistaken, but am inclined to believe that the object of the exercise is to convey zest.

The health and fitness hype has, by and large, been accepted uncritically, and the woman who does aerobics or, more especially, weight-training, is presented as a powerful free spirit, a strong, active, 'modern' woman who can and does take care of herself. I choose to dissent from this viewpoint and suggest that the current fitness vogue has little to do with health, that, on the contrary, it is a sign of psychological ill-health, and that far from being 'liberating' for women, the pressure to workout and to be fit constitutes a moral straitjacket that is both limiting and debilitating. In my opinion, the workout craze has more to do with anorexia nervosa than with health. In order to pursue this argument I intend to say a little about the social position of women and about some of the important features of women's psychology appertaining to my thesis, and then to develop this idea by concentrating on two contemporary phenomena, body-building and aerobics dance.

Women always have it tough, but over the past 20 years or so things have been getting tougher and tougher. The idealistic, collectivistic spirit of the sixties, which was buoyed on the wave of a sexual revolution and booming economy, has eroded to leave a depressed, 'realistic' and individualistic ethos. Mass unemployment, urban decay, the threat of nuclear war and related ills result in an atmosphere of gloom, hopelessness and cynicism. In Britain, the political consensus that held for so long has been brutally broken. Beliefs in the moral necessity for full employment (never held for women, anyway) and decent housing, education and health-care for all people can no longer be taken for granted. We are governed by a tough, callous new breed who extol the virtues of self-discipline, thrift and competition.

Naturally, in a climate where the market-place rules, the only freedom available to many is the freedom to be poor. Women, as usual, bear the brunt of these times. Beatrix Campbell has written of the harsh realities involved in the lives of northern working-class women.[1] And of course we are again the focus of men's anger as they make us into scapegoats. We are taking 'their' jobs, and should get back where we belong, in the kitchen.

What can women do? It seems to me that basically they can do one of four things: the first is to fight back and resist, as the miners' wives have done; the second is to opt out and, believing that there is nothing one can do, sink on a wave of apathy; the third is to find a pseudo-solution to one's problems, just as a child who is being bullied by an older child retaliates by hitting a child smaller than itself; finally, one can accept the new prescriptions and play by the rules, to be competitive and strong and to despise any sign of moral and/or physical weakness.

It is my contention that excessive aerobics and body-building represent a curious amalgam of the latter two strategies. In order to explain this, I shall first provide an account of aspects of women's psychology that are important.

For many women, the self-concept is synonymous with the physical self. This isn't surprising when one considers that women's bodies are used to advertise virtually any commodity, to sell newspapers and to entice us to watch films and television programmes. Other people tend to evaluate women according to how they look, rather than according to more important qualities. For example, a recent psychological study had actresses participating in job interviews, unbeknown to the interviewers. The actresses behaved in a standard manner at each interview; only the amount of make-up that they wore varied. Depressingly, job offers were more forthcoming for those actresses who were wearing lipstick. No wonder that women tend to use self-control – by, for example, changing their hairstyle and mode of dress – as a poor substitute for political, economic and social control.

Marilyn Lawrence has written about how anorexic women, like their 'normal' sisters, use controlling their bodies as a substitute for controlling the real issues in their lives over which they have no control.[2] Anorexia typically occurs when a woman is feeling somehow at a disadvantage and out of her depth. The ever-lower reading on the weighing scales gives a feeling of being in control. Not only is she able to achieve something that other people find excruciatingly difficult to do, but by starving herself and denying her bodily and emotional needs, the anorexic gains pseudo-control over her life, or at least over one aspect of it.

In addition, she feels morally justified. In the first place eating is seen as being unfeminine in our culture,[3] and in the second, she can draw on the ascetic tradition that the 'sins' of the flesh are bad: to be truly spiritual one should transcend the fallible body. By denying her need for food, the anorexic scores on both counts.

Furthermore, the notion that women's bodies, in particular, need to be controlled is widespread. Unlike men, who are assumed to be rational and logical, women are deemed to be impulsive, irrational and prey to their animal instincts. Women's bodies, while being a source of attraction and fascination for men, are also greatly feared and considered to be uncontrollable, impure and unclean.

Hence, there are powerful pressures exerted on women to control their 'errant' bodies. Not only is it morally 'good' for them to do so; they also gain pseudo-control over their lives and assuage men's fears. It is of the essence that a great many fetishistic fads pay lip-service to an aesthetic ideal but, in fact, have more to do with asceticism, being painful or uncomfortable to endure or wear, at the same time limiting woman's freedom by constricting her movements: for example, the wearing of stiletto-heeled shoes with narrow, pointed toes in the West, or the practice of tight-lacing. In the latter case, it is illuminating to note that in late Renaissance France, a tight-laced bodice conveyed self-control and sexual and social self-discipline. The old adage that one has to suffer to be beautiful is so much more than empty words.

To recap, women are treated as a commodity; their worth is judged in terms of how they look. There are moral and social gains to be had from controlling their bodies, an act which also fosters the illusion that they are controlling their lives. When these factors are considered in the context of a climate of increasing hardship, where women are experiencing a decreasing ability to control their lives, one would expect more and more women to respond by attempting to control their bodies. The pervasiveness of dieting and increased incidence of eating disorders, notably anorexia and bulimia, are undoubtedly partly attributable to these factors. When one considers this along with the current political, ideological stress on individualism, the need to fight and to be competitive, the necessity of standing on one's own two feet, and the notion that it is only harsh medicine that can make us better, activities like 'going for the burn' and 'pumping iron' take on wholly different meanings.

It is probably a truism to say that the relationship between weight-training, its more extreme counterpart body-building, and feminism, is somewhat equivocal. Some feminists see the trend towards women developing muscular bodies as a very positive one. Not only does the muscle-bound look challenge assumptions about how women 'should' look, the very existence of women who are strong, capable and powerful challenges contemporary notions about female sexuality. Superficially, weight-training and body-building might appear to be ideal sporting pursuits for women. They are highly personal and individualistic, and, claim their advocates, non-competitive. Each woman can decide how much muscle she wants to build and which muscle groups she wants to develop. The woman who weight-trains feels strong and confident, presenting an image that is dictated by how *she* wants to look, not by how men think she should look.

Other feminists, however, see the current fashion for bulging muscles as yet another move towards denying women's sexuality, and one that therefore undermines their right to self-determination. I endorse this latter viewpoint, and would go further: I believe that far from being a healthy, positive thing for women to do, excessive weight-training and body-building represent a kind of 'macho' anorexia; that like anorexia they are a mode of response to the pressures associated with being a woman in our society.

If one examines a cross-section of contemporary magazines aimed at young women, it becomes glaringly obvious that the muscular body is well and truly in. Articles abound on the subject of weight-training, models in the ads and fashion and beauty spreads are big and athletic, and numerous interviews can be found with 'beautiful' women who detail their fitness regimes.

Sadly, some of the more serious publications that one would expect to adopt a more critical and responsible stance towards the new vogue have also jumped on the 'muscles are good' bandwagon.[4] One of them, *New Society*, for example, contrasts today's 'taut, toned and tanned' look with that of the 1950s, as exemplified by Monroe, when women were meant to look 'soft, feminine and fleshy'. The article ends by stating that 'physical assurance can be alluring . . . equality can be sexy'. There are, I believe, two fundamental errors of logic here. First, it is implied in the article that the current aesthetic ideal is intrinsically worthy and physically and morally superior to the hour-glass curves that the fifties dictated. No acknowledgment is made of the fact that muscles represent little more than the current stereotype of female beauty, that far from having revolutionary connotations, muscular women represent the new 'ideal'. It is instructive that the following week a letter appeared in response to the article from one of Britain's top women body-builders. It states that 'body-building is the only way in which one can reshape one's own physique into the form one desires'. In fact, the same old story: in the fifties busty curves; in the sixties and seventies emaciation; the eighties, Charles Atlas. What is 'liberated' about women being supposed to change their body-shape with little more regard than when discarding last year's earrings?

Any 'new' look that is marketed as being 'right' desexualises women, as only a tiny minority of women will typify it. The rest can reject it for the nonsense that it is, wait hopefully for 'their' look to come into fashion (although many 'looks' are unlikely ever to receive the adulation of the fashion and beauty gurus – lumpy bottoms, short, sturdy, hairy legs, etc.), or try to change their appearance to fit the new shoe. Sadly, many women find themselves doing the latter two things, and either getting incredibly depressed and hung-up about the way they look or embarking on a never-ending course of 'self-improvement', trying to change their bodies and appearances to suit fashion.

The second fundamental error is contained in the sentence about physical assurance being alluring, equality being sexy. The mistake here, which is one that other publications sympathetic to women's issues have made,[5] is in equating physical prowess with equality, and confusing power with brute strength. Being able to lift heavy loads and to 'vault over fences, get away from – or even fight – attackers'[6] has little to do with freedom and self-determination for women. On the contrary, it represents a capitulation to the masculine ethos that might is right and an endorsement of the current ideological stance that urges us to stand on our own two feet and to be tough and competitive. The image conjured up is not one of equality but of survival, a veritable tableau of nature red in tooth and claw.

Further evidence that the muscular look has little to do with women's emancipation comes from the fact that the image we are being pressurised to emulate is a masculine one, and a gross parody at that (how few men have bulging muscles and stand-up veins). Most women have breasts, stomachs and hips, albeit in different shapes and sizes. At puberty the percentage of body fat in females increases markedly, so that adult women typically have a higher fat to lean tissue ratio than men. This is no mere fluke, no consequence of female conditioning: it has been proposed that for the onset of the menarche, fat must constitute an estimated 17 per cent of body weight, with a body composition of 23 per cent fat being necessary for the maintenance of regular ovulation.[7] The cult of the muscle would have us deny our biological bodies and substitute hard, manly muscle for womanly fat (one wonders if this is why fat is so despised in our culture)? What is more, many of the purveyors of the cult of body-building who would have us swap womanly fat for macho muscle are men. In an article that appeared on the *Guardian*'s Women's Page, a male fitness instructor asserted his belief that more women are now attracted to body-building as an 'end product of Women's Lib'.[8] Later, the article focused on '. . . Moreen, slight, blonde and feminine . . . [who] for the past eight months, talked into it by her husband Mark, . . . has trained with weights for two hours each night, usually five nights a week.' The irony of having a statement about body-building for women being a result of 'women's lib', followed by information about a woman being persuaded by her husband to spend a considerable portion of her time changing the shape and form of her body (presumably to a physique that he would find more attractive) appeared to be lost on the female author of the article, who failed to comment on it. Yet again we are supposed to reject and control our dangerous bodies.

What about my suggestion that body-building has anorexic qualities? On the face of it, the muscular, strong, woman body-builder appears to be the antithesis of the emaciated, weak anorexic. But this notion only holds true if one believes, erroneously, that anorexia is about weight, dieting and female 'vanity'. It isn't. Earlier, I touched on some of the fundamental issues for the anorexic: control, denial of bodily and emotional needs and the sense of moral goodness that doing this brings. When viewed in this way anorexia and body-building have a number of important features in common.

Body-building, like anorexia, is a time-consuming, painful enterprise. Both activities completely structure and dictate the life style of the individual concerned. The anorexic's life focuses on food and her relationship to it. She is constantly preoccupied with it. Similarly, the focus for women body-builders is the gym. I've already mentioned the *Guardian* article which detailed that Moreen trains for ten or so hours a week.[9] The same article also cites the case of Jackie, who is 'even more committed and, prior to competitions, puts in about three hours, seven nights a week' (she has a full-time job). No doubt, the professional women body-builders, who do not have full-time jobs or who actually work in gyms, put in even more hours than this. As the anorexic's world revolves around food and eating, so the body-builder's world is encompassed by the gym and training.

The ascetic appeal of anorexia is readily apparent. Anorexics vehemently deny their bodily needs, most notably for food. They also tend to put themselves through punishing exercise schedules, often becoming *more* active when their bodies start to collapse under the strain.[10] They deny their need for warmth and frequently go out in the coldest of weather wearing only light clothing.

This desire to do battle with the body and to transcend it is also present in women body-builders. They steadfastly deny the bodies that they were born with and try to emulate a masculine ideal. They try to subdue their bodies, to bring them under control, make them do what they want. Just as the anorexic is driven almost mad with hunger, the body-builder mercilessly pumps iron, trying to push her body beyond the pain barrier, to lift yet heavier weights, day in, day out. Like the anorexic, when she achieves her goal and successfully 'masters' her body, she gains a feeling of 'strength', of moral superiority, of being 'good'. The anorexic cannot imagine living without her 'illness'. I get the impression that women body-builders cannot imagine living with non-muscular bodies.

Further evidence linking anorexia with women's body-building comes from the observation that both groups of women detest and loathe body fat and work fanatically to reduce if. And, I should point out, by 'fat' I don't mean obesity but the perfectly normal amount and distribution that the average woman has. Often anorexics will claim that they feel fat and bloated, even when they are severely emaciated. They fear that if they eat a single chocolate bar it will immediately be converted to fat, and probably sit tauntingly on their stomachs or hips; that every pound of weight gained is a pound of fat which threatens to pollute them and must be got rid of. Women body-builders will claim that their dislike of body fat arises because the dreaded material masks muscle definition, a catastrophe when taking part in competitions. They therefore watch what they eat, consuming a high-protein, low-fat diet, with some carbohydrate included to provide energy (hardly what is now known to be a healthy diet). Dieting is intensified before competitions to reduce their fat levels still further. Indeed, one woman body-builder actually likened this intensive dieting to a 'sort of athletic anorexia'.[11] This does not seem to me to be an adequate explanation. What needs to be explained is the hatred of fat, and therefore womanliness, that drives them to masculinise their bodies in the first place.

If you're still not convinced on this point, perhaps the following will persuade you. Some time ago I read an interview with a female weight-trainer. She justified what she was doing by saying that working with weights was a positive thing for women to do, giving them self-confidence, etc. All well and good, until she started to compare the 'active', 'positive' presentations of women in body-building competitions with the passive, sorry presentation of women in the Miss World contest, and to say that when she looked at *them*, all she could see was fat. Her revulsion at the 'fat' traditional beauty queens was barely concealed. But surely something is wrong here? The typical Miss World contestant has the figure of a model – tall, thin and small-breasted. The majority, if not all of them, are considerably underweight when compared to population norms. Yet, like the 70-pound anorexic who believes that she is grossly obese, this woman saw these thin women as being covered in fat.

Finally, more damning evidence for the anorexia–body-building connection comes from the fact that both anorexics and women body-builders do not menstruate. It is generally accepted that menstruation ceases in cases of anorexia nervosa because the individual is well below the optimum weight/ideal body ratio essential for normal menstruation. The reason that I have seen given for the cessation of periods in women body-builders is that they are under physical and mental stress with their training. Maybe, but they are also drastically reducing their percentage body-fat, which is probably the more important factor. Physically and psychologically healthy women menstruate.

Somehow, the woman who does regular aerobics does not seem to be as 'extreme' as the woman who pumps iron, and it is easy to categorise aerobics as a harmless, if silly, thing to do, a con-trick resulting from the ideology that it is good (and chic) to be 'fit'. A deeper examination of the issue, though, reveals that there is a sinister aspect to aerobics, but that, unlike body-building or weight-training, it is much more covert, and only really comes to light when one talks to women who do aerobic exercise.

I once observed an aerobics class being held in a London dance studio, an experience that left me feeling bewildered and sad. Sixty or so women of assorted shapes, sizes and ages were collectively working out; a tall, skinny instructress, dressed in fashionable workout garb, was paying scant attention to her students. Maybe she was doing mental arithmetic: 60 times two pounds (not including yearly membership fee), six or seven times a day, five or six days a week is an awful lot of money!

Her stance of poised disinterest contrasted sharply with the scene being acted out on the wooden floor. Some of the women working out had obviously been doing it for some time and went through their paces with relative ease. Others, however, flayed and writhed on the floor, gasping for breath, faces blood-red, sweating profusely. Their mode of dress, like their physical demeanour, tended to be less 'elegant' compared with the seasoned troopers. Some, who probably hadn't exercised for years, were wearing their old black school leotards, many of which stretched inadequately across the ample curves that their bodies had developed. Others

wore old shorts and T-shirts, or aertex blouses, again from
schooldays. A couple were wearing dreadful plastic pants, tied tight
at the ankles and worn over layers of tights and legwarmers. Why
didn't anybody tell them that you can't spot-reduce 'fat' in this way?
Any loss of weight resulting from this personal sauna is immediately
regained once the person rehydrates her body by taking in fluids.
How vulnerable and self-conscious they looked, how utterly
degraded. What could possibly induce these women to put
themselves through this painful and humiliating experience? The
promise of health and fitness? A trimmer body? The challenge of
changing from a rounded, soft, panting, sweating creature, dressed
in dingy ex-school gymwear, into a trim, together trendy in workout
suit with matching headband and legwarmers? Go through the

If you can't beat em....

initiation ritual, perform your rites of passage, and with any luck, the ugly duckling turns into a swan.

Such explanations seemed barely adequate. I therefore decided to talk to women who were doing aerobics, to try to find out what exactly motivated them to commence and maintain classes. The following two brief case histories should indicate the sort of factors that are important.

Wendy is a tall, striking young woman who works as a computer programmer; she is assertive and positively radiates self-confidence. Yet periodically she experiences feelings of gross dissatisfaction with the way that she looks, feelings so strong that they cause her to exercise compulsively. These cycles of activity are usually precipitated by an impending event that somehow makes her feel at a disadvantage – a holiday or important social event looming on the horizon, for example. Wendy typically feels that she is not 'good enough', that she is inadequate and won't be able to cope when the situation arises. Believing that if she is thinner and trimmer she will be able to cope, she embarks on a punishing exercise regime three or four months before the big event.

Daily she'll swim and attend one or even two aerobics classes, often spending a total of two to three hours working out. As soon as she can see the 'benefits' of her efforts in terms of a tauter, 'fitter' body, she relaxes and stops the exercising, her self-esteem temporarily restored. Feeling attractive, happy and in control, she goes on to enjoy the all-important event and completely forgets about exercise until the next big event comes into view. By this time, of course, she's effectively back to square one, her body no longer lithe and 'fit', so the whole process has to start again.

A similar pattern emerges when we look at the case of Edwina, a 29-year-old woman who works as a cashier in a large supermarket. Edwina comes from a family where educational achievement for girls is not held in high regard. Never having received encouragement from her family to do well academically, she left school at 16 with no qualifications and has had a string of boring, poorly paid jobs. She has no interests of which to speak, few friends and never questions or reflects on the emptiness of her day-to-day existence.

Her one pleasure in life is spending time and money on her appearance – buying clothes and jewellery, having expensive hairdos and so on. This is hardly surprising, since looking pretty and trendy is the one thing she can do which evokes favourable comments from her family. She has only ever had one boyfriend, John, whom she has been going out with for five years. Last year

John instigated a break in the relationship: he was bored, felt stifled and wanted to have more contact with his male friends. Edwina was devastated. She had no close friends and felt desperately lonely and insecure. To attempt to counteract these bad feelings, and to give herself 'something to do' in the evenings, she started going to aerobics dance classes.

She threw herself into this with gusto, going from doing no exercise whatsoever to attending four or five classes a week. She rapidly lost weight and inches off her body, and the dance sessions came to replace John by providing a focus for her life. Ten months later John returned. At first she continued with 'her' aerobics. Gradually, however, she has been doing less and less and she thinks that she might stop altogether soon.

Both these cases illustrate how the initial push to do exercise can be initiated by feelings of being at a disadvantage or inadequate. Low self-esteem, feelings of insecurity and self-doubt are projected on to the body, which must be disciplined and 'improved'. Instead of examining the social circumstances that provoke such bad feelings, and why they are so threatening, these women internalised all that was bad and focused it on their bodies. As self for many women is synonymous with physical self, the logical corollary is that they change the offending body. In Edwina's case, for example, she did not question the nature of her relationship with John, or reflect on how empty her life was, why it was empty and what positive steps could be taken to improve the situation; she thought, 'He's gone, which means that I'm not good enough, so *I'll* have to change'.

In order to further illustrate these points and to examine the factors and circumstances that provoke women to exercise excessively in greater depth, I shall recount one more case-history in more detail.

Jo is an attractive 22-year-old postgraduate chemistry student who appears to be self-confident and extremely capable. On the two occasions that I have spoken to her about her excessive exercising, however, it became apparent that she really feels insecure and has a very low self-esteem.

She tries to swim five days a week (30 lengths of a big pool) and attends two aerobics classes weekly. Eventually, she hopes to build up to doing four aerobics classes each week. At one stage she was also doing weight-training.

What motivates her to be so active? 'Fear,' she answers with a wry smile. This fear stems from two basic sources. Firstly, she does not feel in control of her body: she smokes, likes getting drunk and has been experiencing an appetite that she feels is excessive. By disciplining her body and getting fit, she hopes to be able to lose weight and to stop abusing her body so much. The second reason is that her mother, who is the same height as her, weighs 12 stone. Jo fears that she will get like her mother, which she associates with being old and unattractive. Exercising will prevent this from happening. A further advantage is that, lacking a steady boyfriend at the moment, she is, in a sense, 'preparing' herself, by making herself more attractive should one come along.

As we talk I can see that although Jo perceives her body as being out of control, it is in fact her life that is chaotic, and that controlling her body substitutes for controlling her life. It also becomes apparent that, like many women, she does not respond to adverse circumstances only by disciplining her body but sometimes fails to care for her body and is very self-destructive.

At 16 Jo went through an anorexic episode. She was extremely wound up after doing her O levels. When she found out that her boyfriend, who was her first ever, was going out with another girl, she responded by stopping eating, an action that she now feels reflected her inability to deal with the fact that you can't control other people's behaviour. Luckily, this episode didn't develop into full-blown anorexia, and she recovered and went on to do 'A' levels before going to university.

Whilst at university, when aged 19, Jo had her first serious relationship with a man, Ian, whom she moved in with. Although the 'closeness' of the relationship brought her much-needed security, it also brought problems. Ian had only two 'O' levels and was employed in a fairly menial job. On one level he felt quite proud of Jo's academic success but on another he resented it, as it made him feel very inadequate. He reacted by putting Jo down at every opportunity, when alone and when with other people. This had a dramatic and negative effect on her self-concept and she began to experience severe depression.

Jo first began to exercise when she thought that she and Ian might be splitting up. At this time, Ian had an affair with Linda, so Jo went off on holiday, by herself, to think things over. While on this holiday, she had a brief and enjoyable affair that was purely sexual. On being told about this when she returned, Ian castigated her and said that he found it quite sordid that she could enjoy a casual, no-strings-attached fling of this nature. When Jo pointed out that *he* had had an affair, he retorted that his one was 'nice and romantic'. The old double standard rears its ugly head yet again!

By this time, it seemed obvious that Jo and Ian's relationship was in its death throes. There followed, however, a bizarre two months in which Ian, waiting for Linda to return from abroad, continued to live with Jo and to act as if nothing was happening. During this period he was constantly comparing Jo and Linda: how they looked (in quite specific details), how they performed in bed and even how they danced. Jo realised that she couldn't really compete, that Linda was scoring more 'points', and so began to accept reluctantly that the relationship was over. In retrospect, she now says that she feels there was a little part of her wanting to get out of the relationship and so she probably 'pushed' Ian. At the time, though, she was frightened to admit to herself that it was only insecurity that was binding her to him.

Immediately following the break-up, Jo stopped exercising but spent a great deal of time thinking about her appearance, buying clothes and so forth. She had fantasies about bumping into Ian when she was looking so incredible that he would be struck with feelings of remorse and regret. She felt lonely and was very self-destructive, spending a full two months continuously stoned out of her head. Eventually, she began to realise the futility of behaving like this and decided to do something positive about her health. She began therapy, stopped smoking and started exercising again. Unfortunately, as part of this 'health' kick, she also came off the pill, met a new man, got pregnant and had to go through the trauma of having an abortion. After the abortion, this new male started to be very cold, callous and nasty to her. This reinforced her idea that she was not attractive and so she started exercising even more vigorously.

She now realises that her 'thing' with exercise is related to her relationship with men. I ask if she feels that exercising like she does represents taking care of herself? No, she says. She's only using the exercise as a tool to make her feel physically and psychologically better. Does she see any similarities between exercise and her previous anorexic episode? Yes, she does. When Ian (and subsequent boyfriends) rejected her, she rejected herself. In a sense, both self-destruction (anorexia) and trying to change (exercise) constitute a rejection of herself. It is not the men who are bad and wrong, it is her.

A month or so before I interviewed her, she knows that she could have slipped into an anorexic episode. She'd lost half a stone quickly, was not eating and was 'tense and neurotic' about her looks and the need to exercise. At the moment, she feels okay, but realises that future disappointments or betrayals could tip the balance towards anorexia.

What about when she reaches the optimum level of activity that she hopes to. Will she feel in control or will she feel that she is being controlled? She reiterates that at the moment she's not taking the exercise thing too seriously. It's a new craze; like when you lose weight, she has a new thing about muscles. Because the muscular body is currently being marketed as the latest shape for women? Yes, and, she admits rather grudgingly, probably because Ian used to say that he liked women with sporty, athletic figures.

We go on to speak of the ascetic aspects of exercising. Does Jo feel that it's a moral thing, that she transcends the body? Yes, it makes her feel better when she puts herself through pain. Denying herself food also has moral connotations for Jo. Like many women, she feels that eating is 'unfeminine', and feels embarrassed when she, say, buys a piece of cake in the college canteen. She recalls feeling 'inadequate and unfeminine' because she used to take coffee with cream and sugar, whereas her friends took it straight black.

What of the future? At the moment she has a 'sort of boyfriend'. They meet very occasionally, ostensibly on a platonic basis, but invariably end up drunk and in bed together. Afterwards he uses their drunkenness as an excuse and vows that it won't happen again. It does, of course.

Jo's history demonstrates that anorexia nervosa and compulsive exercising can fulfil the same function: to force the body into moral submission. Both her anorexic episode and the beginning of her exercise phase occurred at times when she was feeling rejected, unattractive, undoubtedly angry and not in control of her life. Starving herself or engaging in exercise makes Jo feel more attractive and 'feminine', and the toughness of the regimes gives her a moral 'high' and serves to punish her. It is, after all, she who is bad and wrong.

Self-starvation and going for the burn are ways of exercising pseudo-control over her life when all around her is crumbling and she feels desperate and lonely. Instead of concentrating on why she feels so insecure, why she has such overwhelming dependency needs, how her needs for love and nurturance can be met, and why she invariably goes for men who can't or won't meet them, she blames herself for her situation and tries to change.

Having read thus far, it is possible that you are feeling angry with me for being so critical of women who decide to work for a masculine physique or to improve their aerobic fitness level. I must stress most strongly that I am not criticising the women who do excessive weight-training or any other form of exercise, any more than I am criticising anorexics for being the way that they are. I am criticising the system and circumstances that bring pressure to bear on women to do these things. I am saying that just as anorexia is not about 'slimming', so the current stress on physical activity is not about 'fitness'. Perhaps echoing body-builder Zoë Warwick you are thinking that I've let the Boy George and Marilyn clones off the hook: why should men who adopt a more androgynous look be condoned while muscular women are criticised?[13] The answer is because the two things are not comparable. Women body-builders achieve an unnatural, semi-permanent change in their body-shape (I say semi-permanent with caution here – we don't know about the long-term effects associated with body-building yet, neither do we know what happens to women's physiques if and when they give up the practice). It is unnatural because women are meant, on average, to have more fat on their bodies than men, and because women's (and, for that matter, men's) muscles do not bulge without being worked and worked over a sustained period of time. It is unnatural and unhealthy because menstruation ceases. Boy George can take off his frock and make-up at night. Zoë Warwick can't remove her muscles and neither can Carolyn Cheshire switch on her menstrual cycle overnight. It would be a different matter if non-transsexual men were, say, taking hormones to develop breast-shaped chests. I would be just as critical of such a practice. But this, of course, is unlikely to happen. When men don women's clothing, it can be seen as mildly amusing and titillating, as in the case of Boy George, or downright 'hilarious', when, for example, comedians dress up as the perennial Mrs Mopp. By doing this, men are lowering their status, which is threatening and therefore antidoted with laughter. Women body-builders are unfunny precisely because they are imitating, and aspiring to the level of, what they perceive to be their 'superiors'.

It could be argued that by concentrating on extreme groups of fanatic aerobic-doers and body-builders, my ideas are invalid. Many women enjoy sport and exercise for its own sake and are not 'abnormal' in their pursuit of it. I agree. But, then again, just as there are many women who would not formally be diagnosed as suffering from anorexia nervosa even though they hold similar beliefs and act in a similar way, so many women exercise and weight-train for unhealthy reasons. A recent study examined dietary and body-shape concerns of females in the 12 to 18 age range.[13] In accordance with other work published in this area, although less than 4 per cent were overweight, over ten times this number considered themselves overweight, and approximately half desired to alter their weight and considered various ways of doing so. In contrast with an earlier study which found that for every one girl who considered exercise as a means of weight control, 2.5 considered dieting,[14] this one found the reverse. More girls in each age-group considered exercise to lose weight than considered the amount or type of food eaten (the ratio being 2:1 in favour of exercising). The authors' conclusion is sobering indeed: 'The "fitness industry", like the "diet industry" appears to have nourished these concerns' (with weight) . . . 'It is therefore possible that as a result young females are exposing themselves to the health risks of over-exercise in addition to the dieting risks already discussed.'

Women typically serve the needs of others at the expense of their own. How well I remember when I was a young child my mother lovingly preparing food for my small brother and me, but rarely sitting down to relax and eat with us. She always had too much to do. How often women fail to take time to ensure that they can give themselves the care and attention that is our right, or balk at asking others to give us care and attention. Recently, my mother, who now lives alone, was rather ill. She did not call the doctor in to see her, even though she had passed out a couple of times, because she 'didn't want to bother him'. It makes me so very angry that she, like other women, is unable to embrace and act upon her right to be looked after, to ensure that she is cared for. It is right and desirable for women to look after themselves; to feed themselves good food that *they* actually like, something few women do; to make sure that their emotional needs are met; to take time for themselves to do the things that they enjoy doing; to keep their bodies and minds fit and healthy. Of course, I recognise the physical and psychological benefits that are gained from taking some form of regular exercise, not to mention the fun that can be had in so doing, and would encourage women to do this if they want to. It's just that deep down inside, I feel that somehow many women are driven to exercise for the wrong reasons, and that the pursuit of fitness borders on the obsessive. Rather than being a means to an end, it becomes the end itself; rather than being part of one's life, it becomes one's life; rather than being enjoyable, it becomes an obsessive demon that 'must' compulsively be exorcised.

This gut-feeling has been supported when I have listened to women talking about exercise. In far too many cases the motivation to work out comes not from a sense of self-worth that demands that women take pleasure in caring for their bodies but from feelings of fear, lack of control and powerlessness, the need to punish and subdue our wicked bodies, to transcend their physicality, to gain acceptance by conforming to the latest 'ideal' shape. Compulsive exercising takes time; 'spare' time causes problems for women. In compulsive-eating groups, for example, it is often apparent that the ritual behaviour surrounding the compulsion can be a way of dealing with unstructured time. Perhaps exercise serves the same function. Certainly, if you followed the beauty regime recommended by the popular actress Raquel Welch, you'd be busy for the greater part of each day.[15] Apparently, she even recommends repeating the dreadful schoolgirl mantra: 'I must, I must, I must improve my bust'. What a hopelessly sad and useless thing to do!

Obsessively following 'fitness' plans can become an excuse for living, a means of avoiding interaction with the world and coming to terms with ourselves, a sterile way of dealing with the time that is ours. Excessive aerobics and body-building, like other forms of physical activity, can represent a desperate attempt by women to compete in the harsh realities of the market-place, to be fitter and more attractive, to gain some kind of control over their lives. Of course I believe that women should be fit and healthy. But the concepts of 'health' and 'fitness' should include some notion of psychological health and fitness, a requirement that at the moment does not appear to be being met.

Notes

1. Campbell, B., *Wigan Pier Revisited*, Virago, London, 1984.
2. Lawrence, M., 'Anorexia Nervosa: The Control Paradox', *Women's Studies International Quarterly*, 1979, Vol. 2, pp. 93–101.
3. *ibid.*, p. 97.
4. See, e.g., 'Muscles In', *New Society*, Vol. 65, No. 1077, 1983, p. 4; 'Battle of the Bulge', *Observer*, 2 December 1984; and 'The Meaning of Muscle', *City Limits*, No. 167, 1984.
5. 'The Meaning of Muscle', *City Limits*, No. 167, 1984.
6. *ibid.*, p. 12.
7. Frisch, R.E. and McArthur, J.W., 'Menstrual Cycles: Fatness as a Determinant of Minimum Weight for Height Necessary for their Maintenance or Onset', *Science*, 185: 949–51, 1974.
8. 'Muscling In', *Guardian*, 27 February 1985, p. 10.

9. *ibid.*
10. See, e.g., Bruch, H., *The Golden Cage: The Enigma of Anorexia Nervosa*, Open Books, London, 1978, pp. 5–6.
11. *City Limits*, *op. cit.*
12. 'Pumping Iron-Maidens', *Sunday Times*, 23 December 1984.
13. Davies, E., and Furnham, A., *The Dieting and Body-Shape Concerns of Adolescent Females* (forthcoming).
14. Huenemann, R.L., Shapiro, L.R., Hampton, M.C. and Mitchell, B.W., 'A Longitudinal Study of Gross Body Composition and Body Conformation and their Association with Food and Activity in a Teen-Age Population', *American Journal of Clinical Nutrition*, *18*, 1966, pp. 325–38.
15. Welch, R., *Raquel Welch's Health and Beauty Book*, W.H. Allen, London, 1984.

12
Anorexia and Bulimia: The Political and the Personal*
Troy Cooper

Introduction

While much attention has been focused on anorexia nervosa, little
has been given to bulimia in its own right. It has been assumed that
an understanding of the dynamics of anorexia entails an understanding of bulimia, even though the two problems and the people
that they affect are quite different. Although both behaviours are
apparently aimed at controlling weight, anorexia involves a public
act that others admire while bulimia is a private act that others pity.
Typically, anorexic women are white, with a high-earning father
and comfortably off background; they come from an apparently
perfect family are high academic and athletic achievers whose
behaviour has always been that of the 'best little girl in the world'.[1]
Bulimic women, on the other hand, do not generally come from one
type of background or one social or economic grouping. Yet both
problems are generally considered under the heading of eating
disorders, and anorexia is often considered the sister, if not the
mother, of bulimia. Consequently, bulimia has been largely ignored
as a topic for original thought or theory.

Because of Western socio-religious history, bulimia has been seen
as a loss of control. However, I shall argue that it is in fact the
method used by the bulimic for keeping control over elements of
her life which she considers would be destructive, disruptive and
frightening if expressed. As bulimia has always been discussed

*The writing of this chapter was supported by a grant from the Society for
the Advancement of Research into Anorexia Nervosa. It reflects the views
of the author only and not those of the Society.

175

alongside anorexia I shall follow the same course, but in doing so I hope to show their fundamental difference: whereas anorexia is a position taken in order to say something loudly and publicly, bulimia is a position taken in order *not* to have to say something. As long as bulimia is viewed as 'failed' anorexia and as addressing essentially the same problem, questions will remain unanswered about why bulimia is useful and necessary to the lives of so many women.

Finally, I shall describe a model of bulimia which proposes that bulimia can be divided into two types: pragmatic and control-oriented bulimia. The model shows how control-oriented bulimia can grow from either anorexia or pragmatic bulimia and that it is psychologically addictive. The implication of the model is that bulimia is not the problem as such: the problem lies in the use of bulimia as a substitute for the solution of other problems.

The history and characteristics of anorexia and bulimia

Anorexia Nervosa

Anorexia nervosa continues to impress and dominate the press and the medical establishment alike. The volume of work on the topic is substantial and increasing. The characteristics of the disorder appear simple: it mostly affects white, teenage women whose fathers occupy social-economic classes 1 and 2. Within that group it is currently reaching epidemic proportions. In the light of the increasing prevalence of anorexia nervosa, these facts show clearly how the eating problem is connected with women's societal position, and particularly with a specific group of women whose social and cultural position makes their individual lives particularly pointed instances of a general problem: the reconciliation of the old and new expectations of women.

The first description of anorexia occurs in the seventeenth century in medical texts and, although writing on the topic continues into the twentieth century, it is described as a rare condition, an experience to be treasured by the clinician.[2] Its rarity continued until the 1950s, when it slowly became more prevalent, taking off completely in the 1960s. This increase cannot be accounted for simply on the grounds that anorexia was not previously recognised. The consequences of restriction of diet in anorexia are such that its occurrence cannot be missed, either by family or by medical practitioner. It would have been impossible to miss large numbers of anorexic girls.

It has been argued that anorexia nervosa has occurred prior to the current epidemic but been diagnosed under a different medical heading, for example, chlorosis or consumption.[3] This, however, is not a convincing argument, as the symptoms of these three disorders are very different. It would seem quite safe to say, therefore, that the occurrence of anorexia in its present proportions is a recent phenomenon. Even if anorexia as a disorder is not absolutely distinct and identifiable, we can at least say what it is not.

The precise and defining symptoms of restricting anorexia have been the subject of some disagreement. However, the criteria used by Feigner[4] are usually accepted in the absence of anything better. These are a combination of the following:

1. a loss of at least 20 per cent of body weight;
2. a refusal to eat without known medical reason;
3. loss of menstruation;
4. hyperactivity;
5. the growth of lanugo hair (a downy body-hair that appears on the victims of starvation);
6. cyanosis of feet, hands and extremities (withdrawal of circulation which makes the affected areas blue and numb);
7. a distorted and implacable attitude towards food and body-image.

Although there is considerable disagreement as to the exact combination of symptoms necessary for a diagnosis of anorexia, there are two criteria that all researchers are agreed upon. The first is a distorted and implacable attitude towards food; the second is appearance – when you see a restricting anorexic, you know her.

Treatment of anorexia has been dominated by certain popular theoretical orientations. These can be split roughly into four categories: the political, the literal, the psychoanalytic, or any mix of these three. Central to all the interpretations is the notion of anorexia as an attempt at control. The doyenne of the study of eating syndromes with the most experience of clinical work in this area is Hilde Bruch, whose own approach covers all three areas. She believes that anorexia is a struggle for personal autonomy in the arena of familial and possibly societal politics. As such it is an attempt at self-determination. She also believes that a sufficient condition of the expression of this struggle as anorexia is an overly authoritarian mother who suppresses a growing child's ability to distinguish between hunger and satiety sensations. This theme of a

178 Fed Up and Hungry

struggle for autonomy by the anorexic has become one generally accepted by clinicians and research workers.

Literal theories centre on the notion that the girl cannot accept either adult sexuality or womanhood. Consequently, the girl attempts to suppress the symptom and symbol of these states by ridding herself of menstruation. Furthermore, her body-image has become so distorted, through the influences of an appearance-conscious family and the images promoted by the media, that dieting becomes an inevitable consequence. The theme is the attempt to avoid sexual maturity and its consequences, and a denial of the inevitability of maturation.

Psychoanalytic theories concentrate on the issues of sexuality as expressed through fear of loss of self-control. These include fear of oral impregnation, rejection of the controlling mother by rejection of notional breast (her nourishment), unwillingness to accept adult female sexuality with all that it implies and a desire to remain in a period of Freudian-type infantile sexuality.

Bulimia

Bulimia has enjoyed neither the medical nor the popular interest that has been aroused by anorexia. Historically, evidence for it is much harder to trace. Certainly, vomiting to control weight has an honourable history, even to the point of being institutionalised by the Romans in their use of *vomitoria* after feasting. It may have been a widespread practice amongst Roman and Greek young women.[5] However, as a 'disease' it did not come to the attention of the medical establishment until recently. A partial explanation of this may be that, unlike anorexia, bulimia can be practised for years without detection. Bulimic women tend to keep their weight just below normal, and their bulimia need not intrude on their activities greatly or incapacitate them. Unless the vomiting habit becomes so persistent that it takes up a great deal of time, or induces some kind of physical crisis, bulimia may never come to the attention of a clinician.

That being so, it is impossible to say that the phenomenon of widespread use of this method of weight control is new. The growing numbers of women seeking help or treatment could be the result of a number of factors. It could be that recently women have come to label their behaviour as a problem and to self-refer, or perhaps it may be that for many individuals the frequency of vomiting has increased so much that it cannot escape detection by the family. However, since the level of press coverage of bulimia has been so small compared to that of anorexia, one can be reasonably sure that the problem is not self-created by greater sensitisation on the part of the public. Conversely, it is indicative of the status of bulimia that there is relatively so little coverage in the media, given current estimates of its occurrence in the college population, for example, and the continuing growth of the symptom.[6]

The definition of bulimia, unlike anorexia, does not present major problems. If a woman vomits regularly to control her weight and there is no other medically defined reason for that vomiting, then she is bulimic whether or not she restricts her diet in between vomiting or has binge–vomiting episodes. It has been estimated that 40 per cent of anorexics become bulimic or bulimarexic.[7] In spite of this overlap between the groups, bulimic women are not as similar to each other as are anorexic women. Geographically and economically, they are more spread out. They are not necessarily academic achievers, the products of enduring marriages, athletic or likely to begin their bulimic episodes at a particular age. However, as a group, bulimic women are more likely than anorexics to shoplift, self-mutilate, attempt suicide, become depressed or become alcoholic.[8]

A brief appraisal of the literature on bulimia shows that theorising on the subject has always been secondary to a theory of anorexia. The titles of such works indicate the fact: for example, Hilde Bruch's standard work on the subject is in a book entitled *Eating Disorders: Obesity, Anorexia Nervosa and the Person Within*. Bulimia is rarely specified in the titles of other clinical books that deal with the symptom.

Within its adjunctive position to anorexia, the most prevalent interpretation of bulimia, with various elaborations, has been that bulimia is an attempt by the bulimic to identify boundaries between herself and her mother – an attempt at separation and individuation. The bulimic feels overwhelmed by another person, her mother, and symbolically enacts regaining control of herself and her life by the ingestion and rejection of nourishment, which represents her mother. The most sophisticated attempt at such explanation has been in object-relations theory.[10] Other explanations have similarly centred on the notion of bulimia as the response of a woman who considers herself not to be under her own control and direction. An example of this has been theoretical attitudes to anorexics who become bulimic. This development usually has been considered a breakdown of the control that anorexia represents; hence, it is a lack of control. In no theoretical interpretation is bulimia examined in a positive light, as something that enables the woman to continue in her current lifestyle. Whereas anorexia is a positive decision, an action of strength, bulimia is a negative action forced through weakness.

Popular views of anorexia and bulimia

The attitude of the press to bulimia is more important than might appear to be the case. As the press began to carry more stories on anorexia, bulimia also became a topic, but almost always within the context of being related to anorexia. Anorexics 'came out' and wrote their stories – both as books and in articles. Bulimic women, with one or two exceptions, did not. There are several reasons for reticence on their part.

Amongst a woman's reactions to telling her friends, her family or her therapist that she is bulimic are fear of the loss of their opinion of her as a 'nice' and 'clean' woman and overwhelming self-disgust. She is frequently ashamed of her behaviour, thinking it dirty, self-abusive and nasty. She does not have the apparent pride of the anorexic woman. Likewise, the press, conscious of their readers' self-image and expectations of other women, do not have a positive attitude towards bulimia. In the belief that their women readers do not want to read stories about women with whom they cannot identify, a magazine does not view a bulimic as the heroine of a piece. They believe that their readers want to read a story in which they can identify with a woman from the middle or upper class, of accomplished background, yet who suffers some mysterious and almost desirable ailment – a subject who is close enough to identify with, yet sufficiently distant to allow fantasy. Furthermore, the anorexic's condition fits in well with the overall philosophy of femininity that the women's magazines reflect and elaborate. Anorexia exudes an aura of self-denial, of silent suffering and self-control in pursuit of subjugation of the flesh. It is a woman's attempt to better herself. These are qualities and a goal which women see as feminine and women's magazine editors seek to reflect.[11]

This may also account for the fact that there is more feminist work on anorexia than on bulimia: the anorexic population is one with which the feminist is most likely to identify. It is worth remembering that a high proportion of feminists come from a well-educated, parentally middle-class background and therefore stand a relatively high chance of having themselves once been anorexic. Furthermore, as I will demonstrate later, the anorexic solution may well be of a kind with which feminists have had most sympathy: an assertion of the personal as political. In contrast, bulimic behaviour appears self-indulgent, dirty and physically unrestrained. For a movement concerned with getting women's work and experience valued more highly, bulimia can be a sensitive issue, especially as women involved in the movement are often those with the highest standards of personal politics, achievement and health.

Culturally, anorexia is admirable because it is perceived in women as control of the flesh and of sinful or dangerous bodily desires, and as a corollary an assertion of spirituality, which appeals to strong social and religious traditions (see Chapter 1). Bulimia, however, is the descent into the flesh. It is the apparent indulgence of the flesh, followed by its manipulation and self-abuse.

Reconsideration of the theoretical approach to bulimia and anorexia

We have seen how bulimia as a symptom in its own right has come to be largely ignored. It has been conceptualised as a breakdown of 'will', as something no woman could possibly want to do. Bulimics, afraid of others' sanctions and bewildered by their own desires and actions, have found it easiest to play the role of 'victim'. While everyone can understand wanting to be anorexic, no one can understand wanting to be bulimic.

This is also reflected in clinical attitudes to the degree of prevalence of the two eating symptoms. Experimental work has established that most women in our culture – probably in the range of 80 to 90 per cent[12] are women who habitually try to keep their daily calorie intake to a certain level and try to eat less than they need to stop themselves feeling hungry. This is technically called restrained eating. Furthermore, a substantial percentage of this group will score just below the cut-off line for diagnosis of anorexia nervosa on the Eating Attitudes Test, a test widely used by researchers to identify people with eating disorders.[13] However, because it is obvious to most researchers and clinicians why most women in the West restrain their eating, i.e. the overwhelming social condemnation of female fat of any kind, no one would dream of suggesting that all these women need treatment. Such women are regarded as people responding understandably to pressures placed upon them. Consequently, a certain degree of dieting or self-restraint is considered normal.

But clinicians have not accepted, or made any acceptance clear, that a certain degree of bulimic behaviour is acceptable on the same pragmatic grounds. It should be accepted that if a woman chooses to vomit after a heavy meal in which she judges that she has eaten too much, there is no problem *per se*. Physically, frequent vomiting can be extremely dangerous, even apart from the issue of non-absorption of food. It can result in severe electrolytic imbalance in body cells, haemorrhaging, increased blood pressure, heart strain, erosion of tooth enamel and so on.[14] But as an infrequent course of action it need be no more deleterious to health than the use of slimming tablets or other slimming aids, self-starvation with intermittent binges or laxative abuse. In this respect it should be brought out of the closet. It is only one of a range of solutions found by women to the problem of living in a society which promotes an abundance of food but applauds a scarcity of flesh.

The problems arise when bulimic behaviour becomes frequent, in which case it will become physically damaging, and in the need or desire for such punishing behaviour. If, for example, vomiting performs a particular function in enabling a woman to 'cope' with a lifestyle that she finds problematic, stressful or overdemanding, then it is obvious that the behaviour will escalate. To 'cope' in these terms is to carry on fulfilling the demands that are made upon her, to not make a fuss and to continue behaving as usual. To 'cope' is seen as remaining in control. It is in this context that bulimia becomes dangerous. As something which allows temporary feelings of relief from the real problems in the bulimic woman's life, it will be used with increasing urgency as the magnitude of the unaddressed problems increases. Furthermore, each time she uses a bulimic episode to help her 'cope' with important but problematic areas of her life, the bulimic feels more of a fraud, more ashamed and less able to deal directly with the issues behind the need for the behaviour.

So now we can go back and look more closely at the idea of bulimia as a loss of control. Examined closely there appears to be a curious doublethink. Anorexic women themselves see anorexia as a question of control: a popular response on being requested to eat is: 'I can't. If I eat I won't know when to stop.' Yet the very nature of that protest gives the game away. The concept of control relies on choice. An anorexic should be able to choose whether to deny herself or not, a choice made each time food is presented. But she allows that she has no choice; that if she eats she won't know when to stop. I do not think that this means that the anorexic feels blind to her own satiety signals. Knowing 'when to stop', means to the anorexic woman stopping eating at the point where her hunger, or the needs that represent themselves to her as hunger, is satisfied and at which she will remain thin by her standards. Of course, the answer to her problem is simple though unacceptable to her: no such point exists.

The anorexic woman seeks a solution to this problem by trying to persuade herself that she needs and wants less and less to eat. This is not an exercise in choice, autonomy or self-control. The woman who needs or desires such thinness in order to be able to continue in her lifestyle must force herself into the anorexic position. It is the onlooker who imputes control to the anorexic, the onlooker who, surrounded by tempting plenty, makes continuous and painful decisions as to whether to indulge herself or not.

For the bulimic woman it is a different story. As we have seen, the bulimic is perceived by onlookers as doing what everybody wants to do (that is, she eats and stays thin). But the way she does it, her apparent self-indulgence, is viewed culturally as a lack of self-control. Furthermore, as no self-respecting woman should vomit voluntarily, the bulimic woman is perceived as compelled to do so by her immoderation. All in all, bulimia seems not to be chosen by the bulimic woman but forced upon her. But looked at from another angle bulimia is quite different. Vomiting is a physically uncomfortable and practically messy business. To impose this unpleasant penalty on oneself for over-indulgence requires as much self-control as to choose not to indulge. This is the choice that the pragmatically bulimic woman exercises, weighing the unpleasantness of vomiting against the unpleasantness of perceiving herself as fat. It is only when the bulimic woman greatly increases the frequency of her behaviour and cannot stop herself, only when her behaviour answers other needs, that it becomes an issue of self-control. But by then it is not because of the behaviour itself but because of the problems it stands for.

It now remains to ask how pragmatic bulimia changes to an addictive behaviour dedicated to helping the bulimic woman to cope with her life, to helping her remain in control. What kind of mechanism changes it from a mechanism of weight control into a mechanism of self-control?

so I made it to 7 stone

The politics of anorexia and bulimia

Politics of any kind are to do with power: the acquisition and exercise of power. Power is the ability to change the environment in a way desirable to the empowered. This may involve affecting objects, events, people or relationships, but it is always within the domain outside the self.

We have seen how anorexia seems to affect a specific group of women while bulimia is more widespread. The two conditions affect women specifically, but not for any physiological reason. There are a certain number of male cases classed as anorexic (currently 10 per cent[15]) and a growing number as bulimic. However, the overwhelming preponderance of women and the immediate cultural relevance of their symptoms strongly suggest that the socio-cultural position of women itself has something to do with both conditions. But it is clear that the power function of anorexia, serving a very specific group of women in a public way, is quite different to that of bulimia, which serves a diverse group of women in a very private way. We can see that while it is the cultural position of women in the West which connects the two problems, the difference in their expression reflects clearly the different needs that they fulfil. Furthermore, it seems likely that as the onset of anorexia is connected with youth and that of bulimia with more mature years, they also represent the different types of response that women make at different stages in their lives. The Western, middle-class, achieving schoolgirl has very particular pressures on her to succeed, which, together with current social conceptions of femininity, can force her to rebel using the only resource at her disposal: her body and others' feelings towards her. Anorexia is a refusal by such a young woman to take onto herself the responsibility for resolving the impossible position in which she is placed. The pressures which adult, Western women face, while of the same source as the schoolgirl, are within a quite different context and produce a different response to the stress. Bulimia is not a rebellion but an attempt to accommodate oneself to resolve the problem.

The social and political position of women in the West has changed more in the last 80 years than at any other time in the last 800. This has been reflected in a new set of expectations of women for themselves. Whereas men can see success as residing in a limited number of roles, namely those at work, women have been exhorted to seek success in many spheres: in employed work, in domestic work, as wives, mothers and lovers, in maintaining the extended family ties and so on. Thus has been born the Superwoman syndrome;[16] the current ideal of the successful and fulfilled woman is the one who achieves in all areas. The impossibility of becoming such a Superwoman produces stress and frustration in all women, but it is perhaps the bulimic woman who does not acknowledge and allow for that impossibility. She believes that she is at fault for not accommodating adequately. The anger, resentment, depression, sadness – the negative emotions – produced by these tensions and frustrations are not owned up to by the bulimic. Their expression, she fears, would be too disruptive, too dangerous. Their strength and intensity bewilders and frightens her. When, therefore, she finds that vomiting can produce a reduction of those feelings, mimic their expression, it becomes a safety valve for her failure to achieve impossible goals.

Feminists have consistently acknowledged anorexia as an expression of the personal as political. Anorexia is seen for what it is: the logical culmination of cultural beliefs about, and attitudes towards, the female body. Unfortunately, as we have seen, bulimia has not achieved the same standing. The problem lies in the fact that feminists of any persuasion live within culture and cannot avoid absorbing at least some of its strongest values. At a gut level, feminists share with other women a sneaking and unwilling admiration for anorexia which mixes with and reinforces a basic ideological viewpoint. There is a strong inclination within feminist theory to regard women as spiritually superior to men because of the injustice and ill-use we have suffered at the hands of a patriarchal society. Because of a tradition of stoic, silent suffering in response to this position, and of self-sacrifice (especially for our children), the stance of the anorexic woman appeals strongly to a sense of what it is to be traditionally feminine, of women's greater morality. Unfortunately, bulimia is not so easily translated into a sympathetic symbol of women's oppression. Its only cultural standing is in an opposite role: as an affirmation of all that is degrading and uncontrollable in women's physicality and their appetites.

Clearly, the statement being made in anorexia is political in that it is a statement of power over others. It is public. Others must see and react to it. Even if the physical condition of the anorexic is ignored, her saying no cannot be. The giving of food and its consumption is one of the most basic and public of nurturant and social activities. The anorexic woman's refusal of sustenance from her family asserts rejection of them at many levels: she is refusing food, dependence, communication, nurturance. The power that the anorexic takes is that used by Antigone in Greek tragedy. It is the power of saying no to the demands or impositions of others. This is clearly demonstrated in the extremely violent emotional responses anorexia produces from those with whom the anorexic woman lives or is involved. Its strength lies in the passivity of its aggression. The anorexic woman is not performing an act which can be effectively countermanded. She is simply refusing to do something. It is the same kind of passive resistance so effectively used in sit-down protests, 'die-ins' and most, notably, hunger strikes. Anyone who has dealt with anorexic women will acknowledge the overwhelming feelings of impotence this stance engenders in others.

The lack of power struggle, of political struggle, in bulimia is apparent in the attitude of the 'failed' anorexic woman and those who treat her. Many anorexic women eventually become bulimic, usually because of the 'remedial' treatment used in hospitalisation, particularly force-feeding. Once she has achieved a target weight, the anorexic woman will be discharged from hospital, often with little outpatient care, nearly always with the problems that turned her to anorexia untouched. For this group bulimic behaviour often begins in hospital, learnt from another bulimic woman,[17] and is typically associated with this involuntary and frightening increase in weight. It is among this group of women that one will find the lowest self-esteem and the most self-destructiveness. It is acknowledged clinically that this group has the worst prognosis.[18] This is because the treatment administered to the former anorexic has broken her power by erasing the public statement of power which affects others so strongly. Her condition no longer commands cultural approbation and no longer has bargaining strength. She is no longer in a position to draw upon cultural and ideological support for her weight loss; rather than being the subject of unwilling admiration, she is now the victim of an unpleasant disorder. For the most part unconscious of this network of support that she has been drawing upon, the now bulimic woman will feel suddenly let down, and this will cause her to cling desperately to the one external focus of her desires, her low weight. In becoming bulimic she has unknowingly colluded in divesting herself of power; she thereby helps to create a crisis of bewilderment and frustration as she realises that while bulimia may preserve her weight loss it is a hollow victory, for the manner of her weight control was at least as important as the control itself. The now ex-anorexic will constantly struggle to regain her lost anorexic state. But while many anorexic women become bulimic, very few bulimic women become anorexic: it is much easier to lose power when everyone is concerned to make one do so than to gain power when everyone is against it.

A model of bulimia that distinguishes pragmatic and control-oriented types

Whereas the infrequent/casual bulimic may vomit in order to be able to eat, the compulsive bulimic eats in order to vomit. Bulimic women themselves often describe their behaviour as akin to an addiction. As vomiting is not inherently pleasurable, it must be rewarding enough in some other way for the bulimic woman to persist in a physically harmful and unpleasant behaviour.

To consider the behaviour as addictive we have to look at bulimia to see if it fits a description of addiction. One such description is called the opponent process model of motivation.[19] It can best be described using smoking as an example.

Smoking is an initially unpleasant event: the smoke makes one cough, the ash smells, the taste of tar is unpleasant and so on. However, this is only a short-term strong reaction and the long-term effects of nicotine are very positive and are cumulative: the more the smoker smokes, the higher the amounts of circulating nicotine, with its attendant sedative effects. What we can see happening for the smoker are two processes: call them process 1 and process 2.

Process 1 represents the first immediate consequences of the behaviour and process 2 the long-term consequences. Let's say that for any addictive behaviour there are always these two processes and they are always in a certain relationship. First, process 1 is a strong and short-lived set of reactions to the addictive substance or behaviour: in our example, nicotine. Process 2 is a weaker but long-lived set of reactions which are slow to disappear. These sets of reactions can be physical or psychical, but they will always be opposite in value. So, if process 1 was positive physically and/or psychologically, process 2 would be negative, and vice versa. The idea can be thought of as the body swinging like a pendulum between different states. When the body and psyche are in equilibrium, the pendulum is at rest. But when process 1 is tipped off by addictive behaviour, the pendulum swings to one side or the other, a positive or negative state. Process 2 then follows as the pendulum swings the other way, and its value will be opposite. The nature of the two swings is different, however. Although the first is quick and strong, the second slows down and takes longer to complete its path, with the depth of the swing diminished. So the first process is quicker and stronger than the second, but shorter lived.

The opponent process theory of addiction, then, stipulates that in any two processes of the type above, while the body/psyche can quickly get used to the first process, it does not get used to the second. So eventually the effects of the first process wear off and no longer really affect the person involved, but the effects of the second process remain strong and active. If we consider smoking again we will see how this description works. The first process is negative in effect: it is unpleasant and uncomfortable, except perhaps in terms of social acceptance. However, if the effects of the first process are quickly got used to, then the positive second process becomes the only process with any effect. As the effects of process 2 are quite slow to dissipate, repetition of the addictive behaviour (i.e. smoking tobacco) will make process 2 effects accumulate and so become even stronger. In smoking, the initially negative effects can be got used to quite quickly if – for whatever reason – the smoker persists in smoking. With this persistence, process 2 gains in strength as circulating levels of nicotine in the blood build up. Thus the 'buzz' from each cigarette becomes stronger and stronger as dependence builds up.

So now the important question to be settled concerns the reasons why someone will keep engaging in an addictive behaviour with a negative first process until habituation occurs. Although the second process in itself may be rewarding, the strength of its effect is often much weaker than the primary process. It would be difficult for it initially to be a strong enough motivation to continue doing something unpleasant and even painful. So it seems certain that other factors must be helping the smoker to persevere in 'learning' to smoke, for example. Perhaps if the sedative and relaxing qualities of nicotine are extraordinarily rewarding to one particular group of people because of the stressful situations in which they live, these people will be considerably more motivated to overcome the initial discomfort than people who are not so stressed. Their desire for the process 2 effects of nicotine will be greater; consequently, the effects will have greater psychological value.

I believe that this is the kind of process that occurs in bulimia. Bulimia has a negative first process and a positive second process. For the pragmatically bulimic woman, the factor that outweighs the aversive process of vomiting is the pleasure of eating as much as she wants without becoming fat. Bingeing, as experienced by habitual binge–vomiters, usually involves the consumption of large quantities of food for which the binger often has no active preference and which she may actually dislike. The food is consumed not for the pleasure of the food itself but for the various feelings/states that follow its consumption, and the type of food chosen depends on how easy it is to 'bring up'. Consequently, for the group of pragmatically bulimic women, bingeing is rare because food consumption provides the sole motivation for the activity, not the affective and physical consequences of vomiting. It is for the control-oriented bulimic woman that bingeing becomes important. She has become used to the initial discomfort of vomiting. The feelings and states that constitute the secondary process now become very important to her, as they answer other needs that she has which are *not* to do with eating. It is these other needs which can turn pragmatic bulimia into control-oriented bulimia.

Control-oriented bulimic women were often once pragmatically bulimic. Whereas previously the bulimia was occasional, now it has become constant. Vomiting as the primary process is unpleasant and violent. The after-effects of vomiting are weakly positive: feelings of purging, expiation, exhaustion, cleansing, somnolence and so on. The remaining unanswered question is what circumstances could make these after-effects become so desirable that it is worth carrying on long enough with the unpleasant first process for habituation to occur.

The bulimic woman's life will contain demands and drains upon her that she resents, for which she feels guilty. She may not be able to express her anger, resentment or hostility directly to the appropriate source. She may experience her feelings as illegitimate, may think that their expression would harm others who would not be able to cope. Furthermore, the expression of these feelings could alter her life in ways that seem very frightening. Her upbringing may forbid the expression of such feelings. Bulimic women often have extremely busy, successful and tidy lives in which there is no space for the expression of these feelings. Consequently, vomiting and its after-effects can act as a substitute for the expression of these feelings. The process and after-effects involved can mimic the expression of her negative feelings and the ensuing catharsis. The bulimic may well feel that she has discovered the perfect solution: she can carry on 'coping'. However, as it is not the real problems that are addressed, this solution can do little more than provide temporary relief. Consequently, the bulimic woman will need and want to resort to it again and again. Despite her shame and self-disgust, it makes her feel better. Also, as habituation to the unpleasant process of actually retching occurs and its negative value decreases, the second process becomes more accessible.

It is clear that control-oriented bulimia relies on the second process in the bulimic episode becoming strongly rewarding. This is possible because of the Superwoman syndrome, because of the high goals and expectations bulimic women set themselves. The second process can be seen as so strongly positive because the social shaping and training which women receive militates against the expression of messy and negative feelings. Lastly, and perhaps obviously, it is because of women's special relationship to food as providers and consumers, that it is food which is used for the relief of stress or conflict.

Summary and conclusions

I have tried to demonstrate fundamental differences between anorexia and bulimia nervosa. I believe that the two symptoms have been treated very differently for cultural reasons, and that this difference of view has affected clinical treatment of bulimia nervosa adversely. Anorexia has a cultural mythology behind it; it is almost fêted as a mysterious 'and exotic condition, while bulimia is not. Furthermore, whilst anorexia is seen as an attempt to gain and exercise self-control, bulimia is seen as a loss of self-control. I have argued that, on the contrary, anorexia is a political issue, an attempt to alter the balance of power between the anorexic woman and others. Bulimia, however, is an attempt to cope, an attempt by the bulimic to *maintain* self-control despite being under great stress in her life.

I have proposed that bulimia be understood within the context of a theory of psychological addiction. Like smoking, it alleviates stress; unlike smoking, the point is not the induction of relaxation and sedation but the release of a very specific type of tension. Bulimia allows the expression (with ensuing catharsis) of forbidden rage, resentment, fear and other negative feelings, which are the product of demands made on the bulimic by others. The physical and emotional states achieved after a vomiting episide become very positively valued and the bulimic comes to crave them.

While anorexia is an attempt to change a woman's life, bulimia is an attempt to allow her to carry on. Therapists must help the bulimic to identify those areas of her life causing so much tension, which is forbidden expression. Specifically, the techniques used in co-counselling may be useful: the idea is to name felt but unexpressed emotion and act it out (discharge). As bulimic behaviour has become psychologically addictive, a behavioural approach is also required, so that the (often ritualised) patterns of behaviour preceding a bulimic episode can be identified and specific interventions planned for the bulimic to use to break the cycle. The most important task of treatment, however, must be to make visible what is invisible: the 'coping' that bulimia makes possible and the positive attempt at control it represents.

Notes

1. Levenkron, S., *The Best Little Girl in the World*, Warner Books, New York, 1978.
2. Bruch, H., *Eating Disorders: Obesity, Anorexia Nervosa and the Person Within*, Routledge & Kegan Paul, London, 1974.
3. Ehrenreich, B., and English, D., *Complaints and Disorders: The Sexual Politics of Sickness*, The Feminist Press, New York, 1973; Compendium, London, 1974.

4. Feigner, J.P., *et al.*, 'Diagnostic Criteria for Use in Psychiatric Research', *Archives of General Psychiatry*, Vol. 26, 1972, pp. 57–63.

5. Bruch, *op cit*.

6. Halmi, K., Falk, J., and Schwartz, E., 'Binge Eating and Vomiting: A Survey of the College Population', *Psychological Medicine*, Vol. 11, 1981, pp. 697–706; and Fairburn, C.G., and Cooper, P.J., 'Binge Eating: Self-Induced Vomiting and Laxative Abuse: A Community Study', *Psychological Medicine*, Vol. 14, 1984, pp. 401–10.

7. Garfinkel, P.E., 'The Heterogeneity of Anorexia Nervosa – Bulimia as a Distinct Subgroup', *Archives of General Psychiatry*, Vol. 37, pp. 1036–40.

8. Garner, D.M., and Garfinkel, P.E., *Anorexia Nervosa: A Multidimensional Perspective*, Brunner/Mazel, New York, 1982.

9. Bruch, *op. cit.*

10. Sugarman, A., and Kevash, C., 'The Body as Transitional Object in Bulimia', *International Journal of Eating Disorders*, Vol. 1, 1982, pp. 57–67.

11. Ferguson, M., *Forever Feminine*, Heinemann, London, 1983.

12. Button, E.J., and Whitehouse, A., 'Sub-clinical Anorexia Nervosa', *Psychological Medicine*, Vol. 11, 1981, pp. 509–16.

13. Garner, D.M., and Garfinkel, P.E., 'The Eating Attitudes Test: An Index of the Symptoms of Anorexia Nervosa', *Psychological Medicine*, Vol. 9, 1979, pp. 273–9.

14. Neumann, P.A., and Halvorsan, P.A., *Anorexia and Bulimia*, Van Nostrand Reinhold, New York, 1985.

15. Bruch, *op. cit.*

16. Rose, A., 'The Adequacy of Women's Expectations of Adult Roles', *Social Forces*, Vol. 30, 1951, pp. 69–77.

17. Neumann and Halvorsan, *op. cit.*

18. Vigersky, R.A., (ed.), *Anorexia Nervosa*, Raven Press, New York, 1974.

19. Solomon, R.L., and Corbit, J.D., 'An Opponent-Process Theory of Motivation I: Temporal Dynamics of Affect', *The Psychological Review*, Vol. 81, 1974, pp. 119–45.

13

'Poison is the Nourishment that Makes One Ill':[1] The Metaphor of Bulimia

Mira Dana and Marilyn Lawrence

In this chapter we set out to examine the real meanings of the problems women have with eating. All eating problems are significant and can only be understood as an expression of underlying issues and difficulties. We shall therefore spend some time looking at anorexia and compulsive eating. However, our main emphasis is on bulimia – eating followed by self-induced vomiting. Many women who have this problem, and the professionals who treat them, find their particular patterns of eating bizarre and impossible to understand. There seems to be no point to it; it doesn't seem to achieve anything. Our contention here is that, like other forms of disordered eating, bulimia contains a message that goes beyond the limits of the behaviour itself. It is with this meaning that we will be concerned and with its implications for the kind of therapy we offer.

Eating, taking nourishment, is a fundamental human concern. It is not, like breathing, a reflex action, but it is an activity in which we must all engage if we are to survive. As babies, we are entirely dependent on being fed by others. As adults, a wide range of social, cultural and symbolic meanings are attached to the activity of eating. By observing people's eating habits, we can learn a great deal about their attitude towards themselves, towards others, their social world and their status within it. Eating is never a mere physical function: it contains and carries much more than is evident on the surface. This is why any disturbance in the eating function is bound to fascinate and appal us. The almost obsessive interest of

193

the media, of literature and of the medical and helping professions can also be attributed to the fact that these symptoms are powerfully symbolic.

When we talk about a metaphor we have in mind a situation, an incident or a piece of behaviour which represents or correlates directly to another situation which has the same meaning. If we look at one, we can learn and understand more about the other. To relate this more specifically to eating disorders – bulimia, for example – we can look at the actual eating behaviour and attempt to see from it what is happening in the woman's inner world. To be of any use therapeutically, our understanding must be based on more than mere hypothesis or theory. In fact, it is derived from work over a number of years with women who suffer from these difficulties and who have discussed the connections with us.

The literature on women's eating problems has two distinct areas of focus: one is the *results* of the disordered eating pattern; the other is the nature of the disordered eating itself. The first focus would describe anorexia in terms of a wish to avoid weight gain, perhaps as a way of avoiding physical maturation. Compulsive eating can be understood in terms of the woman's need to stay fat in order to protect herself from certain conflicts. In the case of bulimia, this kind of approach doesn't take us very far. The bulimic woman is usually fairly 'normal' in appearance, looking neither particularly fat nor especially thin. In our more recent work with bulimic women we have become convinced that we need to focus on the second area, disordered eating, if we are to understand the problem. If we ignore the meaning of the eating pattern, we miss the essential symbolism of the problem.

Eating and its meanings

We can generalise by saying that a woman's eating pattern symbolises that woman's capacity for self-nurturance, her capacity to take nurturing in and her ability to nurture others.

The woman who eats compulsively feels under pressure to take in everything; she cannot discriminate. She is aware that she needs something, that something is lacking, but instead of finding out what these needs are and attempting to meet them, she swamps herself with all sorts of things that she doesn't really need at all. She tries to limit herself, to ration herself, but she always ends up greedily gobbling up everything she can find. A woman who eats in a compulsive way is actually very bad at asking for appropriate things for herself. She may experience herself as demanding, greedy and insatiable, but she usually ends up doing the nurturing rather than receiving it.

An anorexic woman, on the other hand, feels that she has to deny that she has any needs at all. Nothing can be taken in and there is little to give out. Or at least, this is what is being proclaimed by the symptom. Relationships are experienced as intrusive and dangerous. The only hope lies in self-sufficiency – a denial of any possibility of dependency or nurturance by self or others.

The woman who is bulimic, who eats quite large quantities of food and then makes herself sick, is using her symptom to say something rather different. Symbolically, she is able to take things in (unlike the anorexic woman). However, unlike the woman who eats compulsively, she is not able to hold on to it. What bulimic women can take in varies. Sometimes it is everything, without discrimination, sometimes it is more measured amounts. But whatever the quantity, once it has been taken in, it is no use. It is not experienced as nourishing but rather as poisonous. It is not satisfaction but danger that the bulimic woman associates with her food. This is indicative of her inability to hold on to anything good, and not only at the level of food. Bulimic women often find it extremely difficult to allow themselves to really have something which is good, such as a caring relationship, a compliment or some success at work.

We now need to take a careful look at the underlying social and psychological dynamics which are being so powerfully dramatised in women's eating problems.

It is certainly true to say that, in our society, women experience much more difficulty and conflict about meeting their needs and having their needs met than men do. Very many women find it hard to ask for what they want, difficult to assert what they don't want and feel confused and guilty when they experience their own needs for care and nurturance. Jane Flax[2] suggests that the nature of the mother–daughter relationship itself makes nurturing baby girls a much more difficult and conflictual task for mothers than caring for baby boys. The closer identification of the mother with the baby girl means that a girl is likely to stir up in her mother all the mother's unresolved conflict about her own needs and how or whether she gets them met.

Eichenbaum and Orbach[3] suggest that mothers unconsciously know that one of the things they have to teach their daughters is not to expect too much. The mother 'prepares' her daughter for the fact

tomorrow my life will be transformed

that as an adult woman she will not receive very much care and
nurturance by limiting the amount of care she receives as a baby.
They suggest that the mother's own unmet needs may add an extra
complication. The mother may unconsciously believe that the baby
daughter can meet some of her own need and longing for care.
Thus, at least in fantasy, there is a reversal of the nurturing role or
at any rate an expectation of reciprocity of caring. This might mean
that the baby girl will not be allowed to have an adequate amount of
emotional care within the earliest symbiotic relationship. It may
well be that this very early withholding of a certain amount of care
from baby girls is, even at this stage, symbolised in terms of food. It
seems likely that the mother will not encourage her daughter to be
'greedy' with food, while she may delight in the 'healthy' appetite of
her baby boy. In this way, the links between emotional nurturing
and the taking in of food to meet bodily needs are being made for
the little girl.

   In adult life we find that women are attuned to meeting the needs
of others and often perceive their own needs in terms of other
people. But still the 'food' symbolisation remains powerful. Hilary
Graham[4] gives many examples of the ways in which women put
their families' needs before their own in present day Britain if there
is not enough food to go round. She quotes a woman from

Marsden's study *Mothers Alone*[5]: 'I'd rather the children had the food than I did. It seems to satisfy me more.' Here we see again that physical and emotional satisfaction are being confused – or rather that they are experienced as inseparable. Clearly, the mother's *hunger* is not being satisfied by feeding her children, but something which is more important to her than hunger may be.

What we have been suggesting here is that women's problems with food and eating are the symptoms by which women express difficulties in the area of meeting their emotional needs. We have every reason to believe that the socialisation of women as carers, the ways in which women are encouraged from an early age to care for others rather than themselves, will make women much more likely than men to suffer from problems in this area. It also seems likely that women learn when they are quite young to symbolise these difficulties in the relatively 'safe' arena of their relationship to food. This means that instead of a woman taking the risky step of telling those who are close to her that she needs more emotional support, more signs of their care and concern, more attention to her as an individual, she is likely to keep all this to herself and to 'play out' the problem in her relationship with her food.

The metaphor of bulimia

We can now look at the special case of bulimia. Until quite recently, bulimia was usually considered to be a variant of either compulsive eating or anorexia. It was thought to be merely a way of controlling weight in the face of overeating. Often, in fact, bulimia was and still is regarded by practitioners as a kind of 'failed' anorexia. The woman is deemed to be unable any longer to control her weight by abstinence and resorts instead to self-induced vomiting. Many bulimic women also feel that they would much prefer to be able to resist food altogether. It is only when they begin to unlock the symbolic meanings of the symptom that they begin to understand why they have chosen their particular way of expressing distress and what this 'choice' says about their internal world. Unlike compulsive eating, bulimia does not usually result in the woman becoming fat. It differs from anorexia in that nourishment is actually taken in and there is none of the reward to be gained from self-denial, the feelings of strength and control. On the contrary, the overwhelming feeling is of loss of control. But unlike the woman who eats compulsively without making herself sick, the bulimic woman does not show that she is out of control. Her guilt and shame are not on public show. Rather, she passes as normal. Yet she always has the sense that her normality is a fraud and a sham. It is the hidden nature of the symptom which gives the first clues to what is being stated symbolically. The symptom says that although the woman is thought to be normal, attractive, well-organised and successful at what she does, she herself knows that really she is alone and starving. It may appear that she can deal with her needs openly and realistically, that she can express them and get them met. In fact, though, underneath it all, she feels she is a greedy baby; her needs are too huge ever to be met, too destructive to even allow other people to see. She cannot eat but only, as she would call it, binge. Bingeing is an important concept in our understanding of how the bulimic woman understands herself. Bingeing is not eating; to binge is not to nourish oneself. On the contrary, it is to make a mockery of the whole process of self-nourishment. Bingeing is 'sick' eating. And it is followed by quite literally being sick.

Unlike the anorexic woman, the woman whose symptom is bulimia knows that she has needs. They are not always suppressed or denied, but she perceives her own neediness as a great, monstrous sickness, entirely out of keeping with the rest of her life. It is quite clear that for bulimic women the throwing-out part of the symptom, the vomiting, is just as important as the taking in. They are twin aspects of the same problem, and if we are to understand the metaphor, we have to understand the symptom as a whole. The symptom as a whole represents the woman's ambivalence towards nourishing herself, towards finding a way of getting what she needs. When she takes in good things, she can only do so in a way which is violent and self-destructive. She takes them in in such a way that she is overcome by guilt and horror at her own neediness and can only find relief by giving up the nourishment and returning to a state of emptiness and isolation. The shame and agony involved in vomiting up the nourishment is a compensation, a suitable punishment, for having greedily swallowed it in the first place. It is not just that too much food has been eaten and the fear of becoming fat makes vomiting inevitable. That is too simple an explanation. It is that needs have been perceived which are so terrifying that they must simultaneously be denied.

Perhaps we can now look more closely at the actual behaviour of the bulimic woman and the contradictions it embodies. She consumes an enormous amount of food. She eats whatever is in sight. She might eat raw food which should be cooked, frozen food without waiting for it to thaw, animals' food. She eats without any control over how much, what, where or when. Then she goes to the bathroom, locks herself in and in secret she vomits it all up, throws it all out. Then she cleans herself up, cleans the mess up and goes out relieved and empty of all the food which has become so bad and poisonous inside her. Some women spend hours cleaning up after themselves so that others will not discover the secret, messy part of them.

The contradictions embodied by bulimia can be summarised in the following way:

the eating behaviour is all about ambivalence;
there is an obsession with food and an obsession with vomiting;
she eats massive amounts – much more than she can handle – and then throws it *all* up. The good, nourishing food gets thrown out along with the excess. The baby goes with the bath water;
she fills herself up and empties herself out immediately afterwards;
she desperately seeks nourishment, yet harms her body at the same time;
she deadens her feelings, and at the same time enlivens her physical sensations – with the pain of the vomiting;
bulimia is compulsive consumption but at the same time it is the inability to hold anything in;
it is desperately wanting, but also violently rejecting;
it is submitting to the urge, but controlling its consequences;
pulling and pushing;
all or nothing.

If we begin to translate some of these conflicts and contradictions and to look for the meaning of the symptom in the woman's inner world, we can see that the essence of the conflict is the good versus the bad inside herself. It is about having a clean, neat, good, unneedy appearance, which conceals behind it a messy, needy, bad part, which must be kept secret. Another aspect of this conflict is shown in the way in which the food, once consumed, becomes bad and poisonous and must be thrown out and rejected.

The good and the bad

All of us as human beings have to live with the reality of the existence of good and bad things and feelings, both inside us and in the external world. All of us want to have 'good', pleasurable, positive feelings about ourselves and our environment. In our fantasy we long for a situation where only good feelings exist; in reality we have to reconcile the good and the bad. One of the ways to deal with our bad feelings is to split them off from the good ones and put them aside in a well-defined corner of our lives. This corner we then label 'bad' and we can choose to ignore the feelings there which would be in the way of or mess up the rest of life. This is what the bulimic woman does. If we look at the action of locking herself in the bathroom and throwing up her binge, we see that she is getting rid of the bad food she has just consumed, or that which has turned bad inside her. At a symbolic level, we see that the mess, the badness, is kept in one room in the house, one part of her life, the bulimia. It is the bulimic behaviour which deals with all her feelings of badness.

The function of the bulimia can then be seen as encapsulating the messy, dirty and disgusting part of her in the hidden scene in the bathroom, behind locked doors and in secret. It is a way of diverting unpleasant and painful feelings which are the result of hurtful interactions with the external world on to an internal object which is familiar and safe. This enables the woman to maintain the pleasant, cheerful front which she so values and which she believes others like her for.

It is important for women who have eating problems and for their counsellors or therapists to understand the implications of the symbolic nature of their symptoms.

Therapy itself can be thought of as a nurturing experience. A feminist therapist in particular is likely to offer to women a relationship which is caring and which in many ways replicates the kind of relationship which may or may not have been provided at a much earlier stage of development. The nature of this relationship is such that for the woman, the therapist will come to represent the care-giver, the nurturer, the mother. For the woman with an eating disorder, this is likely to present a problem. The woman who has difficulties with being nurtured, with getting her needs met, with allowing anyone to give her nourishment or with taking in good things when they are offered is likely to find a therapeutic relationship initially difficult. In spite of the difficulties and exactly because it parallels a nurturing situation psychotherapy is the most suitable form of treatment in which some of the issues to do with caring and being cared for can be resolved.

It is therefore both interesting and disturbing that, within the

British National Health Service, psychotherapy is very rarely offered to women with eating disorders. Specialists working with anorexic women will very often delay offering psychotherapy until there has been some gain of weight. What they fail to understand is that weight cannot be maintained or increased until something has changed in the woman's capacity to take in nourishment. Similarly, in the case of bulimic women, behavioural treatments aimed at maintaining a balanced food intake are the most usual treatments offered, ignoring the meaning and significance of the symptom the woman has adopted. This failure to use psychotherapy in the treatment of eating problems is in part the result of a recognition that women with problems of this sort can find psychotherapy difficult and can therefore present problems to the therapist. Women with eating problems may find therapy difficult precisely because their difficulties lie in the area of taking in and making use of good things. But we should never assume that the woman who finds therapy difficult to use is unsuitable for it. The woman with problems in the area of food and eating is, through therapy, offered the opportunity to experience a kind of nurturing, a caring relationship which may help her to resolve some of these very difficulties.

Therapy with women who eat compulsively

Although a good deal has been written on the subject of therapy with compulsive eaters, we would like to look briefly at the implications of what we have said so far for this group of women.

Women who eat in a compulsive way eat more than they are hungry for, yet they have a constant sense of still being empty. Unlike women in an anorexic phase, compulsive eaters do acknowledge their need for food, together with other basic needs they have in their lives. Unlike bulimic women, they experience no relief from emptying themselves of what they have consumed; however much they take in, there is always the sense of being empty, of not having had enough. The nourishment has disappeared somewhere, as though it had never been taken in.

Although she may eat and eat and eat, at the end of it all she still feels hungry. This is not hunger in the physical sense: physically, she may feel 'stuffed' with food. But she has a sense of still being hungry for whatever it was that she yearned for before the binge began. She is left with a sense of being unsatisfied with what has been taken in, as though it is not enough. Of course, it will never be enough, because usually when she reaches for food, it is not food but something else that she is needing. As it is not possible to satisfy her emotional hunger with food, she is always left unsatisfied, empty. The suggestion of a diet to deal with a problem of compulsive eating is not only unhelpful – because it doesn't acknowledge the real issues – but it is positively harmful too. Her initial feelings of emptiness are not attended to, and the fear of feeling empty, which is what drives her to overeat, is magnified by stopping her from eating what she wants. Any treatment which tries to control the eating behaviour without understanding its meaning and significance is bound to fail.

Therapy with women in an anorexic phase

The major difficulty in working with anorexic women is that very little can be taken in, either from therapy or from anywhere else. The anorexic goal is self-sufficiency, the achievement of a steady state within a closed system. Nothing can change. Nothing must enter. The problem is, of course, that a persistent refusal to eat does bring with it very dramatic changes. The end result is the outcome which is so terrifying, and yet so mysteriously seductive to the anorexic woman: force-feeding. The challenge in psychotherapy is to enable the woman to take something in because she feels able to do so, without the therapist resorting to force-feeding. Force-feeding, in the sense of pushing interpretations or insisting on certain therapeutic goals, misses the point. It fails to address the real issue, which is the difficulty the woman has in feeding and nourishing herself.

There is a real sense in which a traditional psychoanalytic technique is not suitable for working with an anorexic or bulimic woman, relying as it does on the capacity of the woman to regulate how much help she needs and is able to take in. Psychoanalysis tends to give to the client a great deal of responsibility for the amount of help which can be 'ingested', allowing the analyst little more than the power to comment on or interpret the client's capacity to take in the things which she needs from the therapy. The kind of therapy which we have in mind will make the therapist a much more active and responsible partner. Understanding the situation and the difficulties of the client, she will attempt to offer what is needed at the kind of rate at which it can be used. Although this has been asserted by a number of writers over the past decade,[6] we still come across therapists who insist on treating anorexic women lying on a couch, failing to appreciate how vitally important it is that she can 'see what she is eating'.

Frequency of sessions is another issue in work with anorexic women. Therapists who are accustomed to working analytically may be tempted to offer to see their anorexic clients several times a week. Indeed, we have heard of child psychotherapy clinics where it is customary to offer therapy four times a week to anorexic young people. These therapists very often complain that their clients are difficult to keep in treatment. It is our experience that a woman in an acutely anorexic phase may find an hour a week a very long time. She may only be able to engage in therapeutic work for a part of the session. The rest of the time may be devoted to a diary of her weekly events or given over to a defensive monologue on the symptom, leaving no space for the therapist to intervene. We need to remember that women in an anorexic phase, as well as managing to survive on very small amounts of food, thrive on small amounts of therapy. What for other clients might seem quite unsatisfying will for the anorexic produce sensations of fullness. It is pointless to try to persuade her to binge; to offer too much therapy is to awaken in her the terrifying recognition that if she allows herself to acknowledge her needs, she will discover them to be insatiable. Until she has experienced in therapy the distinction between autonomy and self-sufficiency, she will be unable to allow herself to be nourished. Self-sufficiency is a denial of needs which have to be met by someone outside the self; it is the assertion: 'I have everything I need within myself.' Autonomy, on the other hand, is the experience of being truly different from and separate from other people, able to act according to internal rather than external demands. But autonomy is based upon the experience of having had needs met, of having got enough from other people in terms of care and concern in order to be able to take care of one's self.

It is only as she begins to experience the therapeutic relationship as helpful and supportive of her attempts at autonomy that she will begin to feel safe about taking in both help and food.

The bulimic woman in therapy

The bulimic woman comes seeking help with her symptoms. She comes in desperation about her patterns of eating, not yet able to fully acknowledge that she may need help with other issues in her life. Initially, she will concentrate very much on her bulimia. Sometimes the therapist may be the first, the only person to know about it, the only person with whom she can talk freely about this secret, messy corner of her life. She will need some time to share this knowledge, to get things off her chest and to see if the therapist can be trusted with that part of herself which she hates to acknowledge. This first period in therapy will be spent talking about food, about her binges and how horrible and disgusting she feels about what she does. The therapist will want gradually to help her move on from this constant and complete concentration on food and eating as the only problem she has. The therapist who allows the bulimic woman to concentrate for too long on her eating problem is doing exactly what she herself does by her eating and vomiting. She is diverting attention from the more painful and serious feelings and conflicts in her life and in her inner world. By moving away from the idea of food and eating as the only problems, the therapist allows her to see her life as a whole in a way which is more real. This does not mean that she should not talk about food, her eating and vomiting at all, but rather that these will become part of her world, not the centre of it, will become one expression of her 'badness', her incompetence, her self-hatred, but not the encapsulation of it.

Therapy itself embodies her contradiction: how is she to take in good things from the therapist when she throws up every good thing she takes in? So she comes to therapy terrified that the other person will be overwhelmed by her needs, her bad feelings and the demands she wants to make. She wants to keep her rubbish, her needs, her baby-self (as she feels it to be) locked away from herself and from the therapist. Her hope is that she will be able to share these feelings and needs as well as her terror of what will happen if she does. Her fear is that she will overwhelm and frighten the therapist, who could not possibly like her and want to help her if she saw the part of herself which is so needy and baby-like, or, worse, that the therapist will perhaps mock and abuse that vulnerable side if she allows it to be seen.

We might say that the central characteristic of the bulimic woman in therapy is her ambivalence. Anorexic women show a very high degree of ambivalence towards giving up the symptom. This ambivalence has to be acknowledged and worked with.[7] If it is not, it will be acted out in the form of missed appointments and the seeking of other forms of treatment. If the ambivalence can be acknowledged, the anorexic woman will generally take what she wants and leave the rest. At times, this will not be enough and the therapist will have to 'tempt her appetite'. The bulimic woman, on the other hand, can appear to be very greedy in therapy. Sometimes she will exhaust the therapist with her despair, with her demands which can seem impossible to satisfy. Then she may go off and manage her life in her customarily efficient manner. It is as though her despair and desperation have been thrown up with the therapist, leaving her free to carry on – until the next time. In this way, none of the sadness and despair which are so apparent in her inner life and in the therapy is allowed to intrude into her outer world. In spite of her obvious and acknowledged neediness, the bulimic woman in therapy is often very frightened to hold on to the care and attention which the therapist is able to offer, and it is very important that the therapist is able to work with the ambivalent feelings which the client brings. The bulimic woman is likely to experience towards her helper the strong, ambivalent feelings of which she is so afraid: sometimes she will feel warmth, love and gratitude towards the therapist for the care which is being offered; sometimes she will feel hurt and rejected because the therapist cannot meet all her needs; then again she may experience the care and emotional nourishment which is being offered as poisonous and will want to 'vomit' it out.

The aim of therapy with a woman in a bulimic episode

The bulimic woman becomes trapped in the idea of 'all or nothing'. She must either eat everything or she must vomit it all up. Either she must not allow herself to have any needs or she must turn herself into a needy baby. 'Good' means thin, self-contained, always coping, never complaining. 'Bad' means fat, ugly, lazy, greedy, demanding and falling apart. There is no possibility of the good and bad being mixed and combined as part of each human being's nature.

She has the same feelings and misperceptions about therapy. Either it must be totally good, the therapist must be perfect and able to meet all her needs, be there for her whenever she needs her or, if it does not give her everything she wants and has always wanted, it will be useless to her and must be got rid of.

For the bulimic woman the principal aim of therapy is to experience that, although it is not perfect, although she will continue to have some needs which it cannot meet, it is still good, it can be held on to and it is nourishing. Because the bulimic woman is so frightened of her own aggression, because she feels that her own negative feelings are bad and dangerous, she will have great difficulty in *talking* about the fact that the therapy frustrates her with its imperfections. She will find it easier to stop coming or to stay away until she feels better. In this way she will keep her bad feelings locked up inside her and will not allow them to intrude into the therapy. She sees these feelings as separate from and not belonging to the therapy. Her aggression needs not only to be explored in the therapy but also to be made real in the therapy. The therapy allows her the freedom she may never have had before to express her negative, aggressive feelings overtly, without fear of retaliation. The aggression needs to be expressed in words rather than through her eating. She is terrified that her aggression, if expressed, will destroy the therapist, will make her run away and will bring forth a hateful response. It is important for her to learn that her feelings of hate for the therapist are not overwhelming and will not destroy all the good in the relationship.

Notes

1. Freud, S., *New Introductory Lectures on Psychoanalysis*, Penguin, Harmondsworth 1973, p. 156.
2. Flax, J., 'The Conflict Between Nurturance and Autonomy' in Howell, E. and Bayes, M. (eds.), *Women and Mental Health*, Basic Books, New York, 1981.
3. Eichenbaum, L. and Orbach, S., *Understanding Women*, Penguin, Harmondsworth, 1985.
4. Graham, H., *Women, Health and The Family*, Wheatsheaf, Brighton, 1984.
5. Marsden, D., *Mothers Alone: Poverty and the Fatherless Family*, Penguin, Harmondsworth, 1973.
6. For example, Bruch, H., *The Golden Cage*, Open Books, London, 1978; Lawrence, M., *The Anorexic Experience*, The Women's Press, London, 1984.
7. Lawrence, M., *The Anorexic Experience*, The Women's Press, London, 1984.

14
Education and Identity: The Social Origins of Anorexia*
Marilyn Lawrence

The key to success?

On a recent radio panel programme an eminent woman in the world
of medicine was asked what she would most like to teach to school
children. Her reply was that she enjoyed speaking to groups of
school girls about medicine and nursing. She felt, however, that her
contribution should be not merely to teach about her own
profession but to make girls aware that in an age of equality *all*
careers were open to them if only they had the motivation and
commitment to pursue them. Education, she said, was the key to a
new and different way of life and it was open to all. Her short
speech was eloquent and rousing (I have by no means done it
justice) and, without doubt, her personal example and obvious
'survival wisdom' would provide encouragement for girls to work
towards educational success. I was left, however, with a vague but
persistent feeling of unease. One can, of course, challenge her
assumptions about the 'age of equality'. Several recent authors on
the topic of women and education have shown that girls are not
equal to boys in their opportunities for educational success. Byrne[1]
offers a careful review of the situation and Curran[2] shows that
especially in the area of science education women fare very badly
indeed. It is also well known that the socialisation of girls often
renders women psychologically reluctant to achieve.[3]

My feelings of unease were not related simply to these issues and

*This article first appeared in *Women's Studies International Forum*, Vol. 7,
No. 4, 1984, pp. 201–11.

were of more fundamental origin. There was something in her enthusiasm for women's educational achievement, something in her belief that success for the individual woman is a necessary consequence of educational success, which I felt unsure about. My inclination was to say that education for women isn't straightforward; it brings with it a whole set of difficulties and contradictions which often push the educated woman into a series of uneasy compromises about herself. At the same time, I felt reluctant to challenge the belief in women's potential fulfilment through equal achievement, because this appears to be a repudiation of the long struggle to provide them with the beginnings of an opportunity for it.

The literature on women and education has rightly concentrated on the issue of equality of opportunity, looking particularly at why women often do not succeed in education. Rather less work has been produced on the effects of education on the women who do succeed at it. There are some interesting personal accounts, such as that by Nancy Friday.[4] Collette Dowling[5] assures us that educational success does nothing to enhance women's capacity for emotional independence and the practical and emotional difficulties of combining a career with motherhood have certainly been considered elsewhere. There is, however, little consideration of the specific effect of education itself on the lives of women. One of the assumptions which is often made in the literature is that education is 'good for women'. This paper puts forward the contention that education can be very bad for them; that it can create not only unhappiness but also contribute in central respects to one of the most crippling psychological disorders of our generation. The discussion focuses on and analyses an acutely important area in which education creates conflicts for women which are often extremely destructive – the area of identity formation. This is an area which is not normally brought into discussion about educational and career choice for girls. Even when such conflicts are being experienced, they often remain unacknowledged.

Educated tastes

My particular interest in the difficulties of educated young women has been aroused by my work in counselling anorexic women. It has often been said that anorexia affects mainly middle-class, young women. Palmer[6] says that 'on the whole, it does seem more probable that anorexia nervosa is more common in the middle and upper classes'. He acknowledges the possibility that this may have to do with referral patterns, or with the biases of doctors or observers. He offers no evidence for his conclusions.

Palazzoli,[7] in her work on anorexia in Italy, suggests that anorexics come from families in cultural transition; in this case, rural families who have moved to the city.

Dally and Gomez[8] mention the importance of social class at adolescence and link the 'pressures' for educational achievement with the 'upper social groups'. In their sample, 77 per cent of anorexics are, by their reckoning, from social classes 1 or 2. It is their contention that family pressure to succeed is an important factor in anorexia, thus making girls from higher social classes more vulnerable. There is no analysis at all of the effect of education itself on young women regardless of social class, and no mention of the educational achievements of the 23 per cent of the sample who do not come from class 1 and 2 families.

My own clinical findings indicate that what we are seeing is not a true social class bias but rather an educational one.[9] The fact that the two often coincide has led to some confusion. Indeed, it may be true to say that in our society educational achievement and social class *generally* coincide. It is, however, important to try to look at the two separately. To state that anorexia coincides with high class status may tell us nothing about the actual process of the genesis of the problem. To understand its links with women's educational success may tell us a great deal. The confusion has been compounded by the fact that the medical experts working on anorexia in special units in London may see an unduly large proportion of middle-class patients. Their willingness to cross catchment areas means that middle-class families are more likely to get their daughters admitted to anorexia units than are working-class families.

My own sample of some 76 anorexics, seen over six years, comes from the North of England, where there are no special units. The particular agency concerned, Anorexia Counselling Service, was a voluntary organisation which took referrals by phone directly from the client or her family, thus reducing the bias built in to the system of referral by GP to specialist. (It did, of course, engender other biases; there is no doubt, for example, that we had a particularly high number of referrals from women who had fallen out with the local medical services.) The sample shows no clear social class bias. There is, however, a very clear coincidence of anorexia with educational achievement. Only two of the anorexic women seen by myself or my colleagues had not achieved at least O-levels in the education system. Most also had A-levels and a high proportion were offered places at colleges and universities. The figures are confused here by the fact that for a number of young women who achieved good O-level results, anorexia itself intervened to prevent them from taking A-levels and going to college. The only surprising aspect of our own figures was the apparently high proportion of women who developed anorexia who were the first members of their family of either sex to achieve highly in education; 19 out of 76. This might lead one to speculate that women who do well educationally but whose families are working class in origin are somewhat more susceptible to anorexia than anyone else. One is left with the impression that the vast majority of young women who develop anorexia have been marked out quite early on in their careers as intellectually bright, unusually competent or even gifted.

Having established that some link appears to exist between anorexia and education, the task begins of analysing more precisely the nature of that link. I am not suggesting that education is the only factor in the genesis of anorexia. If it were, then we should expect a far higher incidence than in fact occurs. Other factors might include unsatisfactory family relationships,[10] certain personality character- istics such as perfectionism,[11] and, in my own experience, a death in the family or close to the family. These things may all *trigger* an anorexic episode. In the same way, Brown and Harris[12] isolate certain life events which may trigger a depressive episode in women's lives. There are other factors in the woman's background which *predispose* her to depression. Whatever the trigger factors in anorexia, we should expect to find a higher than usual degree of educational achievement in the background of the anorexic woman. If we follow Brown and Harris's terminology, we would call education a predisposing factor in the genesis of anorexia.

The following discussion will centre on the effects of educational achievement on the way women perceive and value themselves. The observations should not apply exclusively to anorexic women, but could also refer to women who do well educationally but who do not develop anorexia. Crucial to the discussion is the notion of 'identity', without doubt, a much overworked term. At times, everyone we know or hear about seems to be undergoing an 'identity crisis' or to be 'working through identity conflicts'. This always evokes for me the rather ludicrous vision of a world full of people wandering around not knowing their own names. To attempt to pin down this notion is difficult, and its use by a variety of theorists, in a range of disciplines where it takes on different associations and shades of meaning makes the task no easier. Erikson attempts a definition which is the closest I have found to the sense in which I should like to use the term. He describes identity in terms of an inner sense both of differentness and of being like other people.

The body normally acts as something of a guarantor of identity. One's size and shape guarantees the sense of persistent sameness which Erikson describes. As we become fatter or thinner, or as a result of the normal body changes associated with ageing, the way we feel about ourselves changes too. Our 'identity' is affected. For women, the body acts as an identity guarantor in both of Erikson's senses. It provides a continuing reassurance that one really is oneself, the same person as yesterday. In addition, having the right kind of body provides for women a guarantee of membership of the group of attractive women. The body can, of course also guarantee a woman's identity as a person who is not sexually available, if it does not conform to the prevailing prescription for attractiveness. In any condition in which the primary symptom is a woman's attempts to change her body, we would expect to find an underlying dynamic concerned with the need to sort out or to manipulate an identity.

I should like to look at some of the collective ideas about women and the effects of education on women's capacities to identify with them. I am not, within the limitations of this paper, commenting upon who is responsible for the creation and maintenance of these ideas, nor do I claim to have compiled an exhaustive list. Rather, I have concentrated on those which have emerged most powerfully during the course of my own clinical work.

Different for girls

Adolescence and young adulthood are widely and rightly held to be the stages in life when 'identity' is fairly fluid, when the individual is involved in making choices about what kind of human being to become. Many of the elements which go to make up what we call identity are already fixed – indeed, they are fixed from the time of our birth. These include factors such as sex, race and social class. This makes the decision, the 'choice', as to whether or not to pursue education a particularly crucial one, as it is one area of identity over which she feels that she has some control or choice. The fact that this sense of choice may be largely illusory and that an individual's educational potential may be prescribed by the identity factors mentioned above, does not stop people from believing in it. If it is a myth, then it is a very pervasive myth. The American Dream is based upon it; so too I suspect are some feminist dreams. (We shouldn't overlook, incidentally, that the other identity factor over which women in particular are thought to have control is their appearance.)

This choice, if choice it is, about whether to take education seriously or not, is rarely a conscious one for either girls or boys. It often seems to young people that they either do well at school or they don't, with little awareness of their own motivation as a factor. The issues involved in educational achievement, and thus the issues which affect the motivation of individual young people, are quite different for girls than they are for boys. For boys to do well at school can be status-enhancing or not, depending largely on other status variables. For example, for the middle-class boy with professional parents who went to a grammar school, educational success would have been status-enhancing and educational failure might have brought dire consequences in its wake. For the working-class boy living on a council estate but with status-aspiring parents, gaining a place at a grammar school might have enhanced his status within the family but would probably have spoilt his identity with his peers. Hoggart[14] describes the conflicts of the scholarship boy:

> Almost every working-class boy who goes through the process of further education by scholarships finds himself chafing against his environment during adolescence. He is at the friction-point of two cultures; the test of his real education lies in his ability, by about the age of twenty-two, to smile at his father with his whole face and to respect his flighty young sister and his slower brother.

These issues are clearly not straightforward ones for adolescent boys to handle, but even so, they are much less problematic in terms of identity than those which surround education for girls of the same age. For boys, there are whole areas of identity which are unaffected by educational achievement. For girls there are none. Boys may find themselves 'at the friction-point of two cultures'; girls have struck the friction-point of womanhood. There is no suggestion that boys' decisions about education will affect their ability to attract sexual partners or ultimately to find wives and to be fathers. To opt for education may give the boy somewhat more choice of sexual partner; beyond that, the two areas of life are exclusive. For girls, on the other hand, the decision about whether to try hard at school or not is really a covert decision about her own sexuality. The problem of success is well summarised by Elizabeth Henderson.[15]

> It is painful to imagine that a girl may experience so much confusion and anxiety over shaping a positive identity that she inhibits her own intellectual and personal interests. This is not the motive to be a failure, but the motive to avoid the kind of success that would price a girl out of the boyfriend market and preclude her from following her marriage and sexual aims. This conflict would only exceptionally (and neurotically) be present in a boy. The more a boy achieves the more acceptable he is . . . success does not diminish his masculinity, it enhances it. Popularity with the opposite sex and achievement are not set in conflict with each other for him. For an academic and career-minded girl they may well be.

This should help us to begin to understand the difficulties encountered in trying to piece together the conflicting identity issues in girls' decisions to opt for education or not. At the time the choices are being made, the conflicts are only dimly perceived and never mentioned. The assumption is that the choice for girls involves the same issues as it does for boys. On the face of it, the same old mistake: what goes for men must go for women too. In reality, we are actually dealing with something much more complex and sinister. Education is good for you, but, of course, everyone knows that it's different for girls. For girls, a complex web of double messages surrounds the injunction to do well at school.

This year's model

The search for an identity in which all young people must engage inevitably involves a glance at the viable alternatives. Young people look to older people with a view not to imitating them but to sharing a collective identity with them. They may reject all available models and attempt to create something new, but this too is always a reaction, a refusal to identify with what is around. Identity is a not a notion which has any meaning without reference to a collectivity.

Girls are brought up on concepts like 'maternal instinct', 'natural charm' and '*knowing* when it's right'. They are not encouraged at all to plan their lives in a hard-headed or realistic way. So when girls look forward at the different possibilities for their own being, they do so surreptitiously. Womanhood is a natural gift; you're not supposed to have to work at it or choose between different versions of it. (This is how the cosmetic manufacturers make their fortunes selling us 'the natural look'!)

When girls do dare to glance up ahead at the current models, what is the range? And how well does it measure up when everything they have already learnt about being girls and potential women is superimposed upon it?

The clearest distinction in the models of womanhood is between those women who have careers of their own and those who do not. The education system generally encourages girls to disregard the fact that the vast majority of women will fall into the second group. Education for girls is a 'good thing'. The fact that very few of them will ever use it is ignored. This is especially true at all-girl schools, particularly those which are selective, where a girl's success may be measured in terms of an activity which she is expected to abandon for marriage, or certainly for motherhood.

All girls are socialised into a sexual identity centred on motherhood, regardless of whether they later also have the opportunity to achieve educational success and make their own careers. Having been taught that only motherhood will make them feel complete, women 'naturally' tend to feel incomplete without it. If a girl's present sexual identity rests on some future necessity for motherhood, then this will clearly impose some constraints on choices in the present which have implications for the future. To take education seriously not only contradicts the injunction that motherhood is the primary component of female sexuality, it actually threatens the girl with a sexual identity which is negative and almost universally disapproved of.

There are two central identity stereotypes of the woman who takes education seriously. The first is the director of IBM, the Business Woman – hard, ruthless, selfish, promiscuous, quite unfit for motherhood, sexually irresistible but unmarriable, who will find just retribution for her misspent youth in a lonely old age. The second is the Blue Stocking – the asexual woman, isolated, plain, dedicated, who spends a lifetime sublimating her womanhood (sexuality), into some dry and ultimately unrewarding academic or professional pursuit. Interestingly, it is (or was) often women teachers who provided a living version for this second stereotype. At my own school, an all-girl direct-grant school (the type of school in which anorexia nervosa was and still is particularly prevalent), the vast majority of our teachers were unmarried, dedicated and seemed to us to be very odd women indeed. We were being offered education by women with whom we didn't feel at all free to identify. On the whole, the fact that these women were totally different kinds of human beings from our mothers was ignored. Just once, some of us asked our geography mistress why she wasn't married. She was a beautiful woman, about 40 probably, seeming totally dedicated to her job – us – but she dressed smartly, wore make-up and we knew that she *smoked*! Perhaps the reason behind our question, was the acknowledgment that in some ways at least we *could* identify with her, and this I think must have made us uneasy. In reply to our question, she said that she liked to do things properly and she couldn't do the job and look after a family. She had chosen the job. This answer should have been completely terrifying. It should have confirmed our worst fears about ourselves and what we were doing. We defended against this remarkable and possibly honest piece of information by disbelieving it. We still speculated about her lover who might have 'died in the war', or wondered whether perhaps deep down she was 'a bit odd'. To this day it disappoints me that in spite of all she knew, she still only taught us geography.

There is, of course, one further identity model for the girl who takes education seriously – Superwoman, the most terrifying of all. Superwoman is slender and beautiful, strong yet receptive. She is the woman who manages IBM in her spare time. She organises her day so that all her high-powered meetings are in the morning and she can be home when the children come in from school, waiting for husband, Martini in hand, to ask him if he's had a good day. Absurd as this stereotype may seem, it is nonetheless a seductive one.

The fear of high flying

It is a common pattern, often remarked upon by teachers, for girls in junior schools to achieve rather more educationally than boys of the same age. Some boys will at this very early age show an unusual aptitude for academic achievement, but on the whole it is girls who are inclined to take school work more seriously. This is obviously explicable in terms of girls' socialisation to conformity and pleasing others: we simply transfer the behaviour we have learned at home on to the school. The remarkable yet very common pattern is for this tendency towards achievement to fall off quite dramatically at secondary school. This trend continues with slightly more boys than girls taking O-levels and nearly twice as many going to university.

At postgraduate level, there are nearly three times as many men as women.[16] At about the age of 12 or 13, very many girls lose their seriousness towards school work; they stop trying. By this stage, a clear conflict of expectation has occurred and it is no longer a straightforward matter of applying the same rules to life at school as to life outside it. The usual explanation in the folklore of families is that girls develop a kind of 'silliness' round about puberty. They get interested in boys, in clothes and make-up, and they giggle together, abandoning their previous seriousness and capacity for hard work. In truth, they have discovered a much more crucial component of female identity which contradicts the earlier one. 'Do well at school', the injunction given to boys and girls alike, has always carried after it for girls, 'but not too well'. 'It's good to be clever' has always for girls been followed by, 'but not too clever'. The penalty for ignoring the second, unspoken part of the message is quite simply to be a freak. There is no acceptable identity for the girl who fails to hear what no one has said. The overt part of the message can be followed with relative impunity during the early school years. It is when sexuality occurs and can no longer be denied that the situation must be clarified and something must be given up.

It is unfortunate that so little work exists on the subculture of adolescent girls. This means that the process by which young women change in relation to school and begin to form an adult identity remains something of a mystery. Angela McRobbie[17] throws some light on the subject by pointing out that the subculture of adolescent girls is largely home-centred. The principal elements are the bedroom, the record player, the mirror and, of course, the best friend. (The importance of the best friend cannot be overstated. It has often struck me as ironical that the activity which we therapists have recently discovered and labelled 'co-counselling' is in fact identical to that employed by generations of adolescent girls for making sense of life.) My own observations, based on conversations with young women in therapy, are very much in agreement with McRobbie's.

While boys spend their time actually engaging in activity which both affirms and expresses their identities, girls spend very large amounts of their time *thinking* about such activity and musing and speculating on their possible roles in relation to it. Thus the formation of an identity for adolescent girls is likely to be a very passive process. Unlike boys, they are not involved with *doing* but rather with being acceptable. The girl with homework, the girl who is still involved with education, is likely to spend even more time alone. A 16 year old, recovering from anorexia, described to me a situation in which for months she was literally caught between Shakespeare and eye-shadow, moving alternately between the mirror and the set book. The passivity inherent in the process of identity formation for adolescent girls necessarily brings with it a great deal of self-scrutiny and self-criticism. The mirror tells all. A preoccupation with the body seems inevitable. But it is not the active preoccupation of boys. The questions are not, 'will my body *do* such-and-such', but rather 'is my body acceptable, does it look right?'

Slim-line solutions

I want to turn back now to the young women who develop anorexia. They form part of that group of women who don't solve their identity problems by underachieving – not at first anyhow. They don't conform to the usual pattern of a fall-off in academic achievement after puberty. They are potentially among the most conventionally successful women, when suddenly they embark on a career of self-starvation which often brings their success to an abrupt halt.

The media often refer to anorexia nervosa as 'the slimmer's disease', with the implication that it is the result of young girls slavishly following fashionable stereotypes and mysteriously losing the ability to stop. An alternative explanation which we often hear (given, e.g., by Palmer[18]) is that it is a fear of growing up, an attempt on the girl's behalf to be not so much fashionable as young and boyish. There is probably an element of truth in both of these commonsense explanations.

What must appear strange on the face of it is why educated young women should be either so prone to the relentless pursuit of a cosmetic ideal or so terrified of growing up. It has always seemed likely to me that educated young women are subjected to the stereotyped images of slim women rather less than the young women who abandon education early on. If nothing else they are less likely to read the kinds of magazines which put so much emphasis on slimming. One might even imagine that they have other things to think about than achieving a physical ideal. In terms of growing up, although we might wish to say that turning into an adult woman has little to commend it, it should surely be a less oppressive experience for women who have more choices.

On the other hand, we might point to the model of the successful woman who is always portrayed as slim. (The 'mum', on the other hand, is allowed to be at least 'womanly' if not exactly plump.) So perhaps the girl who adopted an anorexic 'solution' to her difficulties is really asserting something about how she sees her future in the world?

The truth probably lies buried somewhere in the midst of these arguments. The fact is that in our society thinness appears to open almost all the doors that women might wish to enter. It allows admittance to the world of career success; it also clears the way for access to boyfriends and success with peers. One of the things which unites women in the West is their almost universal desire to be thinner than they are. The fact that mothers are permitted a little more leeway in this direction may testify only to their position as social 'write-offs'.

The slimming which precedes anorexia, the kind of limitation of food intake which our society regards as normal for girls, often seems to be an attempt on the girl's part to achieve some semblance of normality. The clever girl may have the feeling that she can never in fact be normal but that she can achieve what normal girls struggle to achieve. (Educated girls, remember, are used to getting what they want by trying hard.) Maybe she can actually beat them at that particular game. It is an attempt to compete in a game in which she cannot legitimately be classed as a player. I am not suggesting that this process is in any way a conscious one; it could never happen if it were. An example: this story was told to me by a colleague, a very perceptive mother who is herself a successful career woman. 'My 12-year-old daughter is obsessed with slimming. She's got menus written out everywhere. I went up to her bedroom to say goodnight and found her writing out what she'll eat tomorrow. She binges every Saturday night. Of course, this all coincides with her coming top of the class and her boyfriend giving her up. He's in the next class up from remedial. When they were 11, it didn't seem to matter.'

This story is a rather tragic example of the girl who can't solve her identity problems by underachievement. She's still coming top of the year. If she could have come tenth, she might still have her boyfriend and wouldn't be feeling like a freak. But instead, she's still achieving her potential and is dimly and painfully aware of having lost half (at least) of her identity. She is now struggling to relocate herself as a young woman by changing her body. *That* must be what's wrong. The fact that at 12 she doesn't look quite the paragon of slim female perfection must be the cause of her unhappiness.

To return to that aspect of anorexia which involves a denial of growing up, the question still remains as to why educated young women should feel the need to retreat from maturity more often than those with less education. Growing up, becoming an adult, requires of young people that they form an identification with people who are already adults. For young women already socialised into 'normal' womanhood, any identity which includes education will entail a loss. The truth of this identity contradiction is not apparent until at least after puberty, when the girl is expected to begin to behave like, and to take on some of the aspirations of, a woman. She may be sufficiently protected either by family, social network or type of school for it not to become apparent even then. It may be that she meets the contradictions head-on when she leaves home, perhaps during her first year at college. (The first year in college is a point at which many anorexics experience their first difficulties with food.) That aspect of anorexia which rejects adulthood, womanhood, is really an attempt to hold together an identity and to avoid the loss of one part of the self which growing up brings with it. It is an unconscious attempt to return to that time earlier in life when it was possible to be a clever and pretty little girl; when people said, 'be good, work hard, do well' – and meant it.

Some writers (e.g. Thomas[19]) have described anorexia as a repudiation of sexuality. (Waller, Kaufman and Deutsch[20] suggest that it springs from a fear of oral impregnation.) In fact, the situation is more complex. Education contradicts women's sexuality; it offers women an identity in which sexuality will be problematic. Anorexia is an attempt to deal with this spoilt identity. It is a response to contradictory injunctions. Anorexia at once exemplifies the feminine stereotype of perfect slimness and repudiates it by making a mockery of it.

Given the foregoing discussion on the relationship between the crisis in identity caused by or related to educational achievement and the incidence of anorexia, an obvious question to ask is 'What kinds of schools are most likely to produce the identity conflicts which give rise to anorexic conditions?'

The current debate amongst both educationalists and feminists about the advantages of single-sex as opposed to mixed-sex education for girls suggests that this educational division may be a highly significant one in the formation of an identity.[21]

The argument in favour of single-sex education for girls is based on evidence that girls tend to achieve better educationally in an all-girl environment. Boys in mixed-sex classrooms use girls as a negative reference group and girls are encouraged to take a less active and aggressive attitude to their learning.[22] The mixed-sex classroom, in short, replicates the 'real world', and it does so to the benefit of boys and the detriment of girls. Single-sex schools, on the other hand, enable girls to learn and to participate in their own learning without reference to boys and without the temptation or coercion to retreat into feminine (i.e. non-achieving) roles.

In answer to the question of which kind of school would we expect to be most likely to induce an anorexic response from girls, there appear to be two possible hypotheses from which to choose.

The first is that identity conflicts which lie at the root of anorexia are likely to be more pronounced in mixed-sex schools. The presence of boys heightens girls' awareness of the contradictions inherent in being both educated and a girl. In all-girl schools, on the other hand, girls are likely to be more protected from the contradictions of their own position by the fact that educational achievement for girls is the norm and is regarded and rewarded as an event in its own right, without reference to boys. We might expect that in a single-sex environment girls would come to terms with their educational achievement without feeling that they had lost their 'femininity'.

The second hypothesis is that anorexia will be a comparatively rare occurrence in mixed-sex schools. This would be due to the fact that comparatively few girls are educationally successful within mixed-sex education and so the number of girls 'at risk' of encountering the contradictions in their identity will be few. At mixed-sex schools educationally successful girls, or girls 'at risk' of educational success, will have a ready-made escape route if the contradictions in their position become too painful; they can simply do the usual thing – defer to the boys and accept a feminine role in relation to them. 'Feminine role' simply amounts to a falling-off in educational achievement.

If we then move on to examine the evidence in support of these two possible accounts, we find that, surprisingly, there is very little evidence. Crisp, Palmer and Kalucy[23] attempted to produce a prevalence study. In the course of this research they produced some evidence which can be no more than suggestive to the debate. They conclude that anorexia nervosa is 'relatively common in the independent sector of education, probably implying a social class factor'. They included seven independent and two (larger) comprehensive schools in their study, and in the period studied 27 cases of anorexia were identified. Of these, 26 were in the independent schools and only one in a comprehensive school. In his own clinic population, Crisp reports that only 15 per cent of his patients attend comprehensive schools. Unfortunately, because he was not looking at the differing impacts of mixed- and single-sex schools, Crisp is less than clear about which of the schools in his study were mixed and which were not. The authors mention that one of the comprehensive schools was mixed; about the other we have no information. It is probably fair to assume that all the independent schools were single-sex, but we are not told this. However, even if there were one or even two exceptions to the general rule that private schools for girls are on the whole single-sex, it is still a fair assumption that the authors found a much higher incidence of anorexia amongst the girls from single-sex schools. It is unclear from the report as to how many of the schools were boarding or part-boarding.

My own observations would tend to support the second hypothesis, though not as strongly as the prevalence study by Crisp,

Palmer and Kalucy[24] suggests. I do not have access to detailed data of the type of school attended by all the anorexic clients seen by the Counselling Service. However, I do have such knowledge about some of the clients. The information I have suggests that a high proportion of women who develop anorexia might be educated at single-sex schools – not necessarily independent schools, incidentally, but sometimes single-sex grammar or comprehensive schools. I must also add that I have at present a number of clients attending mixed-sex comprehensive schools, so the link between anorexia and single-sex education, although apparently strong, is by no means invariable. However, it is disturbing. How is it to be explained?

Clearly, if there is a link between a high level of educational achievement and the origins of anorexia, then we should expect schools which produce one also to produce the other. It could be argued that single-sex schools might protect girls from some of the identity conflicts which education can bring with it. We might wonder though whether even single-sex schools manage in some way to replicate the 'real world'. Perhaps women are taught, albeit covertly, that out there in the real world something different is in store for them. We also need to take into account the tensions created by a school which allows and encourages young women to take themselves seriously and a society which does not. Some of these conflicts are described by Irene Payne[25] in her account of being a working-class girl at a grammar school.

Finally, it may be important to acknowledge that although single-sex schools may offer girls many advantages, they can produce some serious drawbacks as well. There is always an aspect of anorexia which must be understood as an attempt on the part of the woman to take control of her body and, symbolically, her life.[26] There can be little doubt that some of the regimes traditionally associated with single-sex girls' schools do exert a very controlling, even an invasive, effect on the lives of the pupils. Crisp *et al.*[27] say of the independent schools in their sample that they 'were smaller and by their nature (e.g. as boarding schools) had more detailed information on health matters; indeed, the health records in these schools were invariably detailed and complete, and were always complemented by a wealth of information concerning such characteristics as weight and menstrual patterns.' One might want to say, and indeed I *would* want to say, that young women are much better off monitoring their own menstrual patterns! The kind of school regime which habitually makes the private public is precisely the kind of regime which might leave adolescents feeling as though they had little control over their worlds. It would be wrong to blame single-sex education for producing the kind of experience which alienates young women from their own development. This indeed has nothing to do with single-sex education. But it may well have something to do with the development of anorexia.

The observation that education and anorexia tend to coincide could be a dangerous one. It is open to many interpretations. It could provide the rationale for denying women access to educational opportunity 'for their own good'. I had a sobering experience some little while ago which made me realise the possibilities for the misuse of this kind of research. I was interviewed by a journalist for a popular women's magazine who was preparing an article on anorexia. We discussed the relationship between education and anorexia at some length and I thought she had acquired a fairly accurate understanding of my views. However, 'I' later emerged in print saying that girls wouldn't develop anorexia if they were allowed to do the things that all girls really want to do, and that the pressure of education, exams, etc. was too much for them!

It is like the solution of successive governments to the problem of racial disharmony – to limit the numbers of black people allowed to enter the country. They have not tackled the racism itself, both institutional and individual, which gave rise to the disharmony. To discourage young women from participating in education lest they fall ill is a similar non-solution to a wrongly defined problem. On the other hand, to ignore the links is to perpetuate the situation at two levels. At the level of individual young women – those who do not develop anorexia as well as those who do – it is to deny that they are in a difficult situation and to prevent them from giving voice to it. ('Symptoms' only occur when difficulties cannot be acknowledged for what they are.) At the level of the struggle for women's equality and independence, it is to make the false assumption that the battle is won for women when they gain access to education and career success. On the contrary, it may be only just beginning.

Notes

1. Byrne, E.M., *Women and Education*, Tavistock Publications, London, 1978.
2. Curran, L., 'Science Education: Did She Drop Out or Was She Pushed?', in *Alice Through the Microscope*, The Brighton Women's Science Group, Virago, London, 1980.

3. Baker-Miller, J., *Toward a New Psychology of Women*, Penguin, Harmondsworth, 1978.
4. Friday, N., *My Mother Myself*, Fontana, London, 1979.
5. Dowling, C., *The Cinderella Complex*, Summit Books, New York, 1981; Fontana, London, 1982.
6. Palmer, R.L., *Anorexia Nervosa*, Penguin, Harmondsworth, 1980.
7. Palazzoli, M.S., *Self-Starvation: From the Intra-psychic to the Transpersonal Approach to Anorexia Nervosa*, Human Context Books, London, 1974.
8. Dally, P., and Gomez, J., *Anorexia Nervosa*, Heinemann, London, 1979.
9. Lawrence, M., 'Anorexia Nervosa: The Counsellor's Role', *British Journal of Guidance and Counselling*, Vol. 9, No. 1, 1981, pp. 74–85.
10. Bruch, H., *Eating Disorders: Obesity, Anorexia Nervosa and the Person Within*, Routledge & Kegan Paul, London, 1974; and Palazzoli, *op. cit.*
11. Bruch, H., *The Golden Cage: The Enigma of Anorexia Nervosa*, Open Books, London, 1978.
12. Brown, G.W., and Harris, T., *Social Origins of Depression*, Tavistock Publications, London, 1978.
13. Erikson, E.H., *Identity and the Life Cycle*, W.W. Norton & Company, New York and London, 1980.
14. Hoggart, R., *The Uses of Literacy*, Chatto & Windus, London, 1957.
15. Henderson, E., 'Sex Role Dilemmas of Modern Adolescents', in *Adolescence: The Crisis of Adjustment*, Meyerson, S. (ed.), George Allen & Unwin, London, 1975.
16. Curran, *op. cit.*
17. McRobbie, A., 'Working-Class Girls and the Culture of Femininity', in *Women Take Issue*, Women's Studies Group, Hutchinson, London, 1978.
18. Palmer, *op. cit.*
19. Thoma, H., *Anorexia Nervosa*, International Universities Press, New York, 1967.
20. Waller, J.V., Kaufman, R.M., and Deutsch, F., 'Anorexia Nervosa: A Psychosomatic Entity', *Psychosomatic Medicine*, Vol. 2, 1940, pp. 2–16.
21. Spender, D. *Invisible Women: The Schooling Scandal*, Writers and Readers, London, 1982.
22. Sarah, E., Scott, M. and Spender, D., 'The Education of

Feminists: The Case For Single Sex Schools', in *Learning to Lose*, Spender, D., and Sarah, E. (eds.), The Women's Press, London, 1980.

23. Crisp, A.H., Palmer, R.L., and Kalucy, R.S., 'How Common is Anorexia Nervosa? A Prevalence Study', *British Journal of Psychiatry*, Vol. 128, 1976, pp. 549–54.

24. *ibid.*

25. Payne, I., 'A Working-Class Girl in a Grammar School', in *Learning to Lose*, *op. cit.*

26. Lawrence, M., 'Anorexia Nervosa: The Control Paradox', *Women's Studies International Quarterly*, Vol. 2, 1979, pp. 93–101.

27. Crisp, *et al.*, *op. cit.*

15
Food, Need and Desire: A Postscript
Tamar Selby

I would like to look again at compulsive eating here, and perhaps to put in some of the aspects which we often leave out.

As therapists we are often so involved with our interpretations, our attempts to understand the signs and symbols, to get at the reasons and origins, that we sometimes forget to look at what is facing us, to see what is present in front of us. We can be so observant, that sometimes we look behind the thing until we are blind to what is most obvious and available.

When I am with a woman in the room, I may be so engaged with her reasons for saying what she says that I don't pay enough attention to what it is that she says or how she presents herself to me. I try to understand, for instance, *why* she eats rather than looking at *how* she eats and at *why* she stays fat rather than how she presents herself to the world, or what it means to her to be a fat woman in the world.

When what is actually facing me escapes me, my explanations and interpretations are often useless to the client. We sometimes feel redundant if we don't come up with a brilliant interpretation, but while we bombard women with our cleverness, we may be missing the plain, simple story they are telling us with their words and gestures.

In therapy we tend to look at the problem from an analytical standpoint. A client comes complaining of last night's binge and we try to understand this from our own theoretical perspective. If we are using object relations theory, we might try to find out whether food at a particular moment represents a persecutory or a good object. We might wonder whether the woman is trying to achieve the fusion she once experienced in her mother's arms with the nipple in her mouth. Some therapists will see compulsive eating merely as the ability to relate in a concrete way to a concrete substance. Some may even see compulsive eating as an expression of the wish for a penis or the wish for a child, or something of that sort.

All of these ways of understanding have their value, but just as when we are doing a jigsaw puzzle, if we don't stop sometimes and look at the whole, no amount of arranging the pieces will do the trick.

One important aspect of compulsive eating which we often overlook is the way in which the compulsive eater eats.

I sat in a McDonald's one day eating a Big Mac. I became aware of myself sitting there and eating, thoughtlessly shovelling the thing into my mouth. There was a monotonous taste in my mouth, undefined and unchanging. The movement of my hands and my jaws was mechanical; I was a machine in need of fuel. Whenever I finish a Big Mac, I leave the place wanting something else to eat. I never understood why before; I always put it down to the fact that the meat was too adulterated or the bun too small. Now I realise that it has nothing at all to do with the amount of calories in the food. It has more to do with the way I sat down there to refuel myself. I did not really *eat*; I was not engaged with the food; I was not there. Perhaps, when people describe the fast food culture as plastic, this is partly what they mean. It is not only the neon lights, the plastic dishes and the horrible coffee cups. Although this is an inevitable and integral part of the plastic culture, it is more the unengagement with the food, the fact that it is a kind of artificial eating, which makes it deserve the title.

Compulsive eaters don't eat food; they count calories. The nice piece of bread ceases to be a nice piece of bread and turns into so many calories. No wonder diets never work: they make us stop eating and count calories instead. We would still be hungry if we counted 3,000 a day. The woman who is a compulsive eater can never make food her own. It is because it is never her own that she needs more and more of it. She gobbles the lot, quickly and thoroughly, but it is still not hers. Her eating experience is a futile activity – thoughtless and senseless. Notice the way in which the compulsive eater allows herself to nibble from someone else's plate; as long as the food is not hers, she is able to eat it. Because she does not feel involved with it, she need not feel guilty after eating it.

Eating needs care and time and preparation for the food to be enjoyed and to become one's own. Whether we are eating at home, when we have cooked the food for ourselves, or in a restaurant, where a cook prepares the meal, the food needs to be carefully cooked, prepared and arranged, with the table nicely laid, if we are to engage with and enjoy our treat. This is what food really is. And yet as women, while we may be very good at providing treats for other people, we are often very bad at treating ourselves to our food. In popular mythology, we always attribute the French with the real ability to enjoy food. They sip the wine slowly, they serve their food carefully and they taste and enjoy it. In a similar way, we imagine that the French always enjoy sex. Although this is almost certainly a myth, it probably comes from watching the way in which the French eat. We might want to say that it is because they enjoy sex that they don't need to use food as a substitute, but I think this is to misunderstand the situation. It is not that when you start to enjoy your sexlife you stop eating so much; one does not happen at the expense of the other. And yet sex and eating are indeed connected. It is the engagement, the involvement, which allows you to enjoy sex and food, and any other pleasurable activity. It is objectification which turns eating into a compulsive activity and sex into a dull duty.

The woman who eats mechanically does everything in the same way and views herself as an object who goes through life just trying to survive. Is it possible to enjoy making love when you consider yourself as just a body? Many fat women will say they don't get sexually involved with people because they don't want anyone to touch the fat on their stomach or their legs. This way of seeing one's body is detached of all emotions, feelings or thoughts. It is as though the person who touches your body can differentiate between you and the fat. It is as though this fat which no one must touch has a separate identity or life of its own. It is as though touching 'me' and touching a jelly is the same thing, or even the same kind of thing. For a fat woman who is a compulsive eater, they probably do seem the same. The fat woman sees her body as a mere object.

This brings me to take a more critical look at something which has become a familiar notion to us – the idea of the *body-image*. What exactly is the body-image, what does it mean? When I look in the mirror, do I see my 'body-image' or do I see myself embodied? Women who are compulsive eaters never look at themselves in the mirror; they also avoid shop windows. If a fat woman catches sight

he held her gently against him her hair brushing his cheek I love you he murmured......

of herself in the window, she is filled with horror and disgust. Women in therapy often say they experience or see themselves as though there is no connection between the head and the body. The neck is usually the dividing line.

What is happening to a woman who looks at herself and sees her body as a mere thing? It is not enough to say that as women we internalise the way men see us. Certainly men do see us as sex objects. This is true and terrible, but it is only part of the story. If this was all there was to it, all of us would always perceive ourselves as objects and perhaps we would all have eating disorders.

What we are seeing here is a discontinuity in the woman's sense of being which becomes displaced on to what she regards as her 'image'. This 'image', which she can change and manipulate, stands, like food, between her and the world. Food has the remarkable capacity to alter from being a thing in the world to becoming a part of us. For the woman who is a compulsive eater, food is neither a thing in the world nor does it become hers. It turns into an object whose only function is to keep the woman and the world apart. But this, of course, is an impossibility, an illusion. It is like having the fat to stand between her and the world, or the 'body-image', which she can change daily, play with and control.

To deny that one is in the world is precisely this objectification of the body. Under this illusion, a woman can say that she, her 'real' self, is hiding behind the fat, which is not herself. Under this illusion, a woman can say she does not want anyone touching the fat; she can say that she wants people to reach her 'real' self behind the fat. It is this illusion which makes it possible for her to use food as a weapon against the world. It is an illusion of being apart, of not being engaged with the world. Where is this mysterious real self? Behind what does it hide? As long as we talk about hiding behind the fat, we encourage the notion of the body as an object. The idea of peeling off the fat and finding the real self is like peeling an onion and finding its real core.

We cannot look at the fat as a separate entity from ourselves. After all, it is *my* body that is fat, it is me who is fat. I am my body; my body is what I express myself through. My body is in the world. I am in the world. The idea that there is a thin person inside the fat one is not for me a helpful one. Fat women often say that the thin person inside is arrogant, envious, angry, sexual and mean. It is as if one day this thin, mean person will pop out of the fat and be in the world, as if the 'fat', who is not all those terrible things, protects the self and the world from this menacing person inside.

It is not that the 'fat' and the 'thin' express aspects of the person involved, but rather the other way round. Some aspects of the person are translated into 'fat' and some into 'thin' metaphorically. Thus the body becomes a battlefield which is totally split off from the person who does not take any part in the war. She resigns. She is out of control. Her body is controlling her, and it acquires a life of its own.

It is a shaky person, with a shaky and uncertain existence, which is expressed through the body which gains and loses weight from one day to the next. The food and the fat seem to be related to each other in the same way that the woman is related to her body. Eating is private, but the body is public. You can eat in secret, but your body discloses the secret and exposes you. You may eat in order to maintain self-sufficiency, but your body tells your story to the world in detail; it exposes your great need for other people. You may manipulate your environment and attempt to control yourself by eating, and yet your body looks out of control and discloses your great insecurity and vulnerability. You never appear greedy or even hungry. You usually refuse food when in company, yet nobody is deceived. After all, your body tells the public a different story altogether. It is your body that tells your story for you and about you. And yet in reality the story is yours, it is *you*, not just something which belongs to your body.

Compulsive eating is a denial of being engaged, involved. It is rather like perpetual masturbation. When we masturbate we know that this is not the 'real thing'. It lacks the involvement which is so crucial to love-making. It is our involvement which allows spontaneity, rather than the mechanical movement of the hand or the jaws to reach a point of gratification – like me in McDonald's. The person herself hardly takes any part in it at all. A compulsive eater knows no other way of eating but the mechanical gobbling, isolated and secretive. This way of eating is a crime against the self. It involves both a seduction and a rape, which is why it becomes such a terrible secret.

The woman who is a compulsive eater is aware of her own unsatisfied desire. Her hope is to be able to satisfy it. She experiences a tremendous longing and attempts desperately to reach whatever it is she longs for by the only means known to her – eating. As soon as she stops eating, she is stuffed full with food, but feels just as empty as ever. She may be less aware of her longing by now, as she is too busy reproaching herself for the binge. But she is still under the illusion that whatever she desires is within her reach if only she tries hard enough.

Women in therapy often say that it is frustration which drives them to binge. They are frustrated because they don't get what they want and they eat to avoid their frustration. A woman who eats compulsively is frustrated all the time. If she could, she would eat all the time – and indeed sometimes she does. In therapy, as she begins to understand herself better, she realises that it is human contact she longs for, a relationship with another person. When she looks at this longing closely, she may realise that what she once looked for in food she now hopes to get from this other person. She may say she needs the person to be there for her all the time; she wants him or her 24 hours a day and she cannot conceive of any separation, not even for a moment. She wants a relationship with this other person which is absolutely exclusive and in which she has the other person's full attention and preoccupation. She wants the other person's thoughts and feelings.

What she wants is the kind of relationship which leaves no space between two people. Her attempt to get such a thing is futile. One particular need can be satisfied by eating, but desire has no specific object and cannot be wholly satisfied by any means. A compulsive eater always knows that it is not food that she lacks and it is not hunger that she tries to satisfy. What she cannot see is that nothing and nobody can totally fulfil her desire. What she wants from others is something which is beyond reach. It is not a lack that has to be remedied or a need which has to be met. Rather it is the persistence of her notion that her desire can and should be satisfied. It is her belief and hope that frustrates her so terribly; the wish to satisfy her desire by any means and at whatever cost that is so unbearable. By eating she may satisfy a need, but she is wanting to satisfy a desire by gratifying a need.

Our desires are always partially beyond our reach. It is only by accepting this that we may possibly achieve some peace of mind.

A colleague told me about a client who came to a session terribly upset and spoke of all the things she wanted, how hard she tried and how upset she was about all sorts of wishes that remained unfulfilled. My friend stopped her at some point and asked her if it ever occurred to her that she might never fulfil any of these wishes or desires. She looked astonished and somewhat relieved. No, this had never occurred to her. Indeed, even the possibility of such a question had been beyond her. She left the session in a much better mood.

When our clients gain some understanding and insight into their confusion about their needs, wishes, demands and desires, when not every wish is felt as an urgent demand, then desire can begin to be what it is. It is at this point that food too can begin to become what *it* is, something without which we cannot live. We depend on food for our growth, strength and, not least, as one of our most enjoyed pleasures.

Biographical Notes

Carol Bloom

Carol Bloom lives in New York and is a psychotherapist who specialises in working with women with eating problems as well as having a general practice. She is a co-founder of the Women's Therapy Centre Institute (New York, 1981) which is a sister organisation to the Women's Therapy Centre in London. The Institute's aim is to provide a forum for the dissemination and development of new theory and practice in relation to the pyschology of women and to provide postgraduate training and supervision in the practice of feminist therapy. Carol Bloom is a consultant and does training in different parts of the country.

Clair Chapman

Clair Chapman spent five years as a compulsive-eating workshop leader at the Women's Therapy Centre, London, and three years as an abortion counsellor at the London Hospital's Day Care Abortion Service. She is still working with Spare Tyre Theatre Company, and through it has discovered some of the best therapy going. Got a problem? Put in on the stage! Write a song! Then sing it 50 times and see if you feel the same at the end as you did when you first wrote it. She is 34.

Troy Cooper

Troy Cooper is a 27-year-old feminist living in Cambridge and working on a PhD on the psychological basis of anorexia and bulimia. She grew up and went to school in Suffolk and spent a tubby adolescence dieting constantly and unsuccessfully with her mother. When she began research work, she thought anorexia and bulimia were interesting disorders that women became ill with. They were nothing to do with her personally. As she read and thought about anorexia in those first three months of research, she gradually stopped eating and lost three-quarters of a stone. The struggle to stop her weight loss and to come to terms with her appetite for food, and then for the many other things in life, has now become the framework for her views about anorexia and bulimia.

Mira Dana

Mira Dana was born in Israel, where she did her first degree in psychology and worked in a psychiatric hospital with drug addicts. Her interest in eating problems has developed since coming to England eight years ago, and she wrote her MA thesis on the links between anorexia and compulsive eating. She works as a psychotherapist at the Women's Therapy Centre, where she coordinates the work on eating problems. Her own work is mainly with compulsive eaters and bulimic women, running groups, workshops, training and supervision.

Gill Edwards

Gill Edwards co-founded the Anorexia Counselling Service with Marilyn Lawrence in 1978. She has worked as a psychotherapist in the National Health Service for six years and is currently a senior clinical psychologist with a community mental health team in Devon. She is also a feature writer for *Living* magazine. In the past, she has been a freelance journalist and manageress of a Pregnancy Advisory Service.

Bunny Epstein

Bunny Epstein holds a Diploma in Counselling from the South West London College and has also lectured on their course. The twin themes of women's anger and compulsive eating brought together in her chapter reflect a deeply personal as well as professional interest. Her exploration of her own and other women's anger with their children, including research at the Quarry Hill Community of Vermont, led to her MA from Antioch University. Women's anger and compulsive eating have formed the core of much of her individual work with women. Both issues have been the focus of a variety of group workshops she has led at the Women's Therapy Centre and she contributes regularly to the Centre's training course on eating disorders.

Annie Fursland

Annie Fursland has been working as a clinical psychologist since 1980 and has become increasingly involved with women's eating disorders (anorexia, bulimia and compulsive eating). She has worked in the National Health Service and run workshops for the Women's Therapy Centre in London. She is at present studying for a PhD in Berkeley, California.

Jean Mitchell

Jean Mitchell was born in North London in 1957. She left school at 16 and had a variety of jobs before taking a psychology degree at North-East London Polytechnic in 1982. For the past four years she has been researching anorexia and bulimia. A socialist, she lives in Newham, East London, where she is currently involved in a self-help group for bulimic women.

Katina Noble

Katina Noble has been a workshop leader for seven years at the Women's Therapy Centre, where she sets up self-help groups for compulsive eaters. She runs theme-related workshops for women with eating problems on self-nourishment, sexuality and problem-solving. She is also a founder member of Spare Tyre.

Wil Pennycook

Wil Pennycook was born and brought up in Belfast and moved to England, aged 18. She currently works therapeutically with children and adolescents with emotional difficulties and also counsels women with eating disorders. At the moment she is studying part-time for an MA on Women and Education.

Mary-Jayne Rust

Since training as an art therapist at Goldsmith's College, London, much of Mary-Jayne Rust's work has been with women with eating problems, both in community settings (such as Adult Education, Health and Therapy Centres) and on a private basis, with groups and individuals. Most of this work is short-term.

Her interest in this area came about through personal experience of compulsive eating. Self-exploration, working with others and an interest in cross-cultural healing led her to realise the importance of letting the imagination and its images find a language. She sees her therapeutic work as helping each woman to find her own vision or story through images and words from her culture's language.

Tamar Selby

Tamar Selby was born in Israel in 1945. She trained at the Philadelphia Association and the London School of Psychotherapy. For two years she did community work with disturbed adolescents. She has led groups for compulsive eaters at the Women's Therapy Centre and for the last seven years she has worked with individuals in psychotherapy.